Adelaide

INDEPENDENT MONTHLY LITERARY MAGAZINE

REVISTA LITERÁRIA INDEPENDENTE MENSAL

ADELAIDE
Independent Monthly Literary Magazine
Revista Literária Independente Mensal
Year III, Number 16, September 2018
Ano III, Número 16, setembro de 2018

ISBN-13: 978-1-949180-37-4
ISBN-10: 1-949180-37-9

Adelaide Literary Magazine is an independent international monthly publication, based in New York and Lisbon. Founded by Stevan V. Nikolic and Adelaide Franco Nikolic in 2015, the magazine's aim is to publish quality poetry, fiction, nonfiction, artwork, and photography, as well as interviews, articles, and book reviews, written in English and Portuguese. We seek to publish outstanding literary fiction, nonfiction, and poetry, and to promote the writers we publish, helping both new, emerging, and established authors reach a wider literary audience.

A Revista Literária Adelaide é uma publicação mensal internacional e independente, localizada em Nova Iorque e Lisboa. Fundada por Stevan V. Nikolic e Adelaide Franco Nikolic em 2015, o objectivo da revista é publicar poesia, ficção, não-ficção, arte e fotografia de qualidade assim como entrevistas, artigos e críticas literárias, escritas em inglês e português. Pretendemos publicar ficção, não-ficção e poesia excepcionais assim como promover os escritores que publicamos, ajudando os autores novos e emergentes a atingir uma audiência literária mais vasta.

(http://adelaidemagazine.org)

Published by: Adelaide Books LLC, New York
244 Fifth Avenue, Suite D27
New York NY, 10001
e-mail: info@adelaidemagazine.org
phone: (917) 727 8907
http://adelaidebooks.org

Copyright © 2018 by Adelaide Literary Magazine

All rights reserved. No part of this publication may be reproduced in any manner whatsoever without written permission from the Adelaide Literary Magazine Editor-in-chief, except in the case of brief quotations embodied in critical articles and reviews.

FOUNDERS / FUNDADORES
Stevan V. Nikolic & Adelaide Franco Nikolic

EDITOR IN CHIEF / EDITOR-CHEFE
Stevan V. Nikolic
editor@adelaidemagazine.org

MANAGING DIRECTOR / DIRECTORA EXECUTIVA
Adelaide Franco Nikolic

GRAPHIC & WEB DESIGN
Adelaide Books DBA, New York

CONTRIBUTING AUTHORS IN THIS ISSUE

Ryan Johnson, Julia Zwetolitz, Wendra Colleen, Alberto Ramirez, Matt Spangler, David Weinberger, Geoffrey Heptonstall, Clive Aaron Gill, David McVey, Ron Singer, Eric Stevens, Elaine Rosenberg Miller, Robby Pettit, Ted Morrissey, Ingrid Blaufarb Hughes, Maria Frangakis, Jordan Peralez, Nicolette Munoz, Abby Obenski, Robin Wyatt Dunn, Katie Rose, Marcella Meeks, Darren Demaree, Iain Twiddy, Tucker Lux, Jonathan DeCoteau, Diarmuid ó Maolalaí, Tom Laichas, Mark Taksa, Leslie Philibert, Jan Wiezorek, George Held, Sarah Sherwood, Laura Foley, Lenny Lewis, Katherine Carlman, Kate LaDew, Andres Mesa, Dr. Raymond Fenech, Emily Wanko, M. M. Adjarian, Marc Frazier, Sidney Burris, Jim Bolone, Kate LaDew, Naya Antoun, Megan Sandberg, Teresa Lynn Hasan-Kerr

Revista Literária Adelaide

CONTENTS / CONTEÚDOS

EDITOR'S NOTES

WHAT IS ALCHEMY by Stevan V. Nikolic   5

FICTION

THIS IS SOMETHING by Ryan Johnson   7

IT FEELS LIKE HOME TO ME   13
by Julia Zwetolitz

THEY SELL THEIR SOULS TO STRANGERS   18
by Wendra Colleen

STRANGE FRUIT REVISITED   20
by Alberto Ramirez

SORTING THROUGH CLAMS   26
by David Weinberger

MISS CRAMICKLE by Geoffrey Heptonstall   30

THE THREE-MILE RACE by Clive Aaron Gill   35

THE MISSING MASTER by David McVey   38

FLAGMAN by Ron Singer   42

THE SIREN by Eric Stevens   48

THE BEES by Robby Pettit   51

MEDIEVAL MUSIC FROM MIDWESTERN
UNIVERSITIES by Ted Morrissey   59

THE BIG MOVE by Maria Frangakis   66

THE GARBAGE MAN by Rachael Peralez   69

LET'S MAKE A DEAL by Nicolette Munoz   74

HILLSIDE STREET by Abby Obenski   77

NIGHT OWL by Robin Wyatt Dunn   84

FAST LANE by Katie Rose   86

THE PHOTOGRAPH by Marcella Meeks   91

NONFICTION

IN SICKNESS AND IN HEALTH   96
by Emily Wanko

THE CHURCH by Marc Frazier   99

CLOSING TIME by Sidney Burris   103

FULL CIRCLE by Jim Bolone   110

BECKY AND AMY by Kate LaDew   114

TWENTY FIRST CENTURY SLAVES   118
by Naya Antoun

DISCLOSURE by Megan Sandberg   120

INSANE IN THE NAME OF THE LORD   124
by Teresa Lynn Hasan-Kerr

THE EXTRAORDINARY INFLUENCE
OF THE MOORS ON SPAIN   127
by Dr. Raymond Fenech

BUSHKILL by Ingrid Blaufarb Hughes   131

POETRY

CITY DEER by Darren Demaree   133

THE RIVER IN SUMMER by Iain Twiddy   134

SYNTHESIS by Tucker Lux   136

STEEL PROPHET by Jonathan DeCoteau   138

THIS IS MY EVENING   142
by Diarmuid ó Maolalai

RENAMED by Tom Laichas   146

COMFORT IN A THEORY by Mark Taksa   148

LEMONS FOR CLARA by Leslie Philibert   151

IDENTITY by Jan Wiezorek   153

NEW TESTAMENT by George Held   157

ROAD TRIP by Sarah Sherwood   160

JANUARY by Laura Foley   162

NEWTON'S LAW by Lenny Lewis   165

NEGLECT by Katherine Carlman   167

IT'S THAT KIND OF DARK   169
by Kate LaDew

HAPPINESS by Andres Mesa   171

NEW TITLES

ON BEAUTY: ESSAYS, REVIEWS,
FICTION, AND PLAYS   174
by Wally Swist

MARTYRS, HEROES, AND FOOLS   176
by John Wells

A COAST by N.C. Robert   177

AWAKENING by Laura Solomon   178

Editor's Notes
Stevan V. Nikolic

WHAT IS ALCHEMY

What is Alchemy? Is it magic, philosophy, or a science? What was its original meaning and purpose? For the most of people today the word "alchemy" is associated with the medieval wizards in a dark and ominous laboratories trying to discover the formulas for the transmutation of metals and for the "elixir of life". But the story of Alchemy is much more complex and starts thousands years earlier, extending over three continents, hidden deep in the mists of time.

It is the story of the lifelong devotion of men of different cultures and races, throughout the ages, in finding the answers on the basic and crucial questions of human origin, existence, and purpose. Their devotion was inspired by a vision of the perfection of human beings, freed from all illnesses, ailments, and limitations of both mental and physical abilities, realizing the powers hidden in the deepest levels of their consciousness.

The etymology of the word "alchemy" is mysterious as the Alchemy itself. While most researchers refer to the Arabic word "al-kimia" associated with the Ancient Greek word "chemeia", most likely derived from the Ancient Egyptian "khmi" (meaning: black earth), there are those who believe that the origin of the word alchemy lies in the Ancient Greek word "chumeia" (meaning: mixture).

Trying to define Alchemy is almost impossible task taking into account the immensity of its complex content. Sometimes it seems that the only way to give a proper definition is by perceiving it on three different levels: on the practical level – as both forerunner and the successor of natural sciences; on the spiritual level – as applied system of philosophical teachings; and on the absolute level – as a "blueprint" of Creation and its workings.

As the practical discipline, Alchemy is regarded as the precursor of the modern sciences, but with the mystical or spiritual components. Numerous procedures, methods, formulas, and devices, created and developed by Alchemists, are still in use in modern chemistry, pharmacology, medicine, and physics. They are credited with the identification of many chemical elements and the formation of the basic periodic table. Their contribution to metallurgy was significant as well, particularly in developing methods associated with the use of fire to purify or change physical attributes of the metal. Most of those interested in practical Alchemy today are pursuing research in holistic medicine and much less in the transmutation of basic metals into gold. So, in many ways, practical Alchemy today could be regarded as proto-chemistry. However, new and exiting discoveries of modern physics and Quantum theory are causing that contemporary physicists are turning more and more their attention to the Alchemical hermetic concepts of our inner world and of the universe in order to explain some puzzling aspects of their findings.

On the spiritual level, as applied philosophical concept Alchemy is a process of inner separation, transformation, and new integration. Our minds and our bodies are nothing else but vessels for purifying and transforming many levels of our consciousness. By changing our own consciousness, we change our relation to the universe. Famous Alchemist Paracelsus describes Alchemy as "the voluntary action of man in harmony with the involuntary action of nature". We can say that Alchemy is a broad philosophical vision of the whole creation, built on the universal correspondence system. It is a mystical quest, with the main objective of liberation of the soul from the world. Alchemy teaches about unity of existence underlying mind and body, psyche and matter. It is an art of resurrection of spirit in the realm of matter that raises our consciousness about who we are, where are we coming from, and where are we going. It is a method of aligning ourselves with the whole of the creation.

On the absolute level, as a "blueprint" of Creation and its workings, it is the concept rooted in the ancient Hermetic philosophy, of the complete unity and interactivity of the existence of man and the limitless realities of the vast Creation in all its perfection, beauty, and harmony.

THIS IS SOMETHING
by Ryan Johnson

"ADAM GO!! YOU HAVE TO GO, I'M WORKING RIGHT NOW!!" My voice echoed throughout the noise-rich air of a sunny commerce driven weekday in an attempt to shame Adam in the eyes of the few people outside of their cars, of which there weren't many.

"Come on buddy, give me a cigarette," Adam repeated his mantra. Everyone he had ever needed anything from for free had the name Buddy in common.

"ADAM LEAAAVEE!!"

"Just one cigarette. Come on, buddy." His voice was low, at hardly a whisper. It was as if it was me causing the disturbance, disrupting my work day as a gas attendant because I couldn't part with a fag. He always got what he wanted. I pulled a Maverick Light out of the pack and passed it to him. He put it between his lips and beckoned me closer with two fingers. It took me a moment to understand what he was after. The fucking bastard didn't even have his own lighter. I passed him mine.

Of course he wouldn't have come all this way for just a cigarette and some constantly interrupted fragments of juvenile conversation as I filled cars with gasoline. Adam, he just didn't know how things worked sometimes. Though for never carrying a wallet, he always had money in his pocket. He was just stopping by to check: did I?

It wasn't much of a fight. I guess I didn't have too many illusions about that, but watching the video on Q's phone made it even more clear just how one-sided an affair it really was. I got to throw the first punch, because I hit him in the back of the head as he was walking away. But then he turned around and allowed me to throw a whole handful of punches before finally fighting back. And when he fought back it was just over. Hardly any time for people to gather, whipping out cell-phones and chanting "Fuck him up!" and "Worldstar!" and whatever else you traditionally yell to make a fucking event of it.

When Troy turned around, in the video, he was already done processing that he'd been hit, that there was going to be a fight happening now. He just had this look of malicious glee on his face as I packed in a few more hits. He put his arms up a little bit to defend himself, but it wasn't even like I was landing solid punches on places that would really hurt him, like a kidney, his groin, or anywhere like that. I was just flailing like a jackass hitting extremities at that point. I was just pissed off and had no idea what I was in for. It would have been better to take out my frustrations on a bottle of vodka, I'd soon learn. I worked at a fucking liquor store after all.

He made a grab at me. I evaded him. Tried to hit him again and missed. The delivery of the hit looked like I was trying to swat a fly. It was enough to make his hat fall off which is the only victory I can claim in this fight.

You can see it all online. On Youtube or WorldstarHipHop, your choice.

He made a run at me, and since there was no way I was turning my back on him for a second, I leaned into the hit and watched my whole body jerk in the video as he put me up against the wall. With no actual corners to corner me with, he held me in place with erratic punches. Never knowing where the next one would fall, I threw my arms up in front of my face, chest, even legs at one point, spastically.

"This is getting hard to watch," I finally said. I could see the genesis of a smile forming on Q's face.

In the video Troy threw me on the ground, leaned over, picked me back up by my bloody sweatshirt, using the momentum to put me in a headlock wherein my head was almost right up against his ass. It was so traumatizing to watch that, like when the fight itself was happening, I would drown out most of the background noise. That was the first 5 or 6 times I watched the video. Now I could hear full well the taunts, jeers, and laughter coming from the crowd of coworkers and strangers alike who bore witness, and did the world a solid too by recording on their phones.

I remember being tightly nestled in the crook of his arm, smelling the scent of his natural body odor conquering any man-made deodorant, thinking what if my neck broke? What if he thrashed me around so violently that my neck broke and I could never walk again? How dumb would it be for something like that to happen? Over her. Over a few dumb comments. Over not doing my fucking job.

This guy would come to the gas station every evening. He'd come by way of the crosswalk dividing the gas station from the nearby strip mall, where nearly every store but an Ashley's Furniture had gone out of business. He'd buy two big Poland Spring water bottles, walk out of the mart with them in a bag and head right over to us, or just me if Adam wasn't there. He'd been doing this for almost 3 months now since Adam told him it was ok, and I wasn't happy about it. I didn't even know his name, but Adam said that was alright. It didn't matter much anyway.

"What's going on today boys?" he asked, taking a swig from one of the bottles. He always had on a button up shirt and dress pants, hair combed back, like he should be somewhere besides here. In an office building crunching numbers or something. He spoke with this nasally voice that made me dislike him even more.

"Nothing much," Adam replied, puffing on another one of my Mavericks.

"Can ten bucks buy you anything?" Adam gave me an accusatory glance.

The man sniggered, "Cheap bottle of wine maybe, you serious?"

"Can you give us more time? We can get more money, or, or we can just pay you back another time!"

"You ain't owing me shit," the man said, hardly taking us seriously. "Ten is it then, or are we just going to hold off for another day?"

"No, no, the ten is fine. Just get us a cheap bottle of white wine should be good."

Adam handed him the ten dollars. The man walked away. I pumped gas for this nice old Irish guy who always tipped me a dollar or two. This time it was two. I walked back over to Adam who was standing along the side of the building. He said nothing but I knew what he was thinking.

"What did you want me to do, Adam?"

He turned on me immediately. "I don't know, get behind that register for two seconds, ask him if you can break a 20 yourself, there were so many things you could've done!"

"No I can't, not with Narender, you know he watches that register like a hawk. He's hardly ever short! Besides, only you would have me fucking over my coworkers! Not that I care, but where's your skin in the game?!"

"It's walking down the street! In that guy's pocket, where yours should be!"

"Fuck off, my skin in the game is you doing your dirty underage shit where I work!"

"Look," Adam sighed and exhaled, causing the wispy hairs on his upper lip to tremble. "Are you really going to get all butt-hurt over this? First, you're getting some, for free this time I might add, and second, it won't be long before you're 21 and we won't need to be doing this shit anymore. So relax and go help that Jeep over there."

I turned and walked back over to the pumps where a black Jeep was idling patiently. I was sure Adam had watched it wait there while we argued. Piece of shit. It bothered me that he just assumed I'd be taking over the scheme for our sketchy, nameless friend when I turned 21. What pissed me off was that I would. Just like with the Mavericks.

I wondered why we did this. If it was really worth it. Though for Adam, one way or another, I'm sure it was. For an unemployed stoner, his time was always spent in the pursuit of some goal, though most times that goal was known only to him.

It took a few good punches to the stomach for me to throw up, which elicited just the kind of reaction from the crowd as you'd think. Some got on Troy's forearm which angered and disgusted him enough to let me go and drop me to the ground again with a rough push. He said something I couldn't pick up during the actual fight or in the video. Especially since he looked down as he said it. I could see her standing in the background. I was surprised she didn't have her phone out too. The bitch who had caused all this. I bet she got off on it.

Anyway, then Troy looked up and said something the cell phone microphones were able to pick up a little better. "ARE WE DONE?! YOU STAY THE FUCK DOWN AND WE'RE DONE!! ARE WE DONE?!"

I was on my side clutching my stomach and nodding. A hardly audible and cracked, 'yes', could be heard coming from the back of my head.

"Hahahaaa, yes! Worldstar!" the cameraman said.

"Dude," Q said as the video came to an end. "I would find a new place to work."

"Dude," I replied, feeling ridiculous for what I was about to say. "I don't want to feel like I'm running away from this."

"Dude, a legendary ass beating like that, there's no shame in running. You want to get out and see if the stain is still there from where you puked."

Q had been sure to park as close as possible to the location of the actual fight. I'm sure he had been fighting back the urge to walk over and snap a pic at the angle the cameraman had as he captured the fight, for posterity's sake. I knew I wasn't going to get much from Q in the way of sympathy, he owned a few Tapout shirts, and by watching the video once again at the mere price of a ride to work, I believed I had more than paid my dues.

"Thanks for the ride, Q," I said and got out.

When the fight was over I limped away with a swollen knee, a cut above my right eye that required stitches, extreme nausea in my stomach, and lingering soreness in my shoulder, collarbone, knee, and thigh. I had no insurance to pay for the damages so, aside from the stitches, I let everything else alone, and hoped time and avoiding another run in with Troy would set me back on the right track before long. Since it was nearing a month since the fight happened, my sore collarbone and knee were beginning to worry me, but there was nothing I could do now as I walked across the street to the liquor store trying as usual not to let the pain show.

The automated chime sounded as I entered. I punched in and loitered by the cashier I would be relieving. He hadn't been there that night but I was sure he'd heard all about it and seen the video. Who hadn't?

I watched as he counted out his drawer, nodded for me to do a recount, then punched out and left. A man walked in the once empty store, one of our regulars. A typical 9-5er in a button up shirt and dress pants, no tie, the bastard having shed the first vestige of his white collared existence. He bought the cheapest bottle of white wine we had and put it in a bag that already contained two water bottles. All was per usual except for the purchase. But I could care less about the reasoning for this. I rung him up and he left.

Before I could put 10 minutes behind me on my shift, a voice came from the back: "Hey, bitch, is that you?"

When this behavior started I pushed back with what little means I had. Pretending I hadn't heard, ignoring him to his face, you know, the stuff your mom tells you to do when you're being bullied. But he had kicked my ass and so he wouldn't be ignored, so before long I just had to grimace and swallow my medicine. Not that it mattered, but technically I had started the fight.

"Yeah," I grumbled, just loud enough so he'd hear.

Troy eagerly materialized from the back of the small store. "Hey bitch, I was stocking the shelves back there, didn't strain too much because I figured you'd want to take over when you got here." He walked over to the register and I resisted the urge to flinch as he patted me on the back. "Best get to it then."

I headed for the back. I couldn't take any form of his retaliations and he knew it. I'd started something, he'd finished it, and was taking extra care to prolong my suffering for as long as possible. Maybe Q was right about finding a new job.

I took a drink from the wide mouth Nalgene Adam had filled for me around the back of the building. He was smoking another one of my cigarettes and I was drinking cheap, tasteless, white wine. I didn't even know what kind it was. It was making me start to feel good. Lighter. I lacked the vocabulary to describe a light buzz to myself. Of course Adam had assured that a light buzz was all I would be getting, the Nalgene being less than half full as a result of my only contribution to the venture being the five dollars I'd made in tips that day that we'd handed to the guy when he returned with our wine.

"Jesus Christ man, you have a fucking job, you should be the one paying for this, not me," he said when he handed me the Nalgene after ruefully filling it. "Motherfucker."

The evening rush had both sides of the roads clogged like a fat man's arteries, so I closed off half the pumps with traffic cones to make my life easier. This meant I could still steal time on occasion to drink with Adam. In the moments where I was able to string together minutes or more to drink and bullshit with him I always had to acknowledge enjoying myself. Relishing this time together to be young and do the things young people do with other young people. It was during times like this evening that we really bonded, when it was only the two of us and he wasn't stringing any assortment of strange people of all ages along with him.

"I could grow to like the taste of wine," I said, trying not to lead on that the day's venture was a complete loss. "I don't know, I mean it's not awful."

"Not me. I like beer, and I like women."

My heart sunk a bit an hour later when an old silver Toyota Camry pulled up to the front of the mart and dropped off a girl. I realized why Adam had been drinking conservatively. He had the whole night ahead of him, I was just a pit stop for some smokes and a little bullshit conversation. A guy to surrender tip money to the guy getting him his pre-game alcohol. I was at least glad he hadn't duped me into handing over one of the twenties I had in my wallet.

"What's up Adam?" she asked. She was beautiful. All the girls Adam hung out with were beautiful. She turned to me. "Hey."

"What's going on?" I replied

"Is that?" she pointed at the Nalgene knowingly.

"It's wine," I said.

"Can I?"

"Sure," I replied, handing the bottle over easily. She took a big gulp, nearly finishing what little I had left, and handed it back to me. Turned back to Adam.

"So where are we going tonight?" she asked.

Where did I recognize her from? Also, it was a Tuesday night.

Adam thought about it for a couple seconds. "Hmmmm, well, Maurice is having people over tonight so that might be good, but that doesn't start until later, and we were only able to get this cheap-ass wine for now so I don't really know what to do," he trailed off.

Uncomfortable, I lit a cigarette. Both of their eyes turned on me at once.

"Can I?" she asked. Then she was smoking a cigarette. Adam hadn't asked for one.

"It's a shame that Achilles guy ruined that liquor store for us," Adam complained.

"I told you, his name is Troy and he was just trying to be chivalrous, though I'll take a few lewd comments and the ability to buy underage from that guy who got his ass kicked any day." And there it was. Where I recognized her from. The fight video. Of course.

"Whatever."

"I think Troy thinks I owe him my pussy now after his 'valorous display.'"

"I'd almost be tempted to give it to him if I were you, Amber, for how awesome that fight was."

She smiled and fumbled for a hair tie and tied her shoulder length brown hair back. "Well, it was pretty awesome, but no thanks, he's disgusting." She stamped out the barely half-smoked cigarette and scuffed her Converse on the pavement. "I'm starting to get impatient! What are we doing tonight? I thought you were going to have it all planned out by the time I got dropped off here, that's what you texted me."

They were both on their phones. I was spacing in and out of their conversation. At some point I broke away and filled a truck with diesel using a company fleet card that required a 4 digit passcode to access. I kept having a hard time hearing what the numbers were because the driver left the truck running and had a way of speaking that was all jowls and spit. Then when I came back the Nalgene was empty and Adam and Amber were still talking about the night's plans that I wasn't invited to partake in. I was sure that if I spoke up they'd invite me, but I always seemed to enjoy relishing in their rudeness more.

"Not to be a bitch, but if we did get an Uber, would you pay me back, because you haven't in the past." Women were allowed to be more up front with Adam about his debts accrued 'among friends.'

"Well we don't need to go to Thatcher's, I'm just saying we could," Adam replied, backtracking.

It was interesting to listen to, though sad that their youth's vitality was being entirely spent on where to best get drunk and hang out with other drunk people. Maybe it wasn't so interesting to listen to then. I didn't know. One more swallow of wine and I'd be able to deal with anything. That was always what it came down to wasn't it? That one thing that was just out of reach was the only thing you needed to accomplish anything at all, and therefore served as the excuse for letting things fall apart around you.

"Well I got dropped off here, so what do you want to do?" Amber.

"We can go back to my place until it gets dark out and things start?"

"Yeah right, who's there?" His mom probably, his dad was dead. Then again it wasn't so much about parentage as it was about each location being qualified by how many people were already there waiting to hang.

"No one."

"Am I going to have to get Troy to come over here and kick your ass?"

"God no, come on Amber, I wasn't suggesting anything, you know me."

"Yeah, I do and—"

"You, you!" came a voice from behind us. It was Narender, shooing Adam away. This would happen from time to time and I never saw it as too big of an inconvenience. He spoke in broken English: "You, you always here! You go, now!"

Adam waved, "Ok, ok, I go."

"What the fuck?" Amber muttered.

"Look, let's just get out of here and we'll figure something out, ok?"

"You! Go I say!" Narender let the door close behind him and came a few steps closer.

"Ok? Let's just go!"

"Ugh, fine!"

The two scurried off without saying anything to me. Narender had an annoyed gaze waiting for me once they were gone, but before long he returned inside. The register had a hold on him. He couldn't be more than 6 feet away from it at any given time without feeling its pull. He never mentioned Adam to the manager.

A Honda Pilot pulled up to one of the pumps I'd closed off with a traffic cone. Leaving my post along the side of the building, I walked over and decided I'd just dispense the gas anyway, fuck it.

About the Author:

Ryan Johnson is a writer from Northern Jersey. He holds a B.A. in Literature and Teacher Education from Ramapo College. His poetry and prose has appeared in Hypnos and Trillium magazines.

IT FEELS LIKE HOME TO ME
by Julia Zwetolitz

Home is not just the concrete building. It is also where family is and the memories that occurred in each house. I have moved three times and got to experience many events with my family. I could not say that I could choose a favorite house or a favorite city.

212 Carter's Grove Lane- 1997-2011

I spent fourteen years living in Carter's Grove. It is a small neighborhood in Lynchburg, Virginia off of Boonsboro Road. There are only three streets. The main hill is Carter's Grove Lane and there is also Jameson and Merewether which are cul de sac streets.

Our house sits at the bottom of Carter's Grove Lane. It is a brick house with a pineapple mailbox, a giant oak tree, a windy driveway, a swing set in the back, and woods. The first floor has a mudroom, a kitchen, a piano room, a living, room, a dining room, a foyer, and a powder room. Downstairs is the basement and upstairs are four bedrooms, two bathrooms, an attic, and a laundry room.

Nothing too traumatic happened during my childhood.We celebrated many birthdays, holidays, and religious events in my childhood home. I went to school with the same friends from kindergarten to eighth grade. Lynchburg is small and there is not much to do there. The small airport's only destination is Charlotte. You enter through either downtown or past the airport. Downtown Lynchburg has a few distinct buildings that are the Bank of the James and the Academy of Fine Arts. Our finals dance was at the Bank of the James on the rooftop. Finals is Virginia Episcopal School's version of prom. You have Water stone Pizza, The Depot Grille, the Ploughcroft Tearoom, and Market at Main, for fine cuisine. There are a few shops across the street from the farmer's market. The Craddock Terry hotel is also in downtown as well as a biking and running trail called Percival's Isle. There are train tracks that cut right over the street to get to the trail. The lovely James River flows along the trail and is what you see coming through downtown. Amazement Square and Monument Terrace run up the hill as you leave the Depot Grille. Monument Terrace commemorates Lynchburg soldiers who fought in the civil war. Spanish-American war, World war I and II, the Korea, and Vietnam wars. That is all there is. The turkey trot in 2014 ran through downtown Lynchburg. You run up the beam bridges leading to madison heights and up rather steep incline called Pearl Road and finish by the Monument Terrace.

My friends and I would spend time at each others houses, see plays, or see movies. We had a trailer in the Boonsboro shopping center parking lot called Maylynn's which is where you would get ice cream.. You would get fried chicken from a gas station. Boonsboro Country Club has golf, swimming, and tennis. Boonsboro Road shopping center is home to Isabella's which is the restaurant of choice if you want to be fancy without going to far away from home. There is also Phila Deli in the shopping center where you always run into someone you know especially after back to school night at James River Day School where we all put our books in our lockers and meet our teachers before school starts. There is Kroger which is a gas station grocery store compared to Harris Teeter and Giant Eagle. Some stores such as Francesca's, Talbot's, Gladiola Girls, Chico's, and

Pheasants Eye. There is an outdoor store, pizza hut, and Starbucks. You could go to Rivermont Pizza along Rivermont Road. I liked this small town feel fo shops and restaurants in Lynchburg. There was famiarity everywhere you went.

Along Rivermont Road was Randolph Macon College now known as Randolph College when it became a co-ed school. I attended Holy Cross Catholic Church which is one of two catholic churches in Lynchburg. One year the church had termites and we went to church at Holy Cross Catholic School, which is close to EC Glass and the medical center. We run in the Virginia Ten Miler that starts at EC Glass and finishes at Randolph College for the four miler or back at Glass for the one and ten miler races. I have ran in the four miler and the one milers a couple times and I ran the ten miler once as I was part of the color guard that runs with flags to honor the troops.. Everyone in Lynchburg normally runs in the Virginia Ten Miler races. This section of Lynchburg is not as nice because it is rundown and crime occurs. My sister high school is also not in a nice area that she attended her freshman year. WE stick to our school district and stay away from the bad areas.

Close to the airport is the mall, a movie theater, fast food restaurants, Target, Best Buy, Sam's Club, Wal-Mart, hotels, and Liberty University. There are a few car wash spots, frozen yogurt shop, Olive garden, Chick Fil A, and O'Charley's. When you drive past the airport whose one destination is Charlotte you end up along 29 which is nothings but highways. From Charlotte it takes up three and a half hours to get to Lynchburg and to UVA it will take us four and half hours. I've been back and forth along 29 and always know when the airport will appear or downtown Lynchburg welcoming us back to our hometown. I never knew we would leave our hometown.

I am the middle child in the family. My sister was born in1996, I came along fourteen months later, and my brother was born in 2001. My brother was born on September 29 2001 when my dad was running in the Virginia Ten Miler. My dad originally signed up to just run four miles due to a surgery. My mom, sister, and I were sitting on the sidewalk by Virginia Baptist Hospital waiting for him to run by. My mom motioned for him to come over but he said he was fine and wanted to run the entire ten miles. She continued with the motioning and then he realized it was time for my brother to come into the world.

My sister and I shared a bedroom. We slept in twin beds with Disney princess sheets. Soon she ended up in the bedroom over the garage where she slept in her canopy bed. That room was where my siblings and I would perform plays for our parents. My brother's room was across the hall from mine. All of us used to sleep in that room as babies. Sometimes we would play store in our rooms. We also made embarrassing home videos where my sister was bossy and told my brother and I what to do. I was definitely the worst filmer because I couldn't hold the camera still.

In the basement we would perform a cooking show in which we would make fruit salad, peanut butter and jelly, or another simple dish. We used our miniature play kitchen in the basement. When neighbors would come over we would play Wii or play board games. Hide and go seek in the dark was the most thrilling because when the seeker would come downstairs it would be pitch black and one of the hiders would try to scare them by turning up the TV on full blast or grabbing their foot at the bottom of the stairs. We had white desks downstairs in which we would play school. My brother would always teach about volcanoes letting us know the color of lava and the color of the volcano.

Milestones in that house were first holy communions, eighth grade graduations, permit drivers, and finding out that we would be moving. That move was expected but it was hard on all of us. I was graduating eighth grade in June and my sister just completed her freshman year of high school. My brother would be starting fifth grade. I was upset upon hearing the news because I would not be attending Virginia Episcopal School with my friends that I have known since kindergarten. I also was scared to start high school in a brand new place. My sister held a grudge because she liked her school and didn't want to leave. We left that house with a pizza stain on the carpet.

The news about the move came when my parents sat us down and told us about my dad and his new job in Pittsburgh. I was sad since I would leave behind my friends and not get to go to Virginia Episcopal School, a day and boarding school where we would wear dresses or skirts four days a week and the men would wear jackets and ties. It was sad when I had to write down where I was going to attend high school at my eighth grade graduation. I couldn't write VES and I didn't know where I would be for high school in Pittsburgh. I would have to start over and meet a new group of people. There would be no running into people everywhere I went or being at school in less than five minutes. My mom's family lives an hour from Pittsburgh. I looked forward to seeing them more than twice a year. We also had family friends who would come over on weekends to hang out with us. The shift to high school was hard for me and my sister and I.

I experienced many things between the time I was born and when I turned fourteen. Virginia was all I knew and I was familiar with the everyday routine of a small town. I was going to high school and I had to start fresh.

103 Summer Place- 2011-2013

Summer Place did not live up to its name. It was reached by driving through a cornfield and past the district middle school and high school. It was a brand new neighborhood and our house was built on a plot of land with woods in the back. During hunting season you would hear gunshots in the woods and during homecoming you would hear the sound of the marching band. The only cool part about living in that neighborhood was that our neighbor was Jackie Evancho who got in second place in America's Got Talent. We trespassed in her house as it was being built.

Pittsburgh is big and that first year was tough. We had my mom's family who lived an hour away and family friends away who made our adjustment easier. The house's main features are a catwalk, a living room, a dining room, an office, a kitchen, five bedrooms. five bathrooms, a basement, and a laundry room. My brother got a bigger room than my sister and I which made my sister mad. Her room was small. My sister and I shared a Jack and Jill bathroom.

The kids in the neighborhood were around my brother's age so he made friends quickly. As for my sister and I we didn't meet people until cross country preseason. We trained with the high school in our backyard but eventually went to a private school thirty minutes away. That drive to school was on a highway after the bus picked us up. It was a terrifying experience for us.

During the early days of our move we helped unpack boxes, meet new people, explore the city, and go to preseason practices. Slowly our belonging were unpacked and we got situated. The walls has scruff marks on them and the floors creaked but it was home. Our cousins would come and visit during holidays, birthdays, and on school breaks. We would spend time hanging out in the basement and sleep down there. For birthdays we would have a cake, early Thanksgiving meals were made the week before Thanksgiving and we lost those pounds playing Just Dance. The dark basement provided the perfect place to sleep. We would walk around the city, go to the farmer's market to get pumpkins, run in races together, and see movies. I looked forward to those days. Christmases spent in Uniontown were always fun. My mom was one of seven siblings so our family get together were always huge as aunts, uncles, cousins, boyfriends and girlfriends all squished in a house. My aunt makes the best sugar bomb cookies that have gobs of icing and powdered sugar on them. We celebrate our Polish roots by eating Polish foods and listening to Polish music. There would also be secret Santa for the adults in the house. Little cousins would open gifts and the older cousins would get money. We played Polly pockets and rock band, and drifted between rooms to catch up with each other. We would cram 25 plus people in a house suited for a family of five. We would eat meals, watch football, and look through old picture albums of us when we were little.

As high school started I was nervous. These kids knew each other since preschool and I would be trying to find a group. The nice thing about Sewickley Academy was that we only have four classes a day that would rotate according to the letters of the alphabet. For instance we would have Class A B, C, and D on Monday, classes E,F,G,H on Tuesday, and B,C,D,A on Wednesday. I enjoyed the free time for lunch and cross country. Cross country was popular in Pennsylvania. Most races were in the rain and mud.

Going back and forth between Pittsburgh and Sewickley was tough form a social setting. My sister always wanted to hang out with her friends after school but I rarely did. Those 2 years flew by quickly. I miss being close to family and sightseeing around Pittsburgh. We went to a Penguins game and a Pirates Game. We walked around the strip, ate at Pamela's Diner, went to Mount Lebanon, and explored shops and stores. The smells in Pittsburgh such as the pastries from Dudt's and Soergels, the Italian food from Labriola's, and the aroma of pierogies at the Pierogie Palace were ones I remember the most. Traffic was a pain and people flew down the highways. There were many four ways and six way intersections. I wish we got the chance to stay longer. Recently I was back in July for my cousin's wedding.

Holidays spent there were always fun. We would go to Christmas Eve mass in Uniontown and drive back home to spend Christmas morning in Pittsburgh. Then a couple days after we would go back to Uniontown, eat a lot of really good food, watch football, and relax. I enjoyed seeing them all the time. Now that we are in Charlotte we only see them three times a year.

206 Paddington Court- 2013-2015

We are back in Lynchburg. The rental house was the smallest house we lived in. It was only temporary because we would be moving to Charlotte We shared a driveway with our neighbors and had to make sure nobody was trying to leave the house when someone was returning home. It was mostly my family that kept coming and going down the driveway. I remember when I had my permit and it was snowing in Virginia. I almost caused our car to go off the side of the driveway since I didn't break soon enough. We also had to watch out for our neighbor's dog Buzzy who would run

thought the woods and chase squirrels. Squirrels and der would also sit in the middle of the driveway staring us down so we had to wait for them to move. There was on squirrel that we saw all the time. My cousin hit him with his car and it was a sad day for all of us. Backing out from the driveway caused us to go up a hill into our neighbor's driveway. You could either end up in the grass if you turned the wrong way or head straight up towards our neighbor's garage. I remember I struggled with that part since our family garage was only a two car garage and someone had to park outside. On cold days my sister and I had to start the car before we left for school so we wouldn't enter an icebox at 7:30 in the morning.

I was excited to be back with my friends and finish my last two years of high school with them. This would be my second high school and my sister's third one. I was going to be a junior and my sister was going to be a senior. My brother was going to be in seventh grade at the private school we all have been at since kindergarten. This time we knew we would be back for only two years. We were originally going to head straight to Charlotte but my parents wanted my sister and I to finish high school.

I was excited to be reunited with my childhood friends and finish high school with them. It was strange to be back in our little town after being gone. Everything remained the same. It was sad to drive back to our old house and see it sit in the dark because nobody bought it yet. We caught up with our friends.

It was strange for me to be considered the new student and go through new student orientation. The first year at VES was hard as I had to adjust to a different schedule and curriculum. Wednesdays were spent in the chapel with Bojangles after. Everyone would allow the seniors to leave the chapel first; I was glad to be a senior since I could get Bojangles before they ran out. We had to wear dresses and skirts four days a week and the guys had to wear jackets and ties. On Fridays we would get to wear spirit wear or business casual. We had our own hanging spot for the day students and occasional borders. The day student lounge had lockers and three ugly black couches with dirty red cushions. The stuff that occurred in the day student lounge were the memories that I always remember. In my AP composition class we had to keep a jounrla of funy things that people said and most of my quotes were from people in the lounge. We would procrastinate and suffer from senioritis as soon as we got accepted into one college. At least that was the case for me. I met new friends and kept old ones. After graduation we would all be going our separate ways.

I got my license before I started my senior year. Two high school graduations also occurred in that house.

2437 Ansley Court-2015-now

This is our final destination. I was going to start college at Queens, my sister would start her second year at UVA, and my brother would be starting high school. This house was a teardown. My parents would go back and forth between Charlotte and Lynchburg to check in on the status of our new house being built. Our neighborhood is along Providence Road by Wendover so it is only two miles away from Queens. I liked being close to home so I can go home whenever I wanted. Charlotte has a lot of restaurants and shops that we figured out how to get to. WE have navigated short cuts to get to places.

My brother has his friends, my sister is gone at UVA, I have fraternity friends, and my parents get along with neighbors. I joined Phi Mu after my sister and mom encouraged me to in order to make friends. I signed up that day and went through the three rounds of recruitment. Bid Day was a crazy and exciting day for all the new girls in each sorority. I met many faces and it was an overwhelming experience until I got my big and was initiated. My big and I share many things in common and she was the one I spent the most time around. Soon everyone formed into friends groups. Phi Mu gives me a reason to have fun in college. The only stressful times in Phi Mu are recruitment, philanthropy week, and elections. Being around these girls has taught me to step out of my comfort zone and take on leadership positions. They are my family too. So this move has been easier on us. Summer has been working and internships, camps, and family vacations. My cousin had been living with is for 2 years so he is a help around the house. We also got a dog two years ago. We got him because my mom felt sorry for my brother. Scout is now a two year old English cream retriever.

This is where we will stay.

About the Author:

My name is **Julia Zwetolitz** and I am a senior at Queens University of Charlotte. I am a Professional Writing major with a minor in Organizational Communication. I helped create Queens literary magazine Signet. I am also a member of Phi Mu fraternity.

THEY SELL THEIR SOULS TO STRANGERS
by Wendra Colleen

When the Women of Bourbon Street become ghosts, they are the last to realize it. They've been tossed out and forgotten, yet when darkness returns to the street, so do they.

The ghosts can't resist the lure of yesterday. The daylight hours feel like shadows compared to this life in black and red leather, feathers, hot oil, tight straps, the most exquisite pain.

This street is still home to them, but as ghosts they are not welcome. The hawkers at the Gentlemen's Clubs turn away when they approach, the customers look past them.

One ghost pauses in front of a cabaret, her bare feet floating above the dirty sidewalk. Painted nails and sagging eyes, long, silver-tinged tresses hanging limply down her back. A bright dress flows around her like water. Her 100-yard stare bores through everything, straight into her past.

She recalls leaning back against the black painted frame of the doorway, a reprieve she earned after reaching her evening quota. She never told anyone that she enjoyed luring in customers the most. All expectation and promise, all because of her silky long legs, her full breasts, her long dark hair. She could caress and grind in a way that held men spellbound. Sometimes she tortured them with her large eyes, her lips parted, beads of sweat on her upper lip, pinning them, transfixed, as she let her hand trail between her breasts. Lower and lower, her chest heaving, her cheeks flushed, her fingers brushing her inner thighs, coming closer, closer. Sometimes she closed her eyes and shivered, awash in so much power.

The ghost does whatever it takes to feel alive again, when she reigned as Queen of the Night.

Lost in her memories, she doesn't see the man who was once her customer. Where he lingers, hawkers approach, women invite. He's alive and welcome in her former home.

Like her, his face is worn and his hair streaked with grey. As a wealthy regular, however, he's whisked to a private room for a parade of the club's wares. He watches each young woman, the broken heart, pride, or carelessness of her father. He drums his fingers on his seal-skin wallet, savoring the rich, oily feel, and each moment he can buy. Oblivious to the ghost hovering nearby, he signals for another shot of the 100-year old Scotch that they keep on hand just for him.

He invests every spare penny and moment on Bourbon Street. He lifelessly plods through daylight hours, his dreary family routine, waiting to come alive at night in the sweaty, glaring venues. The music blares so loud he blissfully cannot think beyond commanding attention, where a word, a gesture, a handful of bills can transform him, once more, into a King of the Night.

About the Author:

As a psychologist by day and writer by night, **Wendra Chambers** has published young adult short stories in The Passed Note (October, 2017) and in anthologies such as Dark Tales of Lost Civilizations. She is currently pitching and querying her young adult urban fantasy, Evil Was a Child Once. Wendra has also published adult pieces in literary magazines such as Lunch Ticket(Winter/Spring 2018), in addition to political op-eds and academic articles. Lastly, Women in Film and Video selected her comedic screen musical, A MUSICAL FOR OUTCASTS, for their first Spotlight on Screenwriters Spec-Catalogue for distribution to select producers. "They Sell Their Souls to Strangers" was inspired by a Bourbon Street glance she'll never forget.

STRANGE FRUIT REVISITED
by Alberto Ramirez

"What's in Bisbee?" said Abigail.

"A fair question for a native Bostonian," said Charles

He poured himself a glass of Chardonnay and sat down beside her on the leather love seat.

"It's this quaint little mining town turned artist colony in the heart of Cochise County," he said.

"I know where Bisbee is, but I mean, why there of all places?"

"Because it's just like heaven. My dad proposed to my mom in Bisbee, October 30, 1964. Right on the rim of the Lavender Pit. To hear her tell it, it was magical. Picture this. The Arizona sun painting the sky blood red, the burning smell of jack-o-lanterns in the air, blue-green specks of copper ore stirring at his feet as he got on one knee."

"So what—?"

"So let's go to Bisbee. We haven't gotten away in I don't know how long. We can book the honeymoon suite at the Copper King Hotel, order room service, drink chilled prosecco by the pool, do it missionary style like virgins—"

"And keep our love in fine fettle?"

"Yes, that too."

"So much for the Amalfi Coast."

"The Tyrrhenian Sea! Bah! All the fashionable Scottsdale couples spend the holidays in the Mule Mountains."

"Well, I guess if all the hip White Liberals are doing it."

"Black Liberals, too, Abigail. I don't want you to feel left out."

"How thoughtful. Ok, let's go to Bisbee."

After they'd driven through the mountain tunnel, the road to Bisbee was all downhill. Charles turned up the radio, intoxicated by the Mingus track playing on KBZB-'The Jazz Spot.' The rhythm of it, the tizzy-and-toot of it, made him step on the gas. He liked jazz. It made him feel cool and was an unspoken pre-requisite for dating Abigail. Her father—the Pastor Bartholomew Sutton of the First Fellowship Baptist Church of North Dorchester—had had a hard enough time dealing with the fact that Charles was white. It helped that he liked jazz.

"Look at this splendor," he said. "I mean, have you ever seen such beautiful scenery?"

"I can't hear a word you're saying," said Abigail.

"Red hills, blue skies, air like wine. It's like a postcard from heaven."

"What did you say?"

"I said, ain't it heaven," said Charles, lowering the volume.

"Yes, it's nice."

"Nice? Nice is the duck pond in Bainbridge Park. This is fucking sublime!"

"If you say so," said Abigail. "Wake me when we get there."

Strange Fruit— a ghostly dirge for lynched black men—came on the radio and Charles casually turned up the dial.

"I love this song," said Charles. "The way Billie sings it, it's like she's singing to me."

"You do know what that song's about, right?" said Abigail. Her eyes were closed.

"It's a protest song against racism, based on the poem by Abel Meeropol—"

"Yes, but do you know what that song's about?"

"It's about the horrors of lynching in the South—"

"It's a prayer in the dark. She's singing to my grandfather Leopold who left Polk County, Florida in 1935 for a better life in Boston."

Charles nodded, a little embarrassed, and quickly changed the subject.

"We're here," he said.

He parked on Howell Ave. in front of the hotel. Their car, a new Subaru—Charles called it a 'Japanese Volvo'—was powdered over in red fairy dust from the drive in. Seeing this as she got out of the car Abigail couldn't help but write on the windshield:

Help! I've been kidnapped! Check the trunk!

"Very funny," said Charles. "Trust me, you're going to love it here."

Charles wheeled the luggage up the crooked, green steps and into the hotel lobby, which looked like it did in 1902. It smelled musty, the odor of decay, of dead things.

"Welcome to the Copper King Hotel," said the clerk. "Do you have a reservation?"

"Yes. For Charles Ingram, Esq."

The clerk glanced curiously at Abigail, then back at Charles as if they were a pair of different colored socks.

"We have you in the Honeymoon Suite for two nights. Credit card and driver's license."

Charles handed him his AMEX and ID.

"Are the border towns safe at night?" he asked.

"Depends on the town. Lukeville's ok. Naco not so much."

"Ok, well who's playing in The Saloon tonight?"

"The Snooker Quartet."

"Any good?"

"If you like jazz."

"Who doesn't?"

Abigail's hand went up.

"Bah! Let's get a cocktail, see for ourselves if the Snookers have got the goods."

Charles signed the hotel register and was handed a room key.

"The bellhop can get these, right?" he asked, pointing to the luggage.

"Of course. Enjoy yourselves," said the clerk, gesturing to The Saloon.

"Come now Abigail. It's jazz night at the Copper King Hotel."

The bar was an eclectic dive—1960's London posh lounge chairs, a velvet painting of a naked waif waltzing with a well-hung satyr in a medieval forest, a black and white Philco TV anchored to the wall above the bar, and an All-American, red, white and blue Tiffany inspired Pabst Blue Ribbon neon chandelier. And despite the city ordinance banning smoking in public establishments (a sign on the wall read, if you're smoking you better be on fire) there was smoke everywhere. Light jazz, the boozy Snooker Quartet in the dimly-lit corner of the bar, played a so-so rendition of 'Take the A Train', while the singer— an aging sex pot in a black sequin gown—took a break, sipped her whisky sour.

Locals and regulars—real open range cowboys in dusty Stetsons, bikers, The Desert Huns in their leathers, off-duty border patrolmen, resident artists and secret serial killers alike—held dominion over the bar, so Charles and Abigail sat at a high-top table near the jazz quartet and waited for the waitress to come around.

"What's the verdict?" said Abigail. "Are they innovators or appropriators?"

Charles looked at the band, saw that they were all white musicians, except for the drummer, who looked to be part black, but it was hard to tell in the poor light.

"The drummer's good," he said. "As for the others, it's too soon to tell."

The waitress came spryly from behind the bar—Miss Bisbee 1955, busty, red-dyed bouffant hair-do, candy apple lips and cat-eye glasses—and b-lined to the young tourist couple.

"Welcome lovers," she said. "Name's Gayle. How are you tonight?"

"Pretty good," said Charles.

"Where you kids from?"

"Scottsdale."

"Nice. Staying awhile or just trucking?"

"We're honeymooning," said Abigail, winking at Charles. "Just here for the weekend."

"Congrats! Champagne?"

"Craft beer, whatever you got on tap," said Charles.

"A glass of chardonnay," said Abigail.

"Got it. Be back in a jif."

The waitress returned with their drinks.

"Say," said Charles. "Is this place really haunted?"

"Sure is," she said. "Haven't you seen America's Most Haunted Hotels on TV? The Copper King's top of the pops. It's silly with spooks."

"You ever seen a ghost?"

"All the time. Which room are you staying in?"

"We're in 252."

"Old Mrs. McCrery died of consumption in that room in 1907. You're definitely going to see ghosts tonight."

"That's great Gayle," said Abigail. "We're going to need a few more rounds to make it through the night."

"I'll keep them coming," said Gayle.

She scuttled back to the bar to tame the horde of thirsty regulars.

"To us," said Charles, raising his glass to toast.

"Next year in New England," said Abigail.

The jazz quartet broke into a half decent interpretation of 'My Funny Valentine.'

"Want to dance?" said Charles.

Abigail nodded, went to get up, then looked coyly over her shoulder at the rabble of drinkers at the bar, thought better of it and sat back down.

"What? Them?" said Charles. "Come on, don't mind them. Let's dance."

"I don't know. I feel funny," she said.

"Funny how?"

"Funny, like a mouse in a room of cats."

"Stop it. It's fine. You're fine. Trust me."

"Is that what you tell clients, Mr. Public Defender, so they'll go along with a plea deal?"

"No, it's what I tell my beautiful girlfriend so she'll dance with me."

"Fine," said Abigail. "But I won't enjoy it."

They were good dancers from dancing late nights at the Ironwood Country Club in Phoenix, and moved as best they could in the tight corner. The spot-light shining on the singer cut across Abigail's pretty face, and ran the length of her long legs as they spun slowly across the little makeshift dance floor. He held her close, and started to say, "You make me smile with my heart" when someone at the bar shouted, "Hey! Negro!"

Charles had heard the word before, a palindrome sounding the same way backwards as forwards, in all of its ignorant iterations—once while visiting the Maricopa County jail, an inmate or a guard, he wasn't sure which, had shouted the N-word from the upper tier as he exited a client's cell. Another time while driving cross country through the Deep South, a white lady in a Piggly Wiggly parking lot in Hattiesburg, Mississippi had said the word nonchalantly, as if she were saying good morning. But he'd never heard it quite like this, under these circumstances, while dancing with his lovely African-American girlfriend. The only constant was the visceral reaction he had upon hearing it. It was the same every time—a deep, mournful, sickening feeling. They kept dancing, but Charles was a little lighter on his feet now, weighed down by the feeling.

"Did you hear that?" he asked.

"Yes I heard it," said Abigail. "Let it go. We're guests here."

"Guests, are we? Well, so much for small town hospitality."

"Come on," she said, leading him off the dance floor. "Let's just go up to our room."

He wanted to do as she asked, but was grappling with self-loathing for being white. But he wasn't like the others. Years ago, during a sidebar with a judge in a racially charged trial, the Phoenix District Attorney had pointed accusingly at Charles and said, 'You got a real quixotic sense of social justice, Ingram. I think you read one too many Civil Rights briefs during law school.' If that didn't absolve him for being white he didn't know what would.

"Aren't we good Americans?" he said.

"Yes," said Abigail. "But not tonight. Let's go."

"Fine," he said. "But I'm having one more drink."

"Charles don't! Whatever you're thinking of doing, it's not worth it. Let's just go."

"One more drink," he said, handing her the room key. "Go upstairs. I'll be right up."

"I swear to God," she said, grabbing her purse.

"Don't be mad," he said, but she was already gone, the rickety saloon doors swinging to a standstill.

Charles went to the end of the scuffed, mahogany bar and didn't try in the least to get the bartender's attention. He didn't want a drink. He wanted living proof of the ghost who'd shrieked while he slow-danced with his girlfriend. He wanted to confront it and tell it to go to hell. It was still here, hanging back invisibly on a wonky stool and, like all apparitions, would make its presence known when least expected.

In the corner, the jazz quartet was wrapping up its set, an up-tempo rendition of 'Black Orpheus.' It sounded good to Charles. Forgetting that the place was haunted, he tapped lightly on the brass foot rest.

"They play pretty good," said Charles to the white guy sitting next to him—a pock-faced, middle-aged man with a crew-cut and coke-bottle glasses. He looked like a permanent fixture, installed back in the 1950's.

"Yea," said the regular, not looking at Charles. "They're okay. The other night they had a bluegrass band in here. They were something special."

"You from here?" asked Charles.

"Yea, over on Sieling Loop."

"How do you like Bisbee?"

"This town suits me fine," said the regular.

From the pocket of his red flannel shirt the regular drew a crumpled pack of Red 72s and lit up.

"I used to live up around Apache Flats," he said. "But I like it better in Bisbee. You can do what you like. Everybody minds their own goddamn business. People don't bother you, much."

"Sounds nice," said Charles.

"Yea," said the regular.

Suddenly remembering why he was here, Charles turned and scanned the bar, looked at all of the faces—the tough and rutted, mad, guileful, oblivious, high-spirited faces—and wondered, what does a racist look like anyway? He could not answer the question and decided to mind his own business and go up to his hotel room. He waved the bartender over to settle the tab.

"If you're waiting on Sam," said the regular. "You're going home sober. I've been waiting here for about an hour."

"Sorry, what?" said Charles.

"Sam's a shitty bartender," the regular explained, pointing to the end of the bar, where the pony-tailed barman was engrossed in the classified ads of The Bisbee Observer.

"It's alright," said Charles. "I was just leaving."

"Not until you wet your whistle," he insisted. "Come on now, Skeeter."

The regular pounded his fist on the bar and yelled across The Saloon.

"Hey Sam," he said. "Get off your ass and pour me another drink!"

The bartender looked up annoyed from his want-ads.

"Calm your ponies, Jeff," he said. "I'll be right there."

"Come on," shouted the regular. "Pour me another Negro!"

The word didn't register right away or rather Charles wasn't automatically triggered by it. It was as if his brain had released a heavy dose of opiate to deaden the sound and dull the subsequent perception of disgust and anger he felt when he heard it. But it wore off.

The bartender shuffled to the taps and poured a tall glass of dark stout from a homemade, black-face tap handle. A modern-day, antebellum relic fashioned by an ignorant brewer in some local, homespun brewery. Charles had seen this apparition before, ads with the same face, racist Americana in The Saturday Evening Post, circa 1930. Darkie Toothpaste with monofluoro phosphate. Uncle Remus Brand Syrup. N-Boy's King Sized Licorice Cigarettes. Popularized by appropriators, white minstrel men in dark face. Here it was again. Sudden as an Asphyxiant, the feeling rose up in him again, and he could think of only one thing to suppress it. He wanted to object, like the good public defender that he was, but didn't quite know who to address in that moment, turning first to the regular sitting next to him, then to the bartender, and lastly to his own white, perplexed reflection in the tarnished, antique mercury mirror behind the bar. Speechless and defenseless, he retreated to the corner, to the high-top by the jazz quartet.

It was late and Abigail was rightly furious by now. He reached into the pocket of his sports jacket, pulled out a leather billfold, took out a crisp fifty-dollar banknote, laid it on the table top for the waitress and got up to go. But something wouldn't let him. He needed to make sense of what had happened so he could make things right.

"Excuse me," he said, turning to the jazz singer who was perched precariously on a high-top stool, hitching up her black silk stockings.

"Yes," she said, her voice raspy from cigarettes.

"Could you play a song for me?"

"What'd you have in mind, flutter bum?"

"Strange Fruit," said Charles.

The jazz singer gasped.

"Oh no, I couldn't sing that," she said.

"Do you know it?"

"Well yes, of course I know it," she said. "But I just can't sing it. It's too dark. Sorry, it'd kill the mood in here."

"Thank you all the same," said Charles.

Turning to go, he suddenly stopped and stared out the large, plate-glass window of The Saloon, at the flickering lights of this little desert town.

"Ain't it heaven, though," he said.

Closing his eyes, he felt hot tears streaming down his face, felt a humming deep down inside of his chest. It started way down low, then came welling up, loud vibrations resonating in his throat, becoming words. He was singing now, a protest song for Abigail, at the top of his lungs, with everything that he had in his paladin heart.

"Southern trees bear strange fruit, blood on the leaves and blood at the root, black bodies swinging in the Southern breeze, strange fruit hanging from the poplar trees ..."

About the Author:

Alberto Ramirez graduated from UCLA with a degree in English literature. He has contributed work to Westwind Journal of the Arts, Angel City Review, Drabblez Magazine and LossLit Magazine UK. He is the author of the novel Everything That Could Not Happen Will Happen Now (Floricanto Press 2016), selected by Las Comadres and Friends National Latino Book Club summer reading list 2017.

SORTING THROUGH CLAMS
by David Weinberger

I am sitting next to my father's bed as he sleeps. He is ten days into Hospice care and has become frail since he discontinued treatment for his cancer. I never thought I would find myself staring remorsefully at the man who sometimes treated me so unkindly. His belt would swing, his words would slay, and I would cower in his shadow. And yet, there must have been more because I ache with the thought of losing him.

I take his small, wrinkled, and wiry hand in mine and try to remember that it belongs to my father. I run two fingers across the top of his hand, feeling mostly loose skin and pronounced veins, up his bruised forearm and bicep, and to his shoulder. All are withered and weak and I struggle to make a connection to the vigorous father I knew one August day thirty years ago when he took me out with him on his clamming boat.

On that day, my father raked the bay floor with short pulls and shorter releases. He occasionally let me pull the rake and I felt the floor violently tugging against my efforts. As a diminutive ten-year old, I was not equipped to pull a thirty-pound rake filled with clams, but my father let me continue for a bit, a sly smile on his face as he watched me struggle. After a few inefficient pulls, my father took over and then hauled the rake up hand over hand on the pole, pulled the rake above board and dumped the catch onto the cull racks.

My father was not always a clammer; he held odd jobs for decades before he discovered his true calling. His last job before clamming was as a manager of a rental store where one day he rented equipment to a clammer. They became friends and this friend talked my father into giving up the rental store and starting a new career.

Over the next four weeks, my father outfitted himself with the necessary tools of the trade: boat, steel rakes, aluminium poles, cull racks, and bushel baskets. He purchased new clothes for himself too: an accepted clamming uniform of sorts. Wool cap, knee-high waterproof boots, rain gear, jeans, T-shirts, and flannel shirts. On weekends, he would lay out all the equipment in the front yard and do an inventory to see what he still needed. My siblings and I would swing on the tire swing and watch him check each piece and listen to him ignore our constant questions concerning the equipment. That was not uncommon in our home: my father didn't really speak to us much, regardless of what we were doing. Even though he did not talk during his inventories, I thought it was fun to see him lay it all out, like laying out my GI Joes or Matchboxes to see how the collections were growing.

The largest part of the equipment parked in the driveway, the boat, was actually small and beat up, and I thought, not very fancy or trustworthy. My father repaired it, painted it gray and red, and to my surprise, it was soon ready for the Great South Bay. He got clamming lessons and advice from his rental friend, quit his job at the store, and became a clammer.

It was difficult from the beginning, both in terms of the back-breaking and repetitive work and especially when it came to providing financially for a family of seven people; the commute was long and expensive, he did not make much money, and he was away from home most of the day. But it became easier with experience and as he became more familiar with the better clamming spots, buoy placement, and other tricks of the trade.

After about two years, my father felt comfortable enough on his boat out in the water that he thought it might be enjoyable to bring his kids along for a day of clamming. This was a surprise to me because none of us kids seemed to have a very close relationship with him. We talked and played mostly with my mother, helped her with housework and groceries, shared our problems with her and cried in her embrace. My father was never a part of these activities. He simply seemed to bring money home and discipline us when things went wrong. It was like we were strangers to one another.

It was also clear to me that my father didn't need any help on his boat; he was much too independent for help. At home, help meant finding a missing tool, or handing the right tool at the right time; he never let us do anything that I found meaningful, like hammering in a nail, securing a bolt on the boat, or cutting a piece of wood. If we asked him for help, like with a Wood Derby car or a plastic model, he would usually do the job himself rather than teaching us how to do it ourselves. In spite of these misgivings, I thought that, perhaps, time on the boat with one of his kids may have been his way of getting to know us a little better.

And although we didn't really understand or feel close to our father, we looked forward to these clamming outings: a day off from school, in a boat, alone with our father clamming. We waited impatiently for our turn to come and we were always ecstatic when it came. I was confused as to whether the excitement of working with my father was because I was missing out on a day of school, the imagined fun of clamming, or maybe just being singled out in a large family felt good. It could easily have been finally getting to see that friendly seagull that my father fed on a daily basis and which he constantly talked about.

But it was not all unbridled excitement. I waited my turn with trepidation. I worried about what we would talk about, if we talked at all. I did not know if we would get along all day on the small boat. When my father was at home, an exchange between us was more likely to be an argument than a conversation, a slap rather than a hug. Still, the worry I had was not enough to keep me from anticipating an outing.

When my turn finally came, my father woke me in the morning and it was difficult to find the excitement from the night before: it was early and I still wanted to sleep. My father was wearing his normal clamming clothing. I had the same outfit, prepared by my mother, except with Toughskins instead of Levis, but I was happy I would be wearing my father's clamming uniform. We grabbed our coats, loaded the Suburban, and drove off to Bayview Harbor in Bay Shore. Not a word was spoken between us during this one-hour drive; I thought that I would be good company on the drive but I probably slept most of the way. When we got to Bay Shore, it was dawn, with soft light and a thin fog all around. It was spooky walking out onto the dock to get to the boat, with the strange surroundings in the boat yard and harbor: a rusty sign swinging above a dilapidated door to a small dark building, a mangy dog sleeping in the shadows under an upturned boat, lobster pots stacked all over hiding who knew what, fishing nets strewn here and there. All mysteriously blanketed by fog. My father simply carried out his job and did not seem at all bothered by the spookiness, or notice that I was scared.

Once the boat was loaded, the motor warmed up, and the boat inched out of the slip, I started feeling better. We rounded the bulkhead and I could see the distant bay with fog covering the surface. My father said the fog would be gone by daylight, and later it turned out he was right.

Right away I was in awe of the bay: the grand houses along the coast that I could barely see through the fog, the feel of the boat motoring into the flat, glassy bay. I sat on the floor, leaning against the console while my father stood behind the console steering the boat. I was amazed that he knew where he was going, because of the fog and because the bay seemed like one big open space void of any bearings. Within an hour, we were at the first buoys. I asked when the friendly seagull would show up. He told me not to worry because he would definitely show up around lunchtime. Before the arrival of the seagull, however, it was time to work.

We grabbed baskets, cull racks, and nylon mesh sacks from the cabinet built into the bow. My father started with a six-foot pole section which ended in a T-handle, connected several pole sections together, and then attached the clam rake to the last pole section. He lifted the heavy rake over the side of the boat and let it drop into the bay. I watched the pole disappear in the water as he lowered it hand over hand to the bay floor. Once the rake had sunk into the muddy sand, he started raking. I could not help but stare at my father's muscular forearms and biceps; I had never noticed them before. I guessed that years of clamming had built up quite a bit of muscle. I compared them to my puny arms and wondered if they would ever grow to look like his.

He used those muscles to pull the rake back out of the water, reversing the hand over hand motion he had used before. When he reached the rake filled with the catch, he dumped the contents onto the cull racks, four racks stacked on top of one another, each having different sized gaps to catch different sized clams. My father then gave me a lesson on sorting since I would be in charge of it throughout the day. We started the sort by cleaning out anything that was not a clam. At the time, the early seventies, the bay was still full of diverse life: lobsters, oysters, and horseshoe crabs. Some, like lobster, he kept for family meals, the rest were put back in the bay. We also sorted out the plastic and empty glass bottles that were pulled up. These we put in a garbage bag and left at the harbor.

Once the racks were clear of non-clam items, we shook them so the clams either fell through the gaps or nestled between the rods, separating the clams according to size: little necks fell to the bottom rack, top necks the next, then cherrystones, and finally, the larger chowders in the top rack. We put each sized clam into a separate bushel basket and I watched the baskets fill up throughout the day. When the baskets were full we dumped them into nylon mesh bags. We dumped the smaller clams, the ones that fell through all the racks, back into the bay so they could live to maturity and supply the next generation of clams. We drifted lazy circles around the buoy for a while going through the same work motions: dropping the rake, raking, lifting the rake, dumping, sorting, and beginning again.

After clamming for about an hour, we motored to the next set of buoys and the same work began again. The morning hours passed in this manner, raking, motoring, raking, motoring. The fog had lifted exposing a clear blue sky and a bright sun high in the sky. I sat with my father and we ate lunch. It was the identical lunch that I took to school, peanut butter and jelly sandwich, a piece of fruit, a Hostess Ding Dong, but it tasted better on the boat. My father put a piece of his sandwich on the bow of the boat and a seagull landed and started eating the sandwich. Finally, the famous seagull he always talked about. The seagull did not leave with the sandwich, but instead, ate it on the boat, as if he were an invited guest to a special luncheon. With my eternal doubt, I asked my father how he knew it was the same seagull each day and not just one of the dozens that happened to be around. He laughed at my doubting and claimed that it was the same one, that he could tell by the coloring on the wings. I wanted to believe him because it was a cool story but I doubted that it was the same seagull or that he could tell the difference; he might know about clams but I did not think he knew anything about birds.

After lunch, the rest of the day was spent in the same repetitious manner, with an occasional visit from another clammer to discuss where it was 'hot' on the bay, who was working on the water that day, or what the weather had in store. When the clamming was done for the day and the clams were bagged up, we took the boat to Lincoln Harbor to sell the clams. We pulled up to the dock, unloaded the bags of clams, and climbed out of the boat. The man at the counter weighed the bags and paid my father in cash. It seemed like a lot of money but even with my young eyes I could see how hard my father had worked for it.

We climbed back into the boat and began the long cruise back to Bay Shore. I fell asleep listening to the whine of the motor and when I woke up, my father was unloading the boat and locking tools back in the bow. I helped carry the few remaining items to the Suburban and we headed home.

On the way, instead of sleeping, I stared out the window going over the day. My father and I both smelled of the bay and especially of clams. The job of sorting clams was exhausting over a long day, and a bit slimy and frightening with all those claws that frequently appeared. It was, however, certainly easier than pulling a full clamming rake. I looked at my father driving. He was whistling a tune we used to sing at home. He seemed very happy. I smiled because of that. If I had already learned to whistle, I would have whistled along with him.

About the Author:

David H Weinberger is an American author writing in Berlin, Germany. His stories have appeared in Thrice Fiction, Fredericksburg Literary and Art Review, The Ravens Perch, Gravel, and elsewhere. He holds a Master's Degree in Early Childhood Education and taught kindergarten for eight years in Salt Lake City, Utah.

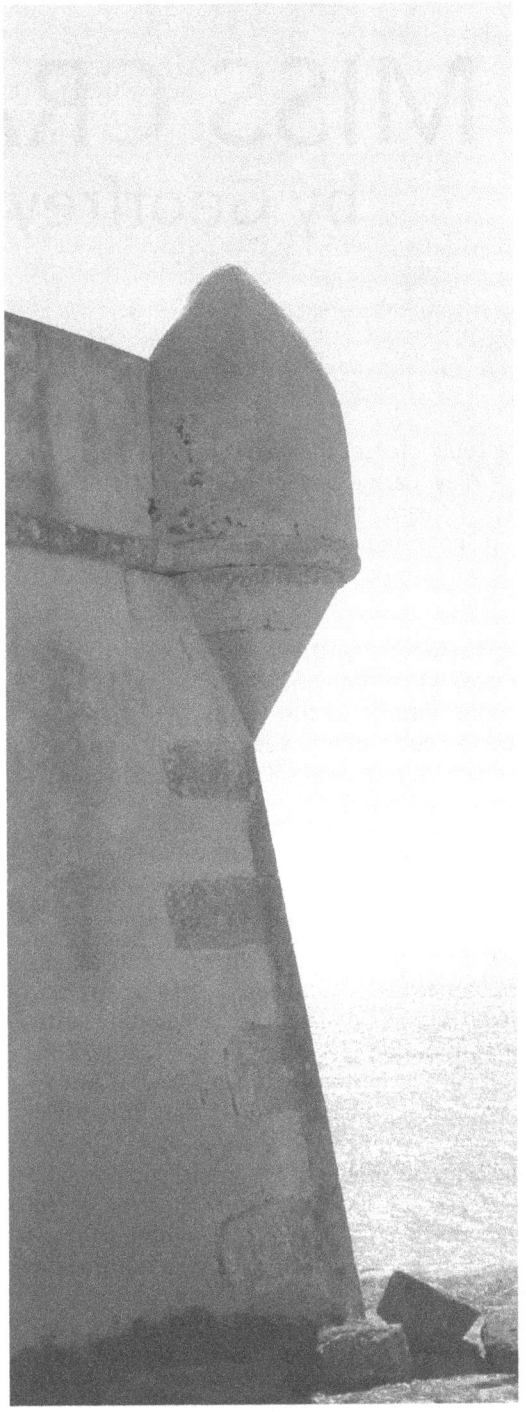

MISS CRAMICKLE
by Geoffrey Heptonstall

ONE

How could I forget the year we were taught by Miss Amy Carmichael? I ask myself this because I heard news of her yesterday. How could I not remember her? But the reply comes back, why would I want to remember Miss Carmichael?

One afternoon there was commotion outside the class when someone went crazy and began shouting threats to the world. We all recognized the voice of Heywood Bennett, the dentist's son who, it was said, took cocaine from his father's surgery.

It was not long before the noise faded as Heywood was taken away. We cheered until Miss Carmichael restored order.

'Well, if we may continue with your education,' Miss Carmichael announced, 'I shall attempt to answer Lauren's question. If you would like to repeat it, Lauren, because I'm sure that by now we all have forgotten what you asked. It was to do with Shakespeare, I think. You see, I did hear you, although there were some distractions both outside and within the room itself.' She paused to look about her as if trying to locate the source of her cold irritation. 'Yes, Nathan, I also mean you and your partner in crime, Miss Angelica Levine.' There was a murmur going round the room. Nathan blushed and Miss Carmichael smiled in victory. 'I'm sorry, Lauren, please go on.'

It was Lauren I remember most of all. Long, straight hair a dark red that appealed to me, although I told myself that nothing about Lauren appealed to me.

Miss Carmichael was talking about Shakespeare, although the book we had on our desks was Moby Dick.

'Well, I don't rem...' Lauren stumbled.

TWO

'Lauren, I believe you asked a question,' Miss Carmichael began again, knowing perfectly that Lauren had asked a question. There was no need for Miss Carmichael to state her belief. It was a fact that Lauren had asked a question. But Miss Carmichael liked to decorate her sentences with elegant formalities, thinking they lent dignity. 'It was,' she added, 'a very interesting question.' Now, that was stated as a fact, but it was Miss Carmichael's belief.

'Lauren,' Miss Carmichael continued, 'Lauren asked if Shakespeare was the author of the plays that bear his name. Now, I find that a truly interesting question. So what do you think?'

She looked at the class with an expression that urgently sought to instill interest. It was a rare time I saw Miss Carmichael vulnerable. In my young wisdom I observed with sadness and glee the desperation that shadowed the life of a teacher of a class like ours. Her life was surely a constant disappointment. What did we think? We did not think anything of questions about the authorship of Shakespeare.

The breeze blew outside, causing the trees to stir. Looking out at the grey sky, we who had lived in this place all our lives recognized the signs of an approaching storm. The weather was more interesting than Miss Carmichael's question. We were thinking also of Heywood

Bennett on his way to hospital where we thought he belonged.

'I don't believe he did.' Lauren replied. 'Because, like, there was this one guy and he wrote so much. And, I mean, really?'

Oh no. But oh yes, this was an opportunity for Miss Carmichael to stand at the lectern and instruct the thousands, if not millions, of her assembled devotees attending on her every word.

THREE

'Well' she began, 'we are confronted with the nature of genius. Shakespeare was one of those rare human beings who can do so much, who can live several lives. Like Leonardo. It is genius. That's all we can say really.'

But it was not all Miss Carmichael had to say on the subject. No, once she had started she found there was always more to say. And then more after that. 'You know, class, if life has taught me one thing it's that there are men and women of genius. They are rare. They walk among us, but we barely notice them. They do not look any different from the rest of us. They do not speak any differently from you and me. But we may see the difference if we look carefully because inside their heads are the differences, the unfathomable, perplexing, marvelous differences that great minds can make in their contribution to the world.'

She paused as if for applause. There was a bored silence, which Miss Carmichael mistook for appreciation, before Lauren spoke. 'To be or not to be. Like, is that genius or just words?'

'That is for you to decide, Lauren,' Miss Carmichael replied in terms of admonition that she would swear was praise.

'Isn't it for you to tell me, Miss Carmichael?' Lauren replied more boldly than anybody else would have dared.

'OK. It is genius,' Miss Carmichael said in a voice that was holding back its irritation.

Lauren persisted, dangerously so, I thought. We all thought the same. You could hear the mind of the whole class begging Lauren to be careful. 'I mean, why?' Lauren asked.

'That's for you to discover, Lauren,' Miss Carmichael repeated.

'It's asking an awful lot of me. I mean, have you ever actually met a genius, Miss Carmichael?'

'Well, here I am,' Ed Garman interjected.

FOUR

Lauren had a response ready for that. She did not like Ed Garman. Nobody liked him, not even Ed Garman. 'Miss Carmichael, should animals be allowed in this room?' Lauren asked facetiously. She was furious that Ed had ruined her moment of challenge. It was to be heroic time, and, jerk that he surely was, had undermined it.

'So I guess there's really no room for you, Lauren,' Ed replied. Nobody laughed. It was not funny. Nothing Ed Garman said was funny even when it was funny, or would have been funny coming out of a less stupid mouth.

Miss Carmichael took control of the situation again. The tension having eased thanks to Ed Garman's untimely intervention, the teacher could command the class once more. 'To answer your question, Lauren, no, I have not met anyone I could call a genius. At least, I don't think so. But I know that if ever I do I hope I shall recognize the genius, or potential genius, within that person. I expect it will happen someday. Maybe tomorrow. Who knows? Or maybe it was yesterday?'

'I don't believe in genius,' Lauren murmured.

'Lauren, my dear girl, you don't have to see what you don't want to see. You don't have to believe anything you don't feel is right. And you don't have to do anything to please me except to be yourself.' Miss Carmichael's final flourish was her moment of generosity and wisdom worthy of Benjamin Franklin [had it been expressed sincerely]. Nothing Miss Carmichael said was generous or wise even when it was so.

Lauren looked like she had nothing further to say. She knew she was beaten. And I felt so sorry for her, truly sorry because her attempt to pin Miss Carmichael down had gone so screwy.

'I really,' Lauren began uncertainly, 'Like, I really don't have anything more to say Miss Carmichael.'

FIVE

It began to rain. I heard the distant sound of the water moving across the whole earth. And we were like creatures of the deep. We went down in the darkness not from choice, not from sense but from an instinct, creatures of the deep that we are.

Miss Carmichael smiled. It was similar to the smile on her face when a younger kid came in one day with a message for 'Miss Cramickle.' The class tried not to laugh. Miss Carmichael smiled her cold smile of superiority that told the world it was stupider than she.

'Class, OK now. I'd like you to pay attention. Let me read you something. And I want you all to pay attention, including you, Nancy. I said, including you, Nancy. Thank you. When you're all quite ready, Arnold, I want you to hear something written by Herman Melville. Now, you all know he wrote Moby Dick. Right? But this is not from Moby Dick. This passage will be a preparation for our study of that masterpiece of our literature. And if you never get round to really understanding this great narrative of the sea , well, at least you will carry through your lives something of the genius, and yes, I say genius, of Herman Melville.'

Miss Carmichael cleared her throat before she began reading from an essay of Melville's on the South Seas. 'In many places the coast is rock-bound....Those parts of the strand free from the marks of fire stretch away in wide level beaches of multitudinous dead shells, with here and there, decayed bits of sugar cane, bamboo and coconuts, washed upon this other and darker world from the charming palm isles to the westward and southward, all the way from Paradise and Tartarus.'

She stopped for a moment of deeper thought that it was her intention to stir in us. Some hope. 'Isn't that beautiful,' Miss Carmichael asked. 'An evocation of a distant shore, of somewhere wild, unknown? Doesn't it stir in you a desire to go out there and find that freedom for yourself?'

SIX

Nobody said a word. This was a class of silences that said so much. We believed Miss Carmichael never heard what we were saying in our silence.

'No, maybe not. OK, you can go now.'

When everybody was out of the room Miss Carmichael spoke to rows of empty desks that did not move and did not speak. I was tying my shoelace in the corridor outside, so I had lingered, and now could hear every word Miss Carmichael was saying. 'Nobody is ever listening to a word anybody says. Certainly nobody ever listens to me. So that you could say my life is a failure. That would be true. But everybody else's life is a failure, too. So I'm in good company. I am in that respect unexceptional. In most other respects, however, I am exceptional.

'So, my dear students, you are so very lucky to be taught by me. And, although you are not listening and have no intentions of ever listening, you can say in later life that you were taught by somebody whose words you never appreciated yet now you know them to be wise. Except that you can't remember for the life of you what those words were. And with that pleasant thought, class dismissed for the summer. Somebody else will be instructing you in the wisdom of the world, for in the fall I shall be long gone from here and from the sight of so many uninterested and uninteresting faces. Thank you. Thank you so much. Your indifference means so much to me.'

Miss Carmichael walked towards the open door. She looked embarrassed when she caught sight of me, for she knew I had heard clearly everything she had said. It was not so much the content that embarrassed her as the fact that she had been overheard talking to nobody.

That nobody was me. She had been talking to me.

SEVEN

'Miss Carmichael,' I said.

Miss Carmichael stood at the open door of her room. To counter her embarrassment, and to shame me, she began to speak softly, as if to herself, although it was not to anybody except me. I was intended to learn and to remember that Miss Carmichael was not the bloodless machine we took her to be. She had feelings within her that she could rarely, if ever, express to a class of teenagers who considered her a diversion in the routine of their high school days.

'The young. Hmmm,' she began. 'Yes, the young. You. That girl – Lauren. So many young people. So many.' What was she saying? What did she mean? 'The young. And we are the old. Not so old but old. Mad and wise, but old. Melville will explain it all. I can't tell you how important that book is, and not just to me. It is written for future generations. It's written for the whole world. For everyone. The whole goddam beautiful world. Such a beautiful, beautiful world.'

That left me with the choice to turn away in contempt or to admit my own embarrassment. I recalled Lauren with her swish of dark red hair, feeling so animated when she challenged the knowledgeable and superior Miss Carmichael. Lauren had come alive. I had not seen her so spirited before. The veneer of cynical indifference had fallen away in her desire to speak her mind and not the words that others had written for her. As she spoke her body gave out such energy that I thought she might rise out of her chair and fly. I knew it was the way Lauren felt too.

Therefore I could never forgive Miss Carmichael her crushing of Lauren's eager, young spirit. I cannot forgive her now as I write this recollection of an afternoon one early summer the year we were being taught by Miss Carmichael.

EIGHT

That Lauren seemed to recover is incidental. Nobody ever recovers from anything, do they? You think they do. Well, think again. Think of Lauren going home, unusually subdued. Think of Lauren at home that evening, tense quarrelsome or anxious. Think of Lauren forever avoiding Moby Dick, for ever going silent when the word genius was mentioned at any place and at any time.

The young. Hmmm. The young. What did Miss Carmichael know about being young?

'I don't believe I'm an angel,' Miss Carmichael said before I turned away. I felt neither contempt nor shame, just confusion. 'No, I'm not an angelic being. But neither are you.'

'What does that mean?' I asked, turning back as I was intended to turn.

'It means that we are both human. You may think you know that already. But it takes a long time before we understand inside ourselves what it means to be human.'

This confirmed for me what I had suspected for a long time. I saw how crazy Miss Carmichael was. At the age I was then crazy old people elicited no sympathy from me. Today I see that she was lonely, sad and desperate. All that was distilled into one word. Crazy.

She had more to say of course. It was more rambling to nobody in particular. 'There are those who deny what is natural. They think themselves above nature. Oh, they have done with all that. They have made their own world. Their creation is greater than anything in nature.'

What was she saying? I could not understand her reason for saying this strange thing. Why speak to me like this? 'I want you to understand. You above everyone must understand. We have to recognize we are part of nature. We are not fully alive if we fail to acknowledge this. It's not an opinion, by the way. It's a universal truth. How do you explain life without an acceptance of the truth that we are part of nature?'

NINE

'Miss Carmichael...' I began. She was not listening.

'Sometimes,' she began, 'you know, sometimes I feel that if we look back we can see the city on the horizon. You know that? If we looked out west we could see the city. I know it's impossible, but you look east you can see the Mayflower. That was only a moment ago. Look closely and you can see the history of the world. You can the formation of the continents, the evolution of life, the first word of Creation.'

Miss Carmichael, I really have to go now.'

'Stay and feel the rhythm of the world as it turns,' she replied. 'You think I'm crazy? I know you do, and maybe you're right, but I'm crazy about the things that matter. That is difficult for you to understand, I think.'

'No, I think I do,' I said, trying hard to understand.

'I think not,' Miss Carmichael retorted, always determined to have the last word. It did not have to be the right word, but it had to be the final, determining pronouncement that would settle everything to her satisfaction, and silence all further objections to her point of view. That was how she had lived her life.

'You know what, Miss Carmichael,' I emboldened myself to say out loud, 'you have no goddam right to tell anybody, including all of us, what we know, think or understand. Because our minds are ours, not yours. And you ought to respect that.'

There was an inevitable silence. Finally she spoke in reply. 'I shall pretend I did not hear that.'

'That's your choice, Miss Carmichael. It's the choice you've always made.'

'I'm going to report this. Curse words, insolence and a threatening manner. You are going to be in serious trouble, young man. Let me assure you of that. And before you say

TEN

anything further, my word will count for much, much more than yours. May I remind you who I am?'

'You are Crazy Miss Cramickle,' I reminded her, and walked away. It was the last day of school for the summer. It was the last time we were taught by Miss Carmichael. She was to become a distant figure for what remained of our high school years.

I spent the summer mostly with Lauren. We never spoke of school much the whole summer. School was out of our minds until September came back like the returning tide on a cold dawn. There was no report, no disciplinary hearing, nothing. Crazy Miss Cramickle kept the conversation to herself. So I was never able to tell the world about her ramblings to an empty room until now.

And now the room of hers is empty for always. Even the echoes and shadows of her presence have faded. Who remembers her but children grown up and long gone from her influence? I can almost hear her voice in the empty room: 'Sometimes I feel that if we look back, you know....'

About the Author:

Author of novel, Heaven's Invention. Several plays performed and/or published. Recent contributions to Bandit Fiction, Fiction Week, the London Magazine, Montreal Review, Poetry Pacific, Scarlet Leaf Review, Sentinel Literary Quarterly.

THE THREE-MILE RACE
by Clive Aaron Gill

Salisbury, Southern Rhodesia, Africa 1959

All year I looked forward to Sports Day at Prince Edward Secondary School.

At the start of the three-miler, I glanced at the winners' podium a few yards away from the finish line, imagining myself on the highest step. As a member of the Churchill Team, I wore a yellow ribbon rosette on my sleeveless undershirt.

A puff of warm wind pushed dry leaves scraping across the track in front of me.

I jogged and skipped, wearing my old tennis shoes with frayed shoelaces, trying to loosen the knot in my stomach.

Rodney, tall and slim with sturdy muscles, was usually the fastest runner, but a week ago, I passed him during a practice run at school. I also ran three miles by myself every weekend for the last month.

Rodney was a member of the Roosevelt Team, and he wore a red rosette. The Churchill and Roosevelt Teams were tied for first place. The winner of the three-miler, the last race of Sports Day, would lead his team to victory. I was determined to be that winner.

The race monitor announced the start of the race and pointed the starting pistol up. "On your marks!"

I spread my hands on the dirt track and took deep breaths. I tried to block everything out of my mind except winning the race.

"Get set!"

I looked in the stands to see if my parents were watching and cheering for me even though I knew they were playing lawn bowls at the Wingate Country Club.

The headmaster and his wife sat with the teachers and office staff, their eyes directed at the contestants.

I saw my English teacher, Mrs. Gerber, who wore dusty glasses, and her 16-year-old son, Sammy, who limped because he had polio when he was eight. They sat in the front row and waved and shouted, "Go Colin. Go Colin. Good luck."

I smiled at them, and for a moment I lost my concentration.

"Bang!" A puff of smoke arose from the starting pistol.

The runners bolted forward ahead of me, and I felt embarrassed to be in the last position.

I remembered my shame at a recent dance party when all the girls I asked to join me on the empty dance floor refused.

The nearest runner ahead of me was Charlie, nicknamed Caboose because he always came last. I ran in long strides that pulled on my quads and hamstrings. My legs felt strong, and a warmth flooded my body as I overtook Caboose.

I caught up to Kenneth, who had a reddish birthmark on the side of his head near his eye, and we raced side by side. Amid the cheering crowd, I heard Mrs. Gerber shout in her high-pitched voice, "Run Colin, run," and I surged past Kenneth.

Rodney was in the lead as I expected. He raced ahead of a cluster of runners, his spike shoes kicking up dirt. He was so far from me that I was reminded of the morning when a current in Cape Town dragged me far out to sea. I struggled in the frigid water to make it back to the beach.

Rodney had a gorgeous girlfriend named Althea. Whenever I saw her, my eyes were drawn to her like a magnet. Rodney and Althea were caught in bed one afternoon by his mother.

A new energy tingled from my feet up my legs. I expanded my chest and tore past Gerald, a skinny, tall boy known as Toothpick, who was breathing hard and wheezing.

I took deeper breaths and my heart hammered.

People shouted, "Go, go, go."

For a few moments, the runners ahead of me seemed to float in slow motion.

Steve, who shared a desk with me in our science class, ran at a fast pace three yards ahead.

Steve, who trained in jiu-jitsu, fought a bully who called me "midget" and "short-ass." That bully left the fight with fewer teeth and never called me names again.

I got a second wind, then dashed past Steve and overtook Fred.

When Fred and I were eight years old, we each pricked one of our fingers and mingled our blood to become blood brothers.

I streaked passed Roy, also known as Baldy because when we changed for athletic exercises we noticed he didn't yet have pubic hair.

Baldy never forgave me after I got sidetracked hunting for birds' eggs and forgot to tell his parents he got stuck in a deep hole where we searched for treasure.

Alan ran in front of me with long strides. He and his family didn't handle money on the Sabbath. He gave me money the day before the championship soccer game so I could buy his ticket on the Sabbath.

I closed in on Alan, but he quickened his pace. While I ran behind him, an intense sense of power flooded within me. I pushed my feet harder off the ground and outdistanced him.

I caught up with Harold, who was gasping. Harold's father was a butcher, and we nicknamed Harold, T-Bone. His family lived in a huge house with a pool and a tennis court that we visited often and named The Club.

I outstripped T-Bone and sped past Edwin. He once threw stones on the tin roof of our house late at night to frighten us until the police arrived to arrest him.

Ahead of me, Gunther slowed, and I ran at a steady pace to pass him. Gunther hid paper money in a book in his father's bookshelf, then couldn't find the money later.

Rodney was the only runner ahead of me. I had to close the gap. I gained on him, running close behind, then we ran side by side, our arms and legs moving in unison. My chest heaved, and I felt as if it would explode as I gasped for air. Sweat dripped into my eyes.

When Rodney ran faster, I had to push myself to keep up. I fought my tiredness to match his pace. Could I pass him? Mrs. Gerber and Sammy wanted me to win. My Churchill teammates needed me to succeed. I couldn't disappoint them. I had to win.

Rodney and I began the last lap together, and the screaming crowd stood.

As we raced around the last bend where no spectators had gathered, Rodney jabbed me in the ribs with his elbow. I tripped and fell with a loud grunt, grazing my face and hands and swallowing dirt.

The runners, including Caboose, rushed past me.

Leaning on my elbow and panting, I tried to get up but swayed as if drunk. I fell, my body shaking.

Rodney ran into the ribbon fluttering at the finish line, and a cheer erupted.

"Get up," someone near me screamed. "Run! Finish the race."

Mrs. Gerber and Sammy stood at the side of the track and pointed at the finish line 100 yards ahead.

I wanted to yell, "The race is over."

"Get up and run," more onlookers yelled.

I struggled to my knees, staring open-mouthed at people who shouted and pointed, my head spinning. I coughed as if something was stuck in my throat.

Walking forward, I stumbled but caught myself from falling. When I saw Mrs. Gerber and Sammy keeping up with me outside the track, tears rolled down my cheeks.

People packed the finish area and cheered for me, almost overwhelming the race monitor. I ran across the finish line and headed towards Rodney, whose proud expression melted into fear. He sprinted away from the track, and I followed him until he left the school grounds.

My legs buckled, and I dropped to my knees. My body shook with sobs and hoarse breaths while I watched Rodney's receding figure.

During the awards for the three-mile race, no-one stood at the winner's position on the podium.

About the Author:

Clive Aaron Gill's short stories have appeared in numerous Internet magazines and in "People of Few Words Anthology."

Born in Zimbabwe, Clive has lived and worked in Southern Africa, North America and Europe. He received a degree in Economics from the University of California, Los Angeles and lives in San Diego.

THE MISSING MASTER
by David McVey

The night before I addressed the conference, I was lying in bed in a tiny room in a Hall of Residence. I picked up my dog-eared copy of McDonnell and began to read.

McDonnell stood in the middle of the street, the fiery background reflected in the filthy pools among the cobbles. The clamour died down; McDonnell, dirty, ill-shod, swathed in poor, tattered rags, looked up at the window. Percival had been looking out at the smoking ruins of his factory, but now turned his gaze on McDonnell's pathetic yet defiant figure. McDonnell, emboldened by the reluctance of the militia to carry out their orders, fixed his gaze on Percival. 'You have lost your factory; you have lost some of your wealth; but you gaze out here on we who have lost everything, rather, who have had everything taken from us. Our dignity, our freedom, our health, our thoughts have been captive while we have toiled and laboured for your mean wages! You have defied God, his Word, decency, justice, fairness. I defy you!'

A thin, pale, bedraggled girl ran to McDonnell in the ensuing hush, and began entreating him to retire to safety. Then both turned to see the militia begin their charge, framed in the fire's ghastly glow.

I stood at the front of the lecture room. Backsides shuffled in seats; a pen clattered onto the tiles. It was time to start.

'James Duncan wrote historical novels after the fashion of Scott, though with a blend of Calvinism and Romance which anticipates Stevenson. He was perhaps the only major Scottish novelist in the period between those two giants, but his most memorable work is unlike anything they produced. McDonnell was the only serious contemporary attempt by a Scottish author to interpret the Industrial Revolution.'

By their faces some of them have never heard of McDonnell, and now they've decided that, because it's not set in London, it's parochial.

'Superficially, it is a lengthy, Dickensian work, employing the familiar thwarted-heir plot. But set in a growing, smoke-blackened Glasgow, a dark pit into which the hope of the working classes is thrown and lost, the novel brings together Irish immigrants, dispossessed Highlanders, rapacious industrialists, and rings with gritty, vibrant Scots dialogue.

'Scottish literature was retreating into a Kailyard haunted by kindly ministers, genial schoolmasters, and mumbling rustics, a world foreign to most Scots. Yet they would recognise the harsh reality of McDonnell; I commend it to you, in closing, as the most neglected great novel of the nineteenth century.'

That shook them; Duncan was harmless when kept in his tartan ghetto, but they resented any attempt to raise him alongside Dickens, Hardy and company. There was polite applause, a handful of desultory questions, and then the lecture-room was empty; I began to stuff my briefcase.

Only Agnes Filey remained. Small and thin and with long straggly grey hair, she was a former colleague who had moved to work in a university down south. Meeting up with her was a pleasure I'd been looking forward to but I didn't feel genial at that moment. She was clearly about to offer me some words of consolation, but I spoke first and snapped, 'That went down like a cold tea-bag, didn't it?'

'You think?'

'I think. They've no interest in Duncan.'

She smiled now, faintly. 'Most of them,' I went on, indicating the empty auditorium with a sweep of my hand, 'have never read any of his stuff, and they won't start now. I might as well have been talking about Desperate Dan.'

Agnes continued to smile and told me she had some news. 'I'm coming back to Scotland, to the University. I just heard about the job this morning.'

'That's brilliant, Agnes! What, back in the department? Senior Lecturer, maybe?'

'No, nothing like that. I just wanted to move back but nobody is taking on lecturers in the arts. I'm to be Academic Liaison Officer with the new Quality Enhancement of Learning and Teaching Team.'

'Oh, hell, yes, the mysterious QuELT.' I remembered the acronym from the subject line of university emails I hadn't opened. 'So, what does your new job involve?'

'I have absolutely no idea,' she laughed, 'They did explain, but…'

The final day's lecture began as a disappointment, and ended as a personal insult. The speaker, an obscurity in brown cords from some provincial English redbrick, was ostensibly covering some abstruse aspects of the Victorian novel. In rambling through his subject he dismissed Duncan as '…a mildly-interesting mid-Victorian writer of pot-boilers.' Afterwards, I went straight to the bar to drown my anger; I was starting to calm down when Agnes appeared at my table. I made a face and she smiled.

'In my more optimistic moments,' I said, 'I like to think that one or two of them might be intrigued enough to actually read the book when it comes out.'

'What - the critical biography of Duncan? Are you still working on that?'

'Yup, The Missing Master, it's called. I hope to finish it next semester.'

'Well, you look like you need that "thin, pale, bedraggled girl" who comforts MacDonnell in the book.'

'His daughter.'

'What?'

'His daughter. Duncan often drew from life; his daughter Christina was in her late teens when he wrote MacDonnell, and he modelled the character on her. He was usually penniless, his wife had died, and Christina nursed him through, like the girl in the novel.'

'Well, you need someone like her. Or maybe you just need a drink.'

Back in Glasgow it was soon Freshers' Week. I was making my way to the department from the library after putting long hours into the book, trying to get the manuscript in shape before the bedlam of the new academic year. It was pouring with rain, one of those September torrents that paint Glasgow a smoky grey. I bumped into Agnes for the first time since she'd started her new job. 'I'd like to stop,' I said, 'But I've got a meeting with the new Professor.'

'A new boss for a new term?'

'Yes. He's only just arrived; I haven't met him yet, so I must go and pay tribute.'

I climbed the stairs, occasionally being flattened against the wall by porters carrying stylish, modern furniture into the Professorial Suite. The retiring Professor had been a kindly, old-fashioned sort, her room a wood-panelled haven dotted with antiques.

Besides the new Professor, I was joined in the meeting by a couple of my senior colleagues; we all stood as the new man entered, a sharp-suited, slightly flabby figure, balding at the temples. He took off his jacket, revealing a crisp shirt of blinding whiteness, and sat down. He welcomed us, and began to speak in measured, affable tones.

'I can only congratulate my predecessor on the fine department she leaves behind her; I look forward to working with you all. Of course, times are changing in the academic world; it is no longer enough simply to teach English litera-

set and achieve targets, win sponsorship but maintain modest expenditure levels. I aim to build on your undoubted expertise, by putting this department on a business footing. It will be a whole new life for us all.'

We listened with growing unease; he outlined the links we were to cultivate with industry and finance ('English literature will survive as an academic subject if it can pay its way'). He went round us individually, identifying economies. He really warmed up when he came to me.

'You're working on this study of James Duncan, aren't you? I was wondering whether you genuinely believe that it represents good use of the Department's time?'

'Yes I do. Duncan is a major Glasgow novelist, and a good publications record reflects well on the status of the Department.'

'I hear what you're saying, and you have a point; but mere status doesn't attract funding. Don't you think making links with potential sponsors, for example, might be more fruitful than researching a minor local novelist.'

I swallowed hard. At the end of the meeting, he asked me to stay.

'Wilson, I was very interested in what you had to say, and I must say I'm very impressed with the body of work you've produced. But I'm sure you'll see that we have to think ahead, read markets, anticipate future demand,' he paused, pouring me a drink, 'So I want you to know that I intend to start withdrawing from teaching Scottish Literature; industry wants thinking people, articulate, well-read - but not parochial. This year will be the last intake. But there's also the question of the Duncan research you carry out here. I'm afraid I can't allow such unproductive work in the department's time. I'm sure you'll understand.'

'But I need our resources to help complete the book!'

'I'm really very sorry.'

I just sat there; my expression must have been idiotic. I suppose he expected some kind of tirade against censorship, a passionate cry from the heart against the tainting of art by commerce; I would have liked to have laid into him, but I was so stunned that I stood up quietly, excused myself and walked stiffly through the corridors, down the stairs, and across the campus to the Staff Club. There I downed drink after drink, cursed the way education was going, saw clearly the day when I'd lecture only on those writers the publishers wanted to push, had a vivid apocalyptic vision of the existing manuscript of The Missing Master being flushed down the professorial toilet, and finally felt that I had sufficient courage to go and articulate my feelings.

I felt myself walking into destiny, but in reality I probably looked like some drunk trying to remember where he lived. I groped my way upstairs, found the professor's door, and threw it open; he was sitting behind his new desk tapping and stroking an iPad while his PA sat opposite. They stopped and looked at me as I grabbed one of the doorposts for support. 'I've come to tell you a few things...' I couldn't for the life of me remember his name, so I banged on, making room for his PA to slip away. 'This is NOT a supermarket; it is a university, and I wish to teach ART, LITERATURE... um... BEAUTY and TRUTH. If I want to sell things I will get a job at Tesco. You people... you people should be fighting for us, not caving in and...' My fine speech, which had come together like a perfectly-played symphony while drinking in the Staff Club, became disjointed in my mind, broke up, and dissolved. I stood open-mouthed for a little while, then fell over. Then I looked up at the Professor and gasped 'Percival!' Or so I'm told, anyway.

Agnes had appeared by then. By all accounts I saw her and cried 'Christina!'

'No, it's me. Agnes.'

'No. We never learn her name, do we?' I said in my befuddlement, 'the pale thin girl'. Some security men had also appeared - in fact I believe I'd attracted quite a crowd - and two of them helped me up and began to lead me out of the door. 'Are you the Militia?' I apparently asked. It was shortly after this that I finally passed out. These days it's a story that always gets a few laughs down the Jobcentre Plus.

About the Author:

David McVey lectures at New College Lanarkshire in Scotland. He has published over 120 short stories and a great deal of non-fiction that focuses on history and the outdoors. He enjoys hillwalking, visiting historic sites, reading, watching TV, and supporting his hometown football (ie, soccer) team, Kirkintilloch Rob Roy FC.

FLAGMAN
by Ron Singer

I must have seen this guy hundreds of times, but I still can't believe him. First of all, he isn't a dwarf or a midget (I think there's a difference), but no way he's over four-foot-something -- closer to four than five. And he's not bulked up, or anything, but sturdy, a fireplug. What could he weigh, one-ten, one-twenty? Gray hair, thick, definitely not a rug. Age, forty-five, fifty? Till maybe a month ago, clean-shaven, but then (I shit you not) he grows himself a little pussy tickler, also gray! Not to toot my own horn, but I notice stuff like that.

Another thing I also can't believe is, he seems to wear practically the same uniform every single day of the year, throughout the four seasons. I guess the garage pays the dry cleaning, and they give him several sets of uniforms: white shirt, black pants, shoes, red tie, all tiny. In the warmer months, the shirt has short sleeves, in colder, long. In spring and fall, they add a black cap and windbreaker, and in winter, gloves, hat (with ear flaps) and parka, also black. The shirt, coat, jacket, cap and hat all have a red logo in large squiggly letters: "ATLAS PARKING," the name of the garage. And, finally, they provide the guy with a big red flag that looks like it's attached to his hand. He waves the flag so hard I can't understand why it does not shred or why the stick does not break. No, he doesn't "wave it," he snaps it. They must replace the flag at least once a month, it always looks new. And he never shouts to would-be customers, just tries to snap them down to the garage (underground). Since the traffic on that particular block usually crawls, those drivers seeking one of the non-existent parking spots on the street have plenty of time to decide to end their misery by springing for the garage.

Who is this strange-looking little dude? Until a couple months ago, his guyrations with the flag made me think it could be a mistake to try and chat him up (although I sometimes do converse with strangers). Because, frankly, he looked like a nutcase! Plus the foot traffic on the sidewalk in front of the ramp down to the garage is so heavy you feel like you better plunge your car right into any opening before the pushy pedestrians clog it up again. ("He who hesitates...") And, on my way back up the ramp, I'm usually anxious to get to the worksite, since I'm usually late.

You see, I was in possession of a monthly parking pass for this place, which is why I seen the guy so much —every day for ten, eleven months. The space set me back three-and-a-half c's per month, which (I shit you not) is a real bargain for this area. Anyways, I make good money, and I'll pay anything to avoid the fuckin' subway ride back and forth to my home in Bay Ridge, Brooklyn —"BR." Why do I hate the subway so much? Don't ask! But I'll tell you this much, it takes maybe an hour each way -- on good days.

Recently, however, I finally decided to stop for a mo' on the way back up the ramp, after handing over my keys to one of the "African-Americans" who park the cars —and collect the tips. See, I overslept that day, so I didn't reach the city till ten, ten-thirty. To my surprise, however, when I come trudging back up the ramp, the flagman was temporarily idle. He looked like he was maybe waiting for the next wave of cars. Or else by then, all the cars that were coming in were in already, and he was just waiting to be informed that his morning's work was over and he could go home to, I assume, his little house and little family for five, six hours (depending on where he lives), till it was time for the cars to be flagged back out and carry their drivers off to their own homes (which I notice a lot of them are in Jersey).

Anyways, last month, my chinwag with the flagman finally occurred, on Monday, July 14th, to be exact, the day after the World Cup final (Germany 1, Argentina 0). Since the Cup was a ready-made topic of conversation, and since I was already late and he was free, I decided to engage him in a brief exchange of views. Actually, I did it just to hear what the guy who had been flagging me in and out of the garage all those days, weeks, and months sounded like. It makes me uncomfortable to see some person three hundred times without so much as a "Hey, how you doin'?" (Not that I am ignorant of what curiosity done to the cat.)

"Some game yesterday, eh?"

"Was no good. Who care? Was shit game!"

Well, well. His voice was high-pitched and nasal, with an accent I couldn't place, maybe Latino. Was he a Mex or Platano (i.e. Dominican)? Probably not an Argentine, however. I say this because men from Argentina, at least judging from the Cup, seem to mostly range from medium to tall. Or maybe he was from Eastern Europe, one of those former Commie shitholes.

"Well, the Germans played great," I replied, determining to pull his chain a little. "Too bad Messi had such a bad day." I heard it said that Lionel Messi, who may be the world's best player (and five-seven), was seen puking before the final. I don't know if this is a fact, and maybe he pukes before every game, but Lionel did look "peeked," or something, without his usual amazing flash. Anyways, as I was saying all this crap to the flagger, I could see from his face that he didn't know what the hell I was talking about. We could of been from different planets.

He just kept shaking his head, with the big flag drooped next to his right knee. By now, his face was a blank, but still with undertones of anger. As I said, although he was obviously p.o.'d at the outcome of the game, I didn't think he was an Argentinian. (I hear a lot of people from the other --excuse me-- spic nations hate the Argentines.) Who knows, maybe he dropped a few shekels on the game. Anyways, I said no more, I just walked away, waving back over my shoulder as I headed for the worksite — another new luxury condo building, my third in the past three years.

In case you're wondering, my specific job entails grunt work --hauling cement and other shit, hosing down the site, whatever. To tell the truth, I don't have any real skills. My only asset is my strength, which, however (if I may say so, myself), is considerable. As the end of a shift approaches, in mid-afternoon, I'll still be hopping on and off the truck beds, while the college boys are bent over clasping their knees and sucking wind. (I refer to the summer employees, many of who are the boss's relations.)

Actually, to tell the truth, I was sucking wind myself that day, because I was still half-wasted from the World Cup bash the day before. Which was like a wake, anyways, since by then the U.S. was history. I wonder if there are studies indicating who drinks and eats more, fans whose teams are still alive, or those who are not. Anyways, in the two, three hours the final took (counting the two fifteen-minute overtime periods), I must of put away a whole package single-handed ("Sadder, Bud Wiser"), plus maybe five pounds of food: cold cuts, bread, potato salad, pie, cake, candy, chips, and so forth. But let's not go there, my heartburn will recur.

Three days after my chitchat with the flagman –it was Thursday, by then-- I was eating lunch with the boys on the stoop adjacent to the worksite. This stoop belongs to a very fancy building, a four-story brick townhouse. The only time we ever see the owners is around 8:30, when we would be having our ten-minute, stand-up, first coffee break out in front of the site. Most days, two young suits carrying computer bags, both of them males, come hopping down the steps, not making eye contact, or anything. Since they never lock the gate behind them, later on, at half-past eleven, we seat ourselves in our "reserved lunchroom" — their stoop-- although I, for one, would guess these guys are the type who might get snippy if they knew we ate lunch on their property every day.

I will say that we leave no litter, however –not

a single bit. Have you ever noticed how construction grunts never leave litter? If I was to hazard a guess as to "why," it would be because, after we work like a bitch erecting a new structure, we want the work area to remain pristine --at least until the job is finished and our backs are turned! In fact, when I see a person spitting out their gum on a sidewalk our men have recently laid, I have to stop myself from charging after the person and cold-cocking him. (Of course, I would not cold-cock a female, I'm not that big an asshole.)

I wonder if the guy couple we see every morning own the whole building or are just renters. My guess is the former, since that building does not have the look of being broken up into separate units. I can't put my finger on the exact difference, but there is one. (I tried to check for doorbells once, but the vestibule was locked.)

Anyways, I was on the stoop with the boys enjoying my usual, which on Thursdays is a hot Meatball Parmigian with a chilled Coke (liter bottle, but I save some for the drive home). As usual, we were shooting the usual shit about the job, the foreman, and so forth, and making our usual pig comments about the passing honeys, of which there are many in this particular 'hood, as well as side-of-the-mouth cracks about all the mutton (of both sexes) pretending to be lamb, of which there is also plenty around here.

During one of our numerous conversational silences, broken only by the sounds of five men glugging, chewing, grunting, sighing, and occasionally breaking wind (from both ends), don't ask me why, but my thoughts turned to the flagman. Since I was aware that at least a couple other dudes on the site also use that garage, I thought I'd ask if anyone happened to know the little guy. But, as I like to do, I came at the question indirectly, from the side, so to speak.

"Say, boys, any of you park your car at that place over on Fourteenth just west of the Square? I think it's called 'Atlas,' or something." Don't ask me why I said that, I know it's called Atlas. And, as I might of guessed, it was Jock, the runty Frenchman, who responded, by cracking wise.

"Let me guess why you are asking us this question, John," he said, in his faintly Frog accent. You could see the ears of the other three get big as they awaited for the inevitable Jockie-ism. "You are going to tell us, 'Sorry, but the place has just burned down,' or 'There was a big crash there this morning.' Or something similar [seem-oo-lah.]. Is this not correct, John?"

That speech was one of Jock's weaker efforts, and it got the exact response it deserved – none. Except from me.

"Very funny, Jockie Boy," I said, "except nobody's laughing. Actually, I was going to ask you guys a specific question, but I better direct it specifically to the other three of you, rather than to this moron Frog."

That got a chuckle. Jock placed his sandwich and coffee container delicately on the stoop next to him. Springing to his feet and hopping down the three steps, he assumed the pugilist position.

"Let us go, John," he said, "let us go right now. Nobody calls me 'Moron'!" By now, he had stopped reacting to "Frog."

I could see that the Jockie was genuinely pissed, but so what? Placing my own food and beverage on the stoop, I coolly stood up, trotted down the steps, and got in his face. But I left my hands hanging at my sides. Since Jock is about a foot shorter than me, the boys all roared. My plan, if necessary, was to bear hug him.

"Suppose I was to apologize, Jock," I ventured. "I take it back, you're not a moron."

"Very well, then, accepted," he said, sounding relieved. He hopped back up the steps and reached for his sandwich.

"No," I said, standing right where I was. "You maybe used to be a moron, but since you got that gavoon haircut last week, now you look like an idiot!" The boys, of course, all roared.

"Asshole!" Jock contented himself with, probably because he didn't want to put the sandwich down and challenge me again, just to get laughed at again.

Returning to my place, I also resumed my meal. But after a few bites and a slug of Coke, I spoke up again. "So. I'll ask my question once more. Is that okay with you, Jock?" He avoided eye contact and did not reply. "So. Any of you bozos happen to know the parking attendant with the red flag in front of the Atlas garage?" Out of consideration for Jock, I did not add, "the little guy."

Well, Jamie did know him. "Jamie" is really "Jaime," pronounced "Hymie" (but no Jewish connection). A young Cuban dude, very good worker, well liked, a carpenter. Plus he can take a joke. For instance, a while ago, one of the other guys told this racist riddle: "What did the Latino fireman name his two sons?" "Hose A and Hose B." Jamie laughed like everyone else, no problem.

Actually, the guy who told that joke, George, is from Uruguay, which will go down in history because their player actually bit an Italian player. (And didn't the Aztecs play soccer, or polo, or something, using a skull for the ball?) George is a decent guy, however, quiet, a hard worker.

Anyways, as I now learned, Jaime's grandfather knew the grandfather of the flagman. The flagman's name, also according to Jaime, is "Raimundo." Back in the day, shortly after that asshole Castro took power, Raimundo's grandpa brought the whole family over to the good old U.S. of A. I think Cuba is the last remaining Commie power on earth. A bunch of fucking ostriches!

Anyways, Jaime told me that much, which satisfied my interest in the flagman, since in light of Jaime's story, the little guy's sour reply to my conversational gamble now made perfect sense. His daddy was probably one of those bitter old Cubanos who still hang out in Miami, playing dominoes and chomping on non-Cuban cigars while they swap lies about returning to the homeland. The apple don't fall far from the tree.

Well, a few weeks later, even if I had still wanted to chat up the little flagman again (which I didn't), the window of opportunity slammed shut: that is, the garage closed. And how! You see, a catastrophe occurred.

What actually happened was this. As usual, I was driving in. A Tuesday morning, early August it was, by then. But just before seven, when I hit the F.D.R., I run into the worst traffic jam I ever experienced. (Which is saying something.)

The night before, as usual, I fell asleep on the couch in the middle of a ballgame. Marie had gotten pissed, as usual, and gone up to bed alone, muttering her usual suggestion that I perform the sex act upon myself. Well, that wouldn't of mattered —what else is new?-- only we both missed the evening news.

Which I realized was a very bad thing, when I became embedded in the cement-like traffic the next morning. What I learned after getting off the Drive and parking the car in a rip-off day garage ($25.33, plus 18.375% tax, total $30), and taking the subway up to the job (same site), was that, in the middle of the night, a 100-year old water main burst, half a block west of Atlas. I first learned this from Jock, actually, while we were hauling sheet rock. The deluge resulting from the break caused big-time damage. Three nearby apartment houses had already rented temporary boilers, because theirs got flooded out. The water was completely shut off in dozens of buildings, and landlines were down for a radius of three, four blocks. (We were lucky --we use cells on the job, and our water comes through a different pipe.) As for the Atlas, it was totally submerged.

What I also heard, later on, from another co-worker who used to park down there once in a while, is that every single one of the vehicles, maybe fifty or more, many of which are really expensive rides --Mercs, Jags, Beamers, high-end SUV's, and E.T.C.-- were completely buried in mud! Actually, the guy who told me this saw the cars being towed up the ramp, one by one, a few days later, on his way to the site from the subway. He said it was unreal, just like a disaster movie. And this mess was going to be at least a six-month nightmare for the insurance agents and the vehicle owners and all others making claims. By the way, did you know that elevators which have their works in the basement and get flooded out are not eligible for coverage? I was told this about the elevators by Peter, our foreman, a knowledgeable guy (but a prick).

Several thoughts entered my head at the time. One: it was lucky my car wasn't down there. Two: would I even be able to find a space now, since the other nearby facilities might also be closed? And, if not, they would certainly not miss this opportunity to gouge the hell out of all the unlucky dislocated parking slobs. For me, personally, it was going to mean months of subway hell.

And then I thought of what's his name, Raimundo. What would the catastrophic event mean to his job? Oh, well, that was his problem, why should I care? But a few days ago, during a lunchtime lull, I did think of the little flagman again. So I asked Jaime, who said he heard Ray (as he calls him) got re-assigned to one of Atlas's places out in Queens --Forest Hills, he thought, or Kew Gardens.

"But what do you care what happens to Ray, John? It's no skin off your ass."

I ignored that. "Good for him," I said, my tone indicating that I didn't give a shit. Jaime gave me a "Well, you asked" shrug.

Which I didn't (give a shit), actually, since I am facing some big new problems of my own. First of all, Marie and I recently underwent another nuclear incident. This one was over her horrible cooking, for which I blame my ulcers on. When she started in with the old crap about my "hereditary disposition," I completely lost it, and flung the offending dish (a big bowl of what she calls "goulash") against the newly painted white wall of our dining tomb, right next to her prize plug-ugly China cabinet. Off to the parental dwelling she stormed, a postwar split-level in Babylon, L.I. –accompanied, of course, by my three kids!

By now, I'm just sad about this incident, which happened three, four weeks ago. And I been on my own ever since. Which means TV dinners and lots of take-out, both of which really fuck with my poor guts. It also means coming home (by subway) to an empty house, no kids. But a peaceful house, however, because no Marie to pull my chain every minute. Silver lining, right? Well...

As if all of that ain't bad enough, the big job near Union Square has finally been completed. Ta-ra! A ten-story condo building, one spectacular unit per floor, at two mill a pop. Actually, we did a beautiful job, if I may say so myself, although truthfulness makes me add (in case you're thinking of purchasing a unit) that by the time of the water main break, it was too late for us move the boiler up to the roof. How does that saying go, "Cavear emptat"? ("Watch out, Buyer!")

So for me and fifty-three other grunts, it's say-onara, back to h.q. to await for the next job. Which isn't so bad, however, when you think of it, since they mostly seem to have several projects in the pipeline. Or, if not, maybe a month or two of Unemployment bennies till the next job call. But still, however, a major hit to my income stream.

And, you might ask, will the city now replace all the rest of the hundred-year old water mains before more of them blow? Are you kidding? Political suicide! And, unless they're indicted, most pols are not the kind of gees who normally fall on their own swords!

Does that last point sound like I'm getting a little cynical, or even morbid? Well, maybe I am. Because, besides all of the aforementioned misfortunes, my own vehicle (how ironic!) is starting to show early warning signs of needing a new tranny (sluggish in first and in reverse, 3.5 K). Plus, I have to get ready to fork over significant spondoolicks for a mega property tax hike, because the city is finally going to replace the ancient sewers in B.R. (also ironic!)

I know, you're asking, "Which of the pols have fallen on their swords, after all?" Do I really know? Maybe our 86 year-old Councilman is among them, finally ready to step back from the trough after eleven terms, and transfer his heroic efforts on behalf of John Q. to a full-time gig out on the links.

Oh, and of course, Marie's salary doesn't cover the kids' school and camp expenses, plus that "certain amount" she feels obliged to fork over to her parents for filling the hungry mouths of three growing kids, plus her own big fat gut!

At any rate, after all this, do I really have to explain why I don't give a flying you-know-what about poor little Raimundo? (Remember him?)

He's probably still out there in Queens, waving his red flag. And if not, for all I care, he could be on his way back to Cuba in a leaky rubber raft with an outboard motor, accompanied by eight other stiffs, each of them armed with an antiquated weapon.

Stop the Press! It's not even ten a.m., and two major events have already transpired today. First, I leave the house (no new job calls) to go get the paper, and I'm blindsided by a huge headline:

OBAMA TO FIDEL: LET'S MAKE NICE!

Well, fuck me! A "thaw!" Does that mean we can forget about poor little Ray in his leaky raft? Then, I get home, and, just as I'm pouring my second cuppa, the phone rings. It's my baby sister, calling to cry on my shoulder because Billy, her son, has decided to become her daughter! Whoa! Maybe, it's time for Y.T. to sell the house and move to a new planet.

Stop the Press (#2)! Get this! The new administration says the Cubanos are poisoning our diplomats. So it's "poor little Refugee-Ray," after all!

About the Author:

The obverse to "Flagman" is **Ron Singer's** work with the immigrants' rights organization, New Sanctuary Coalition. In addition to "Flagman," Singer's recent political writing has appeared at venues including Evergreen Review and Home Planet News. His eleventh and twelfth books are scheduled for release by Unsolicited Press. The Promised End (2019) is a collection of stories about mid-life, old age, and the thereafter; and Gravy (2020), a mixed-genre collection about life after 70.

THE SIREN

by Eric Stevens

The frozen wood of the bench on 7th Street was brittle and burned Steve's thighs while he leaned to one side, watching the cars drive slowly through the icy slush. It was a cloudy night, as always. Steve didn't mind. When it was clear the city lights held the natural wonder of the stars at bay, anyway.

"So, John was it?" Asked the man sitting next to him, in tattered clothes. He didn't look at Steve, but kept his hazel eyes centered in front of him. "You hungry boy?" His pale white hair and beard flowed in the wind, this way and that. The man twiddled a small diamond ring in his right hand, feeling the grooves and silver with his index finger. Steve reached next to him, grabbed another blanket beside the bench and handed it over.

"I'm good Dave. Put this on before you freeze to death." Dave slipped the blanket over his shoulders, edges of brown wool yarn slapping the side of his face while he struggled get it loose.

"Sure could go for a slice," The man said, lifting a liver-spotted hand and pointing to the pizzeria across the street. The interior glowed warmly with white light, the glass doors covered with dirt and character.

"What'll it be tonight?"

"You should know by now John. The works, as always."

"Sure thing Dave." He stood up, stretching, and reached between his thighs in an effort to spread the denim of his Levis apart, mashed together by the icy bench. He approached the crosswalk and waited for the neon sign on the metal beam to give him the all-clear.

"How's he doing tonight?" Asked the cook behind the counter of the pizzeria. He was a big man, bald, with tattoos sleeved on his right arm. He took a ball of dough and started flattening it out while he conversed. "Cold as balls out. Think he'll go in?"

Steve shook his head. "Doubt it."

"What'll it be this time?"

"The works."

"And for you?"

"I'm alright, thanks Brett." Steve stepped back and leaned against the dirty glass window of the pizzeria, glancing out. The night was relatively quiet, no movement except for the flickering yellow streetlight above the bench and the slow-moving sedans of day job workers cruising their way home in the slush. In a way he was grateful for the ice, it kept the traffic calm so he could hear his thoughts better. He pulled out his phone, scrolled numbly through his Facebook feed and checked his email. Meeting at 8 tomorrow? Fuck me, He thought, and sighed.

"Here you go man," Brett said, handing him a paper plate with a grease-slathered slice, covered in toppings. "You stay safe."

Steve walked back, and saw the man shivering. "Dave it's gettin' pretty cold out tonight. Sure you wanna stay out here?"

"Did I ever tell you about the fairy, John?" The man said.

"Nope. But before you do, take this." He stooped and grabbed another blanket lying next to the bench and handed it over. *I should've brought more*, Steve thought. "Put it on and you can eat."

The man slipped the blanket over his current one. His shaking subsided, and Steve handed him the slice. "Thanks John. This is my favorite, did you know that?"

"Sure did Dave. Eat up." The man grinned and pulled a large chunk of the greasy pie away with his teeth and chewed. It was a harsh and sloppy sound. Hearing it gave Steve a warm, tingling sensation that moved across his arms and neck. He smiled.

"Anyways, the fairy."

"Yeah."

"This was about five years ago I think. I was roofing that old townhouse I used to own, you remember that place?"

"Oh right, yeah."

"The place in Cincinnati? Well anyways, I was on the roof, and fell straight on my ass--slid off the roof and fell two stories!" He waved his arms, a drop of grease fell from the wax paper plate onto the blanket. "After I fell, I looked up, and there she was." His eyes went to the sky, still overcast. "She leaned over and said, 'It's alright, everything's ok now.' And she smiled. My god she was beautiful," He exhaled loudly, wheezing a little. "I wonder whatever happened to her."

"That's a pretty nice story Dave." *He hasn't told me that one in a while*, Steve thought to himself. "Look it's getting late. I gotta go, got work in the morning. Wanna come up? It's gonna be a rough night out here."

"Oh that's ok John, I'll be alright." The man's smile faded and he gazed at the brake lights of the passing cars, palming the diamond ring.

Steve made his way down three blocks to the apartment complex on 13th and Carter, rubbing his hands together. His heart sank while the elevator rose. The old pulley system hoisted the rusting aluminum cage slowly towards the fifth floor. Steve pulled out his phone again, browsing nothing.

Night turned to day, day to evening. Steve walked towards the bench once more, cars buzzing along the two-lane road with haste. The ice was gone, the cold remained. He held two warm Styrofoam cups, spilling several drops of hot coffee on his open hand as he walked across the grey asphalt towards the man. "Hey Dave!"

The man turned. "Oh Phillip! Good to see you again!" He smiled. One of the blankets lay next to him, crumpled and damp. The setting sun glowed dimly over 7th Street, casting a hint of orange and red on his white hair.

"Of course Dave, I had to see you." He sat next to the man on the bench. It wasn't icy anymore, and Steve's Levis were grateful for that. So was his ass. "Here, I brought you your favorite." He held out his left hand.

"Oh? Black, no cream?" Steve retracted his left hand, and held out his right instead.

"Of course. So," Steve sipped from the other cup. The sugary brew burned his tongue, but he didn't mind. "See anything new today?"

"A bunny in the clouds. An alligator, too. It looked like it was after the bunny."

"How do you know it wasn't a crocodile?"

"Aren't alligators smaller? Hell I don't know," He sipped the dark roast. "Sure was pretty, though. That too," He pointed towards the sunset. "Always my favorite time of day."

"Yep. Me too Dave. Want some dinner?"

"Starving."

Steve stood up and nodded towards the pizzeria. "The works?"

The man looked at him curiously. "Nah Phillip. Pepperoni, remember?"

"Right. I remember."

Brett wasn't there today. A cute girl he didn't recognize stood behind the register. He leaned against the glass once again, waiting. He checked Facebook, saw a message from someone he hadn't spoken to in twelve years. *Hey man, it's been a while! How've you been? I was wondering if...* Yadda yadda, life insurance. No thanks Adam. Deleted.

He walked back to the bench with the pizza. "Here you go Dave. You need another blanket?"

"Nah I'm not too cold. Thanks," He grabbed the slice, dug in. Steve felt warm again, and relaxed. "The stars are gonna be out tonight, Phil."

"Yep, sure will. Be hard to see them with all this pollution, though."

The man finished his slice. "Yeah, probably. Know anywhere we can see them Phillip? Sorry," He scratched his head. "Steve?"

Steve smiled, looking up. It was faint, but he could make out Orion overhead. "Yeah Dad, I know a place. If you come stay with me tonight I can show you."

"That sounds nice. It's getting pretty cold out here, anyway."

"Sure is." Steve led the man down the three winding blocks to his apartment complex.

"Say Steve," The man said. "I ever tell you the story about the siren?"

"Don't think so, Dad."

"Well I think this was a few years ago. Maybe ten. I was fishing at Lake Michigan, and it was cold--fucking freezing! Anyways, I was sitting at on a stool with my pole in that frozen lake. Freezing my balls off. Had a six pack of Yuengling though, that warmed me up." He reached into his pocket and pulled out the diamond ring, moving it between his fingers. "Anyways, I was just about to call it quits when there she was! Jumped right out of my fishing hole. She just smiled and told me everything would be fine, warmed me right up."

"That's quite the story dad. You remember what she looked like?"

"She had blue eyes, and brown hair. No, no wait," He looked at the ground, grimacing. "Red hair. Definitely red hair. And she was beautiful." He grinned.

"She sure was, dad." Steve's phone buzzed lightly, and he ignored it.

About the Author:

Eric Stevens is a fiction writer from Alabama. He is the author of Tennessee Honey and enjoys writing short fiction as a hobby. He currently lives in Orlando, Florida, where he is working on a new novella. To read more of his work, visit markandrosfiction.wordpress.com.

THE BEES

by Robby Pettit

Detective Earl Smith and his son sat in the cop car. The world outside was green and plastic, awash in yellow sunlight. No bird chirped, no blade of grass moved. The wind stood still. The car's radio provided a muffled soundtrack for the uncomfortable silence. Detective Smith's mind was blank and wordless; had run out of things to say to his son long before they had entered the car.

Detective Smith and his wife were in the painful process of an unacknowledged divorce where they still lived together yet were slowly drifting apart, like shards of a broken window grating against each other before the eventual shattering. Their son was caught between them, slowly being pulled apart by their separating gravities. He and Detective Smith had only exchanged single-syllable words in the past few weeks.

Since today was take-your-kid-to-work day, and since his son got a free day off from school, Detective Smith's wife had made a firm decision that Kevin would accompany his dad to work that day. Detective Smith had not wanted to fight that morning, so he agreed.

Detective Smith shuffled the papers in his lap as he read them. They were that morning's reports, picked up from the precinct along with a donut, still uneaten.

Detective Smith made a noise.

"Kids've been going missing," he said as one word. "So far 8 disappearances."

Kevin said nothing. He looked at the grate in the center of the street. There was a crack down the center.

Doesn't seem to be a pattern. Some kids younger than you, some older."

An animal made a noise somewhere far away.

"Maybe you know some of them. Here . . ." he shuffled the papers, "you know any girls named Cynthia? Cynthia Johnson? How about . . . Alex Keff? David Dundst? Alicia McHallen? The last girl was 6, you probably wouldn't know her."

A car drove by.

Detective Smith returned to the reports. "Looks like they all disappeared outside . . ."

He trailed off. Something in his expression changed, like a tomato souring in time-lapse. He sighed.

"What day is it today?" he asked.

"Friday," responded Kevin. He didn't meet his father's gaze. "Why?"

Detective Smith put the car in gear. "That mean's they're here today."

The car edged out into the street and turned right on the suburban lane.

"Where are we going?" asked Kevin, sighing.

Detective Smith turned left into a neighborhood. "At every crime scene there were the same enormous runes dug into the earth."

"What does that mean?"

Detective Smith shrugged as he pulled into the driveway of a house that looked like every other suburban house in every other cul-de-sac in the country. "It probably means aliens. But I don't know, I'm usually wrong."

Kevin looked his father in the eye. "What?"

Detective Smith got out of the car and walked up to the front door. Kevin followed.

They stood in front of a thick mahogany door.

"Listen," said Detective Smith, "you should probably stay in the car. The people who live here aren't exactly . . . normal."

"It's take-your-kid-to-work day," said Kevin, giving his father a blank stare. "Isn't the whole point to take me with you?"

"Fine," sighed Detective Smith. "Tungsten could use a friend."

"Tungsten? What kind of a name is that?"

Detective Smith knocked on the mahogany door. There was a brief pause and the door swung open. On the other side was a boy, about Kevin's age, with a pleasant face and eyes that protruded out of his head. They were blue and deep like the depths of the ocean, and they seemed to take in the world before them with such voracity it was like watching a hungry cow devour a patch of grass.

"Detective Earl!" the boy exclaimed.

Kevin flinched at the mention of his father's first name.

"Hi Tungsten," said Detective Smith, smiling softly. "Is your dad here?"

Tungsten shook his head. "Not today, sorry. We left him behind. He's getting me a dog."

"Like, from the pound?" asked Kevin.

Tungsten looked at him, and it felt as if he were being memorized. "No, a real dog. One of the ones that roams the plains and drinks from the wild streams."

Kevin was unsure how to respond.

Detective Smith looked defeated. "Oh. Well, tell him I'd love to talk to him when he gets back." He turned to leave.

"Do you need his help?" asked Tungsten hopefully. "With police business?"

Foot on the driveway, Detective Smith turned back. "Yeah. Kids are going missing."

Tungsten made a hmm noise. "Are there runes?"

Detective Smith nodded. "Yeah, there are runes."

Kevin looked surprised. "How'd you know that?"

"I can help you," said Tungsten, smiling.

Detective Smith looked uncomfortably at the ground. "Listen, you're a great kid, Tungsten, and I really appreciate the offer, but I don't want to get in trouble with your dad, and these things sometimes end up being—"

"I know at least half of what my dad knows, and my dad knows everything," said Tungsten matter-of-factly. "Please. I can help. I want to help."

Detective Smith sighed and put his finger on the bridge of his nose. "Fine." He turned to his son. "I'm taking you home."

"What?" exclaimed Kevin. "No!"

"I'm not having you involved in this. It's dangerous."

"Actually," interrupted Tungsten, "it's not. If my theory is correct, the aliens we're dealing with are famously non-violent."

"'The aliens we're dealing with?'" quoted Kevin, eyes wide in disbelief.

"I told you he was weird," sighed Detective Smith.

"Well, if the aliens are non-violent, that means I can come along, right Earl?"

Detective Smith rolled his eyes. "I'm not taking you with us. End of story."

"I don't think Mom would be happy if I told her you ditched me on take-your-kid-to-work day," hissed Kevin. Detective Smith flinched like he had just been stabbed.

"Fine," he exclaimed, throwing his hands up in defeat. "Don't blame me when you crap your pants in the portal."

They drove to the crime scene, Detective Smith in the driver's seat, Kevin in the passenger's, and Tungsten in the back, face pressed up against the window, watching the identical houses blow past with childlike fascination.

The crime scene was in the center of a park. It was taped off, police cones making a sloppy circle around a ring of black, unintelligible scars on the green grass. A swingset and a jungle gym watched from afar as the group of three made their way past the circle of "CRIME SCENE: DO NOT ENTER" tape.

Tungsten bent down and inspected the violent black marks. It looked like someone had been lit on fire and tried to put it out by rolling in the grass. The dark marks had no pattern, no repeated symbols. Tungsten scrutinized the rune, his big Bambi eyes consuming every detail. Occasionally, he would take a piece of charred grass, put it on his tongue, swish it around his mouth as if it were wine, and spit it onto the ground.

"Who is this kid?" Kevin asked, confused and suspicious.

It was now Detective Smith's turn not to respond.

Tungsten stood up suddenly. "I know what happened."

He began to walk around the edge of the rune, picking up various twigs, pieces of grass, bundles of tape and the occasional police cone.

"Our diagnosis was wrong. It wasn't a rune, it was a keyhole. We obviously don't have the key anymore, but—"

Tungsten held up what appeared to be an arbitrarily constructed mess of grass and police tape wrapped around a twig with a police cone on top. He walked over to Detective Smith, took his shoulders, and guided him until he was standing on part of the rune.

He went to do the same to Kevin.

"Wait a minute," said Kevin, backing away, "what is this for? What are you talking about?"

Tungsten frowned. "You don't understand?" he asked, surprised.

"No, you eating grass and making modern art out of random stuff from the park doesn't super make sense to me," retorted Kevin.

Tungsten nodded. "I forgot," he said explanatorily.

He moved Kevin into a position across from his father.

"You forgot what?" asked Kevin, begrudgingly accepting the boy's instruction.

Tungsten looked him in the eye. "The way the world presents itself to you is not the same way it does to me. Dad always tells me that, but it's so hard to remember something you can't experience."

Once again, Kevin didn't know how to respond.

Tungsten placed himself so that the three of them were making a triangle on the edges of the rune. He held up the mess of cone, grass, twig and tape.

"It's happening," he said simply.

"Kevin, look at me," said Detective Smith, meeting his son's gaze. "What's about to happen may be very . . . alarming, but trust me, we are going to be perfectly safe."

"What are you talking about?" asked Kevin.

"Just try not to freak out—"

The black marks suddenly glowed purple, and the next moment, the group of three found themselves pulled upward into the sky.

It was as if they were in an elevator moving at a million miles a second with no floor, ceiling, or walls. Kevin watched as the moon flew past and the earth shrunk to a blue marble beneath their feet. Space flew by them, so fast they could barely comprehend it. Occasionally, they passed a planet, there one second, gone the next. Kevin caught a glimpse of Jupiter and a smidgen of Saturn, but blinked and missed Uranus.

After a few seconds, Kevin realized he was still breathing.

He looked at his father, eyes wide in awe as he viewed the celestial world speeding past—awe, but not surprise. Tungsten, quite out of character, seemed bored with the incomprehensible majesties flying past. Instead, he was staring at Kevin, watching his reaction to the sudden change of scenery.

There was something separating the three of them and the cold vacuum of space. It was thin and glittered slightly, barely there, hard to notice, like trying to see if it's raining outside without looking for a splash in a puddle. The thing surrounding them resembled a long, translucent silk curtain, like the skin of a bubble.

Kevin reached out and touched it. It flowed through his fingers like water, no texture, no sensation. His fingertips went through it and touched the outside world. It was cold and painful—

Detective Smith grabbed his son's hand and pulled it back within the translucent veil. He shook his head.

"You don't want to do that," he explained. "Space and exposed skin don't go well together."

Kevin heard a noise and turned. Tungsten was laughing at him.

A series of planets he had never seen before passed by in the blink of an eye. After what felt like a thousand years and, at the same time, six seconds, the group of three suddenly landed.

The translucent silk curtain dissipated into nothingness. Somehow, they had landed feet-first, even though they had started facing the opposite direction.

Kevin looked around, opened his mouth to say something, and threw up.

Detective Smith stretched his arms and rolled his neck. "Just for the record, I warned you. You insisted on all of this, not me."

Tungsten watched Kevin intently.

"Are you okay?" he asked.

Kevin looked up at him. A brilliant purple sky shone behind Tungsten's head. He could see two moons and another enormous planet in the distance.

"Oh wow. Wow. I . . . Okay, this is . . . huh . . . what, um, where are . . . wow . . ."

They stood in tall golden grasses that swayed in the breeze. The golden grass was smooth and parted around the three figures like water.

We are on the planet of the Marsineans," said Tungsten. "Obviously, the Marsineans are the one who made the passage to Earth."

"They're the ones kidnapping children," said Detective Smith. "What are they?"

"Um," interrupted Kevin, "is no one going to talk about how we just flew through space onto a different planet in a different galaxy? What's that all about?"

"Tungsten and his family are different," said Detective Smith. "They help us with . . . this type of thing."

Kevin stared at the seemingly normal boy in front of him.

"I don't understand any of this," he whispered.

Tungsten was still staring at him intently. The shining purple sky, flowing golden grass, two moons and planet behind him not only didn't catch his attention but seemed to actively bore him.

"Wait a minute," hissed Kevin, turning to his father, "you've done this before, haven't you? That's why you weren't freaking out. You knew about all of this—" he waved vaguely at Tungsten, the flowing grass, and the planet in the distance, "—and didn't tell me?"

"I've only travelled through space a handful of times," responded Detective Smith, "and mostly with Tungsten's father. I didn't tell you because Tungsten and his family are assets of the police department. They value their privacy."

"So what are they, Uber for space travel?"

"We call them when we deal with situations we can't handle, like this one," explained Detective Smith.

"But only on the weekends," added Tungsten. "Friday through Sunday. Including Sunday. And Friday."

"Only on the weekends?"

Tungsten nodded. "We're only visiting."

Kevin shook his head. "This can't be really happening."

"To answer your question," Tungsten said to Detective Smith, "the Marsineans are a telepathic, helium-based people. They feed off the plants native to this planet and are renown for being non-violent."

"Non-violent, huh?" murmured Detective Smith. "Why would non-violent aliens kidnap children from Earth?"

"I think I might know why."

Tungsten made his way through the silky, golden grass, beckoning them to follow. Soon, the ground rose up into a hill in front of them. After a few minutes of hiking, they made their way to the top.

"What is that?" exclaimed Kevin.

Beyond the hill was a valley filled with enormous trees. The trees had orange trunks and were each the size of a ten-story building. They were dripping with huge, juicy fruits the size of entire houses. The fruits were blue and resembled huge, sagging grapes bejeweled with glittering seeds.

"Those are the Marsinea trees. The Marsineans eat their fruit to survive." Tungsten inspected the enormous orange trees and frowned. "There aren't as many of them as there were last time I was here."

"When was the last time you were here?" asked Kevin.

Now it was Tungsten's turn not to respond.

"Hey, look over there," pointed Detective Smith. There was a building, about the size of one of the trees, just a few football fields away. "That's where the children must be."

Confirming this fact was the sound of children screaming, echoing across the plain from the ominous building.

They made their way down the grassy slope, through a clump of the enormous orange trees, until finally they reached the building. It was nondescript and white. The only feature was a sliding door through which Detective Smith purposefully strode. Tungsten and Kevin followed quickly behind.

As soon as they entered, they realized what the noise they had heard was.

The room was filled with young children, mostly toddlers. The toddlers were laughing and playing, running around screaming, falling over, and getting back up again. Various toys were splayed across the floor. The walls were dotted with slots that opened every few seconds, revealing new toys to replace the ones the toddlers had been playing with. The toys that had been replaced were picked up from the floor and tossed into a chute in the corner, never to be seen again. The toddlers were completely enamored with the constant supply of new toys. They didn't even notice the sliding door open and the three figures entering.

"This was not what I was expecting," said Detective Smith, inspecting the chaotic scene in front of him.

"They're . . . playing," said Kevin. "Having fun."

Detective Smith walked through the room, making sure to avoid stepping on any toddlers or their toys. There was another door at the opposite end of the room.

He pushed it open and entered. The room beyond was, once again, filled with playing children. This time, the children were older. The room was bigger than the first one, housing an enormous, complex jungle-gym system. There were monkey bars and slides, poles and bridges, pits full of bouncy balls and tall towers mounted with plastic binoculars. The kids, now around 6 or 7, were running around the playground joyfully. It appeared that a game of tag was in full effect. Somehow, the kids were having even more fun than the toddlers in the first room.

"I'm beginning to sense a pattern," said Detective Smith, pushing through to the next room.

This room was full of kids age 10 to 15. It was filled with screens and complex gaming systems. Each kid had their own screen; some were watching TV, others playing video-games, others sleeping in luxuriously padded chairs with noise-cancelling headphones and eyeshades. There was a fully stocked snack bar filled with every candy and drink a kid could desire.

"This . . . this is like kid heaven," Detective Smith said, confused. "Why would aliens abduct kids and bring them here?"

Tungsten nodded. "Just as I suspected."

Kevin looked at him, then at his father. "Is there something I'm not getting?"

"The Marsineans, they're a telepathic race. And their trees, there aren't nearly as many of them as there used to be—they're obviously having some sort of famine."

"What's your point?"

"Don't you get it? The trees are telepathic, too. They run on happiness. It's like bees and pollen, except with emotion."

Detective Smith's eyes opened wide. "That's why they wanted the children. What's purer than the happiness of a child?"

"They made a child-happiness factory," stated Kevin. "Who would've thought."

"So that's why they need children from Earth, to bring them here and make them happy so they can grow more trees."

"But you can't just kidnap children," Kevin added. "That's not okay. We have to get these kids home, to their parents."

"Why would we do that?" asked Tungsten.

Kevin and Detective Smith looked at him.

"It's obvious that they're happy here, and isn't the prime goal of every human to be happy? Why would we take them away from that?"

"But they were kidnapped," said Detective Smith. "Against their will. Separated from their families."

"But their families won't make them happy," said Tungsten. "They'll never come close to making them as happy as this place does. I mean, look at you two. You two seem to only make each other sad."

Kevin's eyes opened wide. Detective Smith cleared his throat.

The room was quiet, except for the defeaning roar of children laughing and screaming.

"Sometimes there are more important things than being happy," said Detective Smith quietly.

"But if it will satisfy them—" Tungsten stopped. He cocked his head to the side, as if listening for something.

His face turned white.

"What's wrong?" asked Detective Smith.

"Dad found me a dog already," Tungsten whispered. "He's coming!"

There was an enormous rumbling noise followed by the boom of something breaking the sound barrier.

Instantly the three ran through the various rooms, pushing past squealing children and emerging out of the prison of happiness.

Searing through the purple sky was a meteor. Its fiery trail glowed a vibrant gold. The meteor seemed to be headed directly for them.

"I'm gonna be in so much trouble," Tungsten whispered. "He's mad. He only takes the meteor when he's mad."

The meteor was getting closer. Any second now it would hit them and completely obliterate them in a maelstrom of fire and flying dirt.

The golden meteor arched over them, so close Kevin could feel the heat of it singe the top of his head. It slammed into the ground a football field away, coming to rest at the base of one of the enormous orange trees.

Nervously, Tungsten made his way towards it.

The meteor was the size of a burial casket. It was made of lustrous silver metal that shone magnificently in the low purple light. The crater around it was still smoldering when Tungsten approached.

"Hey, Dad," said Tungsten nervously.

The meteor cracked in two, both sides heaving apart. Sitting inside it was a man. He had sleek blonde hair and a tight face stretched over angular bones. He looked like the type of man who owned the world, and when he opened his eyes, it was like looking into the face of God right as He sent you to Hell.

"What do you think you're doing, Tungsten?" boomed Tungsten's father. His voice was deep and inhumanly resonant; Kevin felt as if he would die before its echo stopped ringing in his bones.

"You were gone; I was just trying to help them," Tungsten explained quickly.

Tungsten's father rose from the meteor, and in comparison, the rest of the planet shrunk away. "You should've waited for me. You're not ready to do this on your own."

"I am ready!" Tungsten exclaimed. Kevin opened his eyes wide. Tungsten's father did not seem like the type of man you would want to yell at.

Tungsten's father eyed Kevin. "Who is this?"

"He's my son, Quasar," said Detective Smith. "It's bring-your-kid-to-work day."

"This is no place for a child, Earl."

"I'm not a child!" yelled Tungsten. "When will you accept that?"

"You are weak, Tungsten!" shouted Quasar.

There was power behind that voice. Kevin couldn't help but instinctually tremble.

"I helped them," declared Tungsten triumphantly. "I deciphered the rune, I found the missing children—"

Tungsten fidgeted, then, as if a fly had crawled into his ear. His eyes flicked between his father and the ground, somehow drawn to his father's gaze against his will. Kevin had the odd feeling that a conversation was occurring that he was not able to hear.

Quasar frowned, opening his eyes wide. "You were going to leave the children here?!"

"They were happy!"

"I have raised a fool!"

"I'm not a fool!" Tungsten pointed accusingly at Detective Smith and Kevin. "I watched! I listened! Just like you told me to. All they want is to be happy, and that's what the children are."

Quasar's voice changed, then. It was no more angry and furious, it was now full of sadness.

"There are so many things you do not know, Tungsten. So many things you do not understand."

"I understand them," Tungsten said quietly. "I understand what they want."

"No," whispered Quasar simply, "you don't. They are more complex than you give them credit for. Sometimes, the things they want aren't what they need. Sometimes, they themselves don't even know what they want."

Tungsten looked defeated. "Then how can I? What is the purpose of being here if we can never truly understand them?"

Quasar didn't meet his son's gaze. "That is something I cannot teach you. That is something you will have to find out for yourself."

It was apparent that the argument was over.

Turning to Detective Smith, he said, "I'm sorry my son endangered you. It's time to go home, and take the children with us."

The translucent veil once more descended from above. It encircled the two fathers and their sons, lifting them from the ground and lofting them through the sky, across the universe, past the planets and the stars, past the galaxies and the comets, back to the small blue marble and the thin, gray moon.

They landed softly in the park.

"I've returned the children to their respective homes," said Quasar matter-of-factly.

"Thank you, Quasar," said Detective Smith.

"Tungsten and I will be returning home now," he said, putting his hand on his son's shoulders. Tungsten stared at the ground dejectedly. "My wife is making tacos. They're quite delicious."

"Tell her I said 'hello'."

"Will do."

Quasar and Tungsten turned and began to walk out of the park.

"Hey, Tungsten!" yelled Kevin as they walked away.

Tungsten turned, looking at him in surprise.

"We should, I don't know, hang out sometime."

Tungsten's face lit up.

"I'd like that!" he called back.

The father and his son disappeared around the bed.

"I didn't think you liked him," said Detective Smith. "You two aren't the most similar people in the world."

Kevin shrugged. "He's a weird kid, but he took me to an alien planet today. I've never had a friend who could do that. Maybe I should, I don't know, branch out or something."

Detective Smith put his arm around him. Kevin flinched but didn't pull away.

"That's good, son. I'm proud of you."

About the Author:

Robby Pettit is a 16-year-old author living in Minneapolis, Minnesota. In his free time, he loves to write, spend time with friends, and play soccer. His biggest writing inspiration is the author Neil Gaiman. He dreams of publishing a novel before the end of high school.

MEDIEVAL MUSIC FROM MIDWESTERN UNIVERSITIES
by Ted Morrissey

An ER nurse called Frannie's name, and she and Beth walked through the extrawide double doors which then swung closed behind them. He half dozed in the chair. The implanted chip seemed to vibrate beneath his skin but as he became more awake the vibrations ceased. For a time he drifted between the dream of Elizabeth Winters's words humming subcutaneously and the more wakeful sense that they were not. He recalled an electric train set from his boyhood and using the transformer to make the locomotive go faster or slower, and the sensation with the teeming chip was like that—not on or off, rather a rapid rise or fall.

He checked his phone and its battery was on the brink of dying. He hadn't charged it for hours and of course didn't have a charger with him. Maybe Beth did, squirreled in her ample purse, more the size of an overnight bag. Their phones were similar. He sent a last text to Beth—phone nearly dead—and turned it off to conserve what little life he had left.

He dozed for a bit longer in the chair, his head resting against the hard wall, then came around enough to pay attention to others in the emergency room waiting area. It was just as full as when they'd arrived. A few new grimacing faces were mixed in, suggesting a steady supply of patients on this wintry night. It could be hours before Frannie is discharged—x-rays, calling in an orthopedic, setting the bone, making the cast, probably meds to pick up somewhere. He wished that he had Beth's journal of haiku which was still in her purse, now securely behind the ER's giant doors. There were magazines scattered here and there, and sections of newspapers in disarray. No one that he could see was reading, except perhaps a few people whose faces were bent toward their phone screens. Anyone who wasn't content to be gazing inward at their own misery was staring blankly at one of the three flat-screen TVs angled against the ceiling, carefully positioned for optimum viewing. They each displayed a different channel—the local Fox affiliate, the Weather Channel, and The Waltons on TV Land—all muted but with blocky closed captioning moving in black boxes over their highly defined images. He recalled seeing the episode of The Waltons when he was a child: a snowstorm interrupts the family's Christmas plans.

The Waltons TV was nearest so he spent a few minutes reading the dialogue and the stark scene descriptions—sound of truck engine, howling wind, woman crying. He thought of typing the descriptions on his phone's memo pad to create a found poem then remembered his phone was convalescing, its battery near death. After a while he realized there was something not right with the closed-captioning boxes. At first he thought they were simply out of sync with the action on the screen. Then he realized it wasn't the correct captioning at all; it must've been for a different episode, perhaps even a different show. Weirdly, much of the time the captioning made some sort of sense with the scene being played out on the screen. He remembered the episode well enough to determine that at times the erroneous text revealed something profound via its accidental irony: something more profound than the original scriptwriters were able to capture in the first place.

A man's voice at the in-take desk attracted his attention. He was too far away to comprehend.

his words, but the tone and rhythm of his voice seemed familiar. He wore a blue parka, the kind with the hood trimmed in faux fur, except the hood was down revealing a balding head of gray hair. The man shifted his position at the desk and he recognized him in profile: Marian Tate's companion, the fellow with the ice bucket.

With that realization the scene came more fully into focus. Marian Tate was there too, standing behind a woman in a wheelchair. The woman kept the hood of her red coat over her head, blocking a view of her face, and a blanket covered her from chin to ankle.

After another minute or two of discreet conversation with the ER receptionist, the big double doors swung open and Marian Tate wheeled the red-hooded patient in for examination. The man followed, and the doors swung shut. It seemed they had bypassed the normal in-take procedure, perhaps receiving VIP treatment. He turned on his phone. By the time everything initialized he only had four percent battery life. He typed an abbreviated message to Beth—Marian Tate et al in er examining—and pressed send just as his phone faded completely. He didn't know if the message was sent.

He was thinking that he needed to go beyond the double-doors and see Beth and Frannie when the lights blinked once . . . twice . . . then went out altogether.

A hush came over the entire waiting area—the entire hospital it seemed—for the moment or two before the emergency lights came to life and provided some illumination; and with the dim light returned the din, but intensified. A toddler or two who'd only been moaning in discomfort before were now sobbing with anxiety. Whispered discussions were replaced by lively debate. The receptionist at the in-take desk stood and assured everyone all was well—it would no doubt be a brief interruption in power. Subtext: stay calm, be quiet. People's phone screens glowed phantasmally here and there.

He glanced at the dark gray TV screen: the Waltons and their snowcovered mountain were gone for good. He took a final look at his phone's equally lifeless screen before putting it in his coat pocket. Red lights blinked above the various exits. He wondered if Beth received his message about Marian Tate, and if so what she might be able to do with the information, other than extend the antennae of her vigilance.

Suddenly he was feeling isolated, cutoff. Something significant was unfolding beyond the ER doors, and he was barred from it, banished here among the strange lights and enlivened strangers. His hip was bothering him, itching and burning where the chip had been inserted. Could there be some sort of inflammation or allergic reaction? He'd never been prone to allergies or dermal irritations, no eczema nor rashes, not even acne as a teenager.

What if it was Elizabeth Winters on the other side of the emergency-room doors, and the words sensed the nearness of their author, of their mother, and they were trying to return to her? They wanted to claw their way through the confinement of his skin and fly to their source, migratory birds returning to their hatchling grounds.

He rubbed his temples. It was a ridiculous thought, one which may have grown from the shattered remnants of an old Twilight Zone episode, buried in the black soil of his imagination.

He stopped rubbing his temples and turned to a window, where he was met by his own ghostly reflection. Sensing his isolation profoundly, he stepped close to the familiar image and pretended to be watching the snow scene beyond himself, but in truth he studied his oddly lit visitant—familiar, yes, but something strange too. He blinked at the visitant's unshaven reflection and it was in the eyes where the strangeness chiefly resided. There was something penetrating about the other's pupils—and instantly he knew the meaning of the word tattooed on his shoulder: it was just these sort of pupils Elizabeth Winters had described. He was certain of it by a means he couldn't begin to explain.

Pupils—

He turned toward the voice with the Scandinavian accent.

I thought that was you. What are you doing here?

It took him a moment to recognize Too, who was still wearing his colorful stocking cap as he stuffed his gloves into the side pockets of his puffy jacket.

Frannie—Germanness—slipped on some ice when we got back to the hotel. Looks like she may've broken her arm.

Oh no. Too pulled off his cap and immediately began smoothing his thinning blond hair. It is an epidemic. He stepped aside and motioned toward a man in a wheelchair some distance away.

In the subdued emergency lighting he was able to discern it was Deliberately. One leg was propped up by the chair's footrest. That foot was absent its tasseled loafer.

Possibly a fractured foot, said the Norwegian.

Deliberately was filling out information on a hospital tablet. The Aussie, Here, sat in a waiting-room chair next to him. The Aussie waved hello.

How long has the grid been down? asked Too.

Just a few minutes. I'm not sure. I was lost in thought or maybe half asleep.

It must have gone down just before we arrived.

You'll never guess who else is here. He paused. Marian Tate and her gentleman companion and presumably whoever else was in the hotel room. They were whisked to an examining room VIP-style. Then the power went out.

Too stared at the shut ER doors as if attempting to divine something beyond their unwelcoming façade. After a few seconds he looked at Deliberately, who was just finishing his in-take information. We must reconnoiter, said Too. That is the word, yes? In there. He nodded at the doors.

I think so. I'm stuck out here. They only allow one visitor per patient in the ER, unless immediate family.

You must accompany our friend Deliberately then. You have seen the fox. You know who you are chasing.

That casts me as a greater expert than I am, to be sure—but if Deliberately doesn't mind I'll give it a go.

Too required a moment to process the slang before taking him to Deliberately and the Aussie, and explaining the situation. Deliberately, it seemed, was in too much pain to care about the particulars. Deliberately was also complaining of a racing heart and shortness of breath—probably the pain's adrenaline surge—but the symptoms moved him to the top of the triage list, so momentarily they were pushing Deliberately through the ER doors; he hurried on their heels, and wheels.

The lighting was better but still deeply shadowed in the hallway paths between examination cubicles, which were mainly curtains on U-shaped tracks in the ceiling. The nurse or attendant, whatever he was, in maroon scrubs, wheeled Deliberately to a bed and helped him into it, asking him a litany of questions. Other bescrubbed staff were coming and going disrobing Deliberately, taking his vital sign numbers, connecting him to machines, and entering information on their tablets. They seemed unaffected by the power outage. States of emergency, varying only by degree, must have been their natural habitat so the small matter of an interruption of power appeared to barely register.

He didn't want to be an uncaring friend to Deliberately, whom he barely knew, but he was eager to find Beth and to snoop around for Marian Tate's party, even though hospital policy almost certainly discouraged snooping around in the ER. Deliberately's cubicle was quickly crowded and chaotic—at the moment they were more concerned about a coronary event than a broken leg.

I'm going to slip out for a second, he said. Four to six is a crowd. The harried staff seemed to approve of his departure. Beyond the curtain he asked someone speeding past where there was a restroom he could use, and she motioned around the central nurse's station, to the right. On your left. The young woman in light-blue scrubs had an African-sounding accent.

His request had begun as a ploy to move around the examining area unattended, but he decided the restroom wasn't a bad idea. Walking the frenetic path, he attempted to peek, discreetly, into the various cubicles, ones which had curtains that were withdrawn a foot or two. The vibes emanating from the spaces varied from tense to traumatic, from amused to annoyed. The waves of disparate emotions seemed nearly to alter the air through which he moved, its temperature and density, even its scent, although beneath it all was the tartness of antiseptic, and fragile, if not feigned, optimism.

An impression formed. The emergency room was a living organism, but in spite of the medical (and thus biological) subtext, his sense was that the body-ER was driven by personal narratives, not the illnesses and injuries of the patients interacting with the knowledge and skillsets of the staff; rather, the stories of how the people needing attention came to be there at that given moment, combined with the stories of their friends and family who accompanied them, intersected with the stories of the doctors and nurses and other staff: life choices and career paths which brought them to the ER on this overnight shift after a late-season snowstorm, one whose narrative included an electrical blackout. All of these texts tangled and mutated—collided and replicated, reversed and revised, and at times vanished—to make the tale of his being here, now.

He found the bathroom. When he was finished, he decided to take the long way back to Deliberately's exam cubicle. He assumed the ER formed a large square or rectangle, so if he kept walking, turning at right angles, he'd manage his way back and in the process cover the entire room, surreptitiously examining each exam space, as much as he could see at least. He was pricked by a twinge of hesitation: such surveillance felt like a violation . . . a violation of privacy certainly but more than that: a violation of someone else's pain, almost an act of sadism, to peer hopefully into a stranger's personal upheaval, perhaps even tragedy. To poke around in their fear and sadness, even if only for an instant.

He was reminded of Katie's objections to the Logos project. Mainly she objected because she felt Elizabeth Winters was more grandstander than serious artist, but there was also a sense of violation: an author offers up their life, their psyche, for the reader to enter if they so choose—at least, an author worth her salt—but the agreement is that it's a one-way probing: the author is not allowed to probe right back, Katie had said (no, Katie had argued—it was an argument they had had). He disagreed. An author—a masterful author like Elizabeth Winters—is always probing the reader, getting in their head, under their skin, colonizing their psyche and planting their flag. With Logos, Elizabeth Winters was just doing it all more overtly, more honestly even—in fact, educating us about the process.

They'd been cleaning the dinner dishes while having the argument: Katie washing, he drying. He'd become so animated in his defense he was punctuating his points by absentmindedly jabbing with a meat fork, not into Katie of course, but generally at her. For emphasis.

He couldn't see into all the examination cubicles, as some had curtains which were tightly drawn. It seemed likely that Marian Tate's party would try particularly hard to avoid prying eyes, especially if Elizabeth Winters, risen from the dead, was with them, if she was the one requiring medical attention. He didn't believe that Elizabeth Winters was alive, but, still, the fact he was willing to entertain the possibility, even as a remote one, suggested he thought the author could propagate such a hoax, and thus supported Katie's contention that Elizabeth Winters was more entertainer than artist, more showwoman than sage. No, he reminded himself, that issue aside, there remained the beauty of her prose, as crystalline and as piercing as icicles plummeting from an unseen height. No matter whether one viewed Elizabeth Winters as risk-taking or attention-seeking, there remained the work.

Hey.

He turned. Beth was in the hall, her hand still on the curtain of the cubicle from which she'd emerged. Frannie's cubicle apparently.

I came back here with Deliberately, seems to have broken his leg in a fall.

Those loafers.

Those loafers. The Swede brought him in. The Norwegian: Too.

They took Frannie to radiology.

But that's not all. Did you get my text? My phone was dying.

No, but the reception in here is terrible to the point of nonexistent.

He had Beth retreat into the exam cubicle, and he closed the curtain behind them. The lighting was subdued, even more so than the rest of the ER, with its redundantly named emergency lighting. The dimness made him recall how long it'd been since he slept. Marian Tate is here, she and two companions. The one from the room, apparently, came in a wheelchair but I wasn't able to get a good look before they were spirited beyond the ER doors, very-important-person-esque.

Definitely a woman though?

Yes, well, ninety-nine percent yes. I've been skulking about since Deliberately arrived and presented an opportunity to be admitted to the sacred chamber.

Have you checked all the exam bays?

Exam bays—huh. I think of them as cubicles. I like exam bays better. Sounds more sci-fi. But, yes, pretty much—the ones I could peep into.

Ours was open just enough for me to spy you passing by. It was probably too dark for you to see in.

Definitely haven't been able to check them all. Maybe only half.

The lighting just then improved, and a barely audible hum returned: the power had been restored.

That's better, said Beth. Maybe we should both check on poor, ill-shod Deliberately. She batted her eyebrows conspiratorially.

Indeed. Four eyes are better than two—well, not four-eyes. How about, two sets are better than one . . . set.

Please, gentlemen first. Beth held open the curtain.

The light was nearly dazzling in its revived brightness. It seemed to intensify all of his senses, and for the first time he noted the rubbery squeak of the rushing ER personnel through the white-white halls. The chill in the air bit at his bare cheeks. So, too, the antiseptic smell like lemon-infused chlorine, which had been there all along, suddenly catapulted to the foreground, the effect practically vertiginous. His impulse was to reach out and take Beth's arm, for added support, but he resisted and focused on keeping his balance until the disoriented feeling passed. Meanwhile they'd managed to reach Deliberately's bay without any sign of Martian Tate and company.

They checked on their fellow Logos, who was now attached to several machines, including a cardiac monitor. Deliberately's heartbeat spiked and receded across the screen in a regular dual rhythm. He was alone and his eyes were shut, dozing it seemed. He was in a hospital gown, and his leg was stabilized by a plastic splint. He looked thin and frail beneath the ER's blanket. His round face had shed its puffiness. He seemed to have aged. They left him to his peacefulness and returned to Frannie's vacant bay, where at least they could talk. Before leaving Deliberately he had glanced at the heart monitor, and for a brief instant the rising and falling line seemed to form the word pupils—in a cursively blocky script. He'd blinked and the pulse returned to its normal pattern. He didn't say anything to Beth, deciding it was evidence of his need for sleep.

They were almost at Frannie's bay when the door of the restroom he had used earlier opened and Marian Tate's companion emerged. He wasn't paying attention and nearly ran into them. They all paused for a moment to avoid a collision, staring back and forth. The fellow was fairly tall, having half a head on Chris, and likely in his fifties, with white in his dark beard and thinning hair. Bloodshot eyes peered from behind black-rimmed glasses—he looked a bit like Allen Ginsberg at middle age, but better groomed and tailored. He wore an expensive-looking gray suit and a silk tie with a diamond pattern, except every piece was disheveled and wrinkled. He presented the picture of a professional who'd had an unending day of travel and terrible shocks.

Chris felt the pang of guilt again, at disturbing the man's privacy by this more or less accidental encounter. Perhaps the disturbance of privacy had to do with how carefully he considered him, seeking more details than one would normally and naturally do in a typical chance meeting. The fellow was at a disadvantage knowing nothing of his and Beth's intentions.

They each said their excuse-mes and continued on their way. After a moment he and Beth turned to see where the man was going, but the ER was suddenly bedlam, with medical staff moving every which way. One bearded nurse spoke to them as he rushed past, telling them they needed to return to their patient and stay put. We're about to be slammed, he said over this departing shoulder. In the confusion they lost sight of Marian Tate's frayed friend. They did as they were instructed and retreated into Frannie's nearby spot, still vacant.

Well, we know they're around here somewhere, said Beth, leaning against the empty bed.

Yes, somewhere in this tightly managed chaos. He was thinking about seeing his Logos word on the monitor. He rubbed his shoulder and the tattoo beneath his sweater. He had the odd notion that pupils— had escaped his skin and was on the loose in the ER, possibly trying to escape the hospital altogether. He had an impulse to remove his sweater and t-shirt to make sure pupils— was still inked into his skin. He also found himself wondering where Beth's tattoo was on her body: her shoulder, too? her hip? thigh? He sat in the only chair and willed himself to cease his speculation on the whereabouts of Beth Winterberry's radiant tattoo, except to wonder for a moment if it was somehow actually radiant.

You look exhausted, said Beth.

I think the Jameson and everything else have caught up with me.

You should take a siesta in Frannie's bed. In a minute I'll go check on Mr. Practical Shoes, poor guy.

You've talked me into it. I think I've started to dream on my feet.

It's no wonder. It's almost two in the morning.

How are you still going strong?

I'm a night owl. My second-wind kicked in about midnight. Even so, I wouldn't describe it as going strong, just going.

They traded places, and he stretched out on the hospital bed. It felt too good to lie down to fret over its also feeling a little awkward. There was a white blanket on the bed. He didn't get under it exactly but pulled part of it over his chest and shoulders.

At first he thought he would feel too strange to sleep, plus there was the commotion in the hall, just on the other side of the half-drawn curtain, but he slipped off within seconds. Instantly, it seemed, he dreamed of a many-roomed house, every room empty as if the occupants had moved out. The house, with its echoing wood floors, was unfamiliar. Certainly he had never lived in such a large, rambling house. He walked into a room painted light green, the color of a fancy mint at a wedding reception. He was admiring the pleasant color when he noticed a dark smudge on the far wall. He went to see what it was, possibly to wipe it clean. As he came closer, the smudge took the form of a word—closer still, his word, pupils—
—as if written on the wall in indelible black ink. Who would do such a thing? Who would mar such a perfectly painted wall? He was still pondering the question when he walked into the adjoining room, this one painted in a glacial blue, and on the wall was another black mark—his word, he knew—larger, more noticeable. He confirmed his suspicion before moving to the next room, of saffron hue, where pupils— was larger still. He stepped more quickly to the next, mild lilac, larger yet. Fog, cream, sand, the palest pink . . . growing, growing . . . until his word filled a wall, the understated umber framed in the heavy black of the p's' rounded heads, and brimming to the rim of the u's chaliced vessel, and surrounding the i's island dot like a perfect murky swamp. A sudden light distracted him from the word. Shielding his eyes, he walked toward the next room (it was a never-ending series of rooms). A figure stood in the middle of the space emitting a brilliant white light, a feminine figure, radiating the glow that enveloped him—

Beth was speaking to him. The light in the exam bay had been turned up. He squinted against its harshness and also against the pervasive disorientation. Frannie is back, Beth was saying. We need to take her to the hotel. I Ubered us a ride.

Frannie sat in a wheelchair, her arm in a cast and a sling. Her sunburst parka was over her legs. He thought for a second she'd broken a leg too, then recalled that was Deliberately.

What about Deliberately? he asked sitting upright and pulling himself together.

He's going to be awhile. Too and Here are staying with him.

Frannie appeared to be dozing in her wheelchair.

They gave her something for the pain, said Beth, plus I'm sure she's exhausted.

You must be most of all. Sorry I checked out for a while.

It's o.k. I wrote a couple of poems, well, first drafts at least. She patted her large purse. They may be awful. I'll see what they look like after some rest. The Uber chick should be here any minute.

I think the uber chick is already here. He put on his coat and got ready to push Frannie's chair.

Got her all right? asked a nurse in the hall, where Frannie was parked. The nurse looked frazzled.

Yeah, thanks. He released Frannie's brakes and got the chair rolling.

They're having a night too, said Beth quietly. Several gunshot victims came in all at once. That's what all the running around was about before. It's been pandemonium for the last couple of hours.

Holy cow. Is that how long I was out?

You clearly needed it. Looking forward to some out time myself.

I bet. What about Marian Tate et al.?

Don't know. I lost track of them. They may still be here somewhere.

A nurse at the station pressed a button and the ER doors swung open. Be safe! called the nurse. He and Beth smiled their farewells and pushed Frannie into the waiting area. Outside, he saw, it was still fully nighttime, still a couple of hours until dawn. There was of course the city's electric glow, which reflected in its artificiality off the pure white of the snow.

About the Author:

Ted Morrissey is the author of six works of fiction, including Crowsong for the Stricken, Weeping with an Ancient God (a Chicago Book Review Best Book of 2015), and the forthcoming Mrs Saville. His stories and novel excerpts have appeared in more than fifty publications, among them Glimmer Train, PANK, ink&coda, Adelaide, and Southern Humanities Review. A Ph.D. in English studies, he's a lecturer in Lindenwood University's MFA in Writing program. He and his wife live near Springfield, Illinois, where they direct Twelve Winters Press and its imprints.

THE BIG MOVE

by Maria Frangakis

After nine years in San Jacinto, without electricity and indoor plumbing, we were finally leaving. We were moving to la casita hermosa, the beautiful little house, as we called our future dwelling in nearby Río Hondo, the neighboring "big city." The house had been under construction for eight years, even surviving the great flood of 1958 when the water rose above the windows. After the house was roofed, my father asked the mason he'd hired for the construction to move in with his family to prevent theft of building materials. The understanding between them was that he might have to vacate on short notice when the time came for us to move there ourselves.

I'd heard about this impending move ever since I could remember, but it was one of those magical things that would happen "after the next harvest," although it never seemed to materialize. The harvest hadn't been good that year, either, but we were leaving anyway. For the last couple of days my parents had been talking about it more than usual. I heard them talk about it as I went to bed the night before, and were still talking when I got up. That morning they were not only talking, but were getting our worldly belongings crammed into the back of Papá's truck. He was saying something about possession being three-quarters of the law, adding "If we don't move right away, we'll lose la casita hermosa for certain!"

I hated not knowing what was going on, but knew not to bother my parents for an explanation. At seventeen and sixteen, Conchita and David, my older brother and sister, understood perfectly what was going on and seemed to mirror my parents with their talking, giving me ample opportunity to eavesdrop.

The mason wants to keep the house!" said Conchita. "Someone overheard him bragging in the pub about his plans to finish the house himself since my father didn't seem to be in a hurry to do it anytime soon."

"Apparently," David added, "the mason figured that since the contract for water and electricity was on his name, it would be enough proof that he was the rightful owner. He thinks that a judge might rule in his favor because he's been living there for over five years, and is prepared to fight Papá in court to keep the property."

No wonder we were leaving so suddenly. Papá and David left San Jacinto carrying the great cedar wardrobe, the wrought-iron bed and the cots. David said that the mason and his wife were having breakfast and almost choked on their chorizo when they heard Papá announcing that we were moving in. With David's help, Papá began unloading the heavy pieces, placing the wardrobe and the wrought-iron bed in the master bedroom and the cots in the other two rooms. The mason's few belongings were there but Papá didn't seem to mind. As Papá went back to San Jacinto to get the rest of our belongings, David remained in the house to watch over our belongings.

Quickly, Papá filled the truck with the wobbly table and its matching wobbly chairs, two straw hampers, the big tin tub filled with pots and pans, a few buckets and Papá's chair, the one with the owl stenciled on its back. Mamá put every sheet, blanket and quilt we owned on top of the pile so that we could sit safely and comfortably.

At eight, I got to travel on the back of the truck, along with the rest of my siblings except for

Mariana, who was only three and had to sit in the front with Mamá. We were so happy not only because of the move, but also because Mamá had packed us lunch for the road, as she always did whenever we were going on long trips. She made us burritos de frijoles and hard-boiled eggs just in case we got really hungry in the thirty minutes that it would take us to get to la casita hermosa in Río Hondo.

It was the middle of August and Mamá was six months pregnant, almost replicating the previous move to San Jacinto nine years before in July, when she was pregnant with me. Our new house didn't have actual windows or doors yet, just the cutouts on the brick, but it had two bathrooms complete with toilets and spouts where the showerheads would one day be installed. Papá had been right all along: who needed an outhouse when we could have toilets?

Our new house had beautiful tile floors; each room with a different color and pattern that my father had chosen himself without consulting my mother since he was the one traveling to the city on business all the time. I had never seen such extravagance in any other house. But the most amazing thing was that it had running water and electricity. There was one faucet in the kitchen and another one in the patio. Mamá was thrilled that she would no longer have to carry water. We couldn't stop turning the water on and off and flushing the toilets.

Despite the novelty, I knew I was going to miss el monte. There was a huge guamuchil tree in the property that produced pods, like green beans, but curly, which we called "roscas." They were tasty, but gave us terrible bad breath and the tree couldn't be climbed like the old mesquites in tierra de nadie, back in San Jacinto. Over the brick fence that separated the neighbor's property, hung the branches of a mango tree and a real lemon tree. We could eat the mangoes that fell over our side of the property, but were forbidden from climbing the fence to cut any from the branches over it. As for the real lemons, nobody would ever consider eating that awfully sour citrus and so it remained rotting on the ground. There was also a peach tree, but its fruit was

tainted since it grew right next to our very own, albeit condemned, outhouse. Papá had actually built an outhouse on that property for the mason and other workers to use before running water and toilets had been installed. By the time we moved in, it had been treated with large amounts of lime and filled with dirt.

The house was also fitted with one light bulb, which hung low from the ceiling in the dining room. It had a little chain on its side that one pulled to turn the bulb on and off. It was marvelous to think that I'd never again have to clean the glass shades for the oil lamps the way I had to do each afternoon in San Jacinto. In this house I'd just pull that little chain and we'd have light as if by magic.

We took over the house like a swarm of bees. That night, and for the next couple of days, the mason, his wife and their grown son slept on the back porch in their cots. Mamá must have been really happy with the move because for the first time she didn't seem to mind our yelling and screaming—she actually seemed to enjoy it. The mason's wife kept shaking her head and every once in a while, she would cover her ears, making sure we could see her do so. City people were too sensitive, I thought.

After three days, she could bear our screams no longer and the three of them moved back to their own house, a shack on the other side of the canal where the poor people lived.

About the Author:

Maria Valenzuela Frangakis was born in Mexico's Northwest. She moved to the U.S. to attend Graduate School and spent twenty years in the pharmaceutical industry, publishing her work in scientific journals. While raising her three sons, she received her MBA and founded her own company, a Biotech consulting company. Her fiction has been published in Typehouse Literary Magazine. She currently lives in Chapel Hill, NC.

THE GARBAGE MAN
by Rachael Peralez

'Dear Garbage man, Please make sure you get ALL the trash out of the can.

Thanks! The Brewsters'

I stand there just holding the damp piece of paper. The A-L-L scrawled in all capital letters and underlined. The exclamation mark after the 'Thanks.' I look over at the white house nestled among the pruned Spanish oaks and ball the note up. The bathwater rain makes rivulets of space between the white maggots humping up my arms as I hoist the cans in the back of the truck. They feel muscular and clean inching their way under the cuffs of my gloves. My back burns, and the smell of cat urine puffs out of a half-tied bag as it smacks the bottom of the compactor. I grind my teeth and think about how Mrs. Brewster's wrists must be so silky and warm. About how her perfume would just touch the air around my nostrils as I bit into her heavy breast. A drop of my sweat would fall in the deep divot between her collar bones and how she would moan about how strong I am. How powerful my arms are. I pound the side of the truck and give my driver the thumbs up. Next house.

Sometimes, I go home and think about Mrs. Brewster and the lesbian couple with the hyphenated name on their mailbox. In my head I arrange them in order from smallest to largest. Then from happiest to saddest. I keep all the notes. The apology notes. The critical notes. The notes about Christmas. I wad them all carefully into the smallest ball I can and then tuck them in beside one another in a plastic Wal-Mart bag hanging from a nail above my recliner. Sometimes I just lift them in the sack above my head and pretend I am a doctor doing a breast exam on the lesbian couple at the same time. Sandy has peachy, small nipples that contract under my very professional touch. Alma's are aggressive, and she leans into my palm.

I jog beside the truck toward their Colonial style home. There's a tin full of butter cookies with a glossy-eyed Santa beaming at me sitting on top of their immaculate cans. A damp note flutters in the breeze.

'We thought you might enjoy these!

The Rodriguez-Browns'

I turn toward their house with the cedar playground equipment nestled back in the white pines and look for Alma or Sandy, but the porch is deserted. They have a little boy. He looks like he has mirrors for eyes, and I hate him. Before he came, Sandy threw out beautiful trash. I know it was Sandy because she wears blue, Oxford button-ups and doesn't wear any makeup on her freckled face. My momma never went out without her face on. But Sandy. Sandy doesn't care if the neighbors see her. Alma is too sweet for nipple clamp catalogues and ATM receipts from some strip joint in Harahan. I know that joint, and Alma wouldn't be interested in the collagen-pocked flesh there. Too kind. I know it was her who left me those butter cookies. I still have those catalogues wedged under my mattress and sometimes I think about Sandy licking the skin behind Alma's ears.

The driver is honking, and I'm still holding the goddamned cookies. I put them on the curb and grab the cans. Their trash is ordinary now, full of empty baby carrot bags and electric company envelopes. Later, I will eat the cookies in front of taped episodes of Full House until I fall asleep in my recliner where the devil will perch on my chest and keep me from moving. I guess he's the devil. He wears a suit, and I always imagined the devil in a suit. My eyes will pop open, and he'll just have his feet pressing against my ribs and his knees folded under his skinny elbows. His head is too small for his body, and his teeth seem forced into his grayish gums, like shells stomped into the sand. He'll look me in the eye, and roll his tongue behind his lower lip and grin. The television will flick promises of hair in a can or lab grown diamonds. Then he'll be gone and I'll be able to breathe again. But my house will be different. Somehow. I sling the boring trash into the compactor. A stray maggot is crawling over the cookie tin and inches over Santa's right eyebrow making him look skeptical. I take the tin from the curb and jog up to the cab of the truck to chuck them through the window.

"Jennings, If you eat these, I'll kill your duck dogs." I smile at him. "I'll know. I counted them. There are twenty-four cookies," I say.

"Jesus Christ, Hutch. I don't want your cookies. Just hurry the fuck up so we can get done before traffic gets bad."

Next house. I find a dead cat in a white trash bag. It has a piece of string tied around its tail and its matted fur has patches missing. I knot the bag and throw it in the compactor. I imagine the cat's bones crunching and snapping and its guts spurting out like ropy red toothpaste as the metal slab presses and presses. I take my tin of Vicks out and dab my ring finger in the sticky stuff and rub it inside my nostrils. Four more streets then the fill.

When we finish, I get in the truck and open the cookie tin.

"See? I didn't take your cookies." Jennings tosses me a tub of wet wipes. It bounces off my shoulder and rolls to the floorboard.

"Twenty-four. They're all there."

"You sure they aren't for both of us?"

"It just says 'Garbageman.' Plus, I know them."

"Whatever man, they never leave the driver any cookies," he says.

"Maybe you're not as handsome as me."

"Maybe. You are one sexy son of a bitch. Look at that face." He grips my ear and pulls. Hard.

I don't squeal. He wants me to squeal.

Sometimes I wake up and there's nothing. No one. Just the pressure on my chest and I am nowhere. If I could speak, what would I say? No. I would say "no." When I finally can move, sometimes I'm up in the oak tree outside my trailer, and all the dead things I see wrapped in trash bags, stirring with maggots, are stacked on the lumped roots with their paws stretching the filmy plastic until something gives, and the air is filled with flies, and I am not a man, but something bigger. Something more. I leave my tree on wings made of dog food bags and follow the scent on the women's scribbled notes, if only to see Mrs. Brewster dip her fingertips in a pot of cold cream and scour her face with sad, vicious strokes. Then, when I wish like a beggar does, not for luck or a pot of stew, but for too much, for a million dollars, for a slender goddess blowjob, I am transported to right outside Alma and Sandy's four-bedroom, three and a half bath house seated among those heady trees. And I wait. They begin consuming each other from the top of Alma's black curls to the soles of Sandy's feet, and I, in turn, am left with my empty chest, for when they are done there is nothing left. Nothing left for me.

It's Sunday, and I don't have to work today. My dreams sweep in through the morning light, and I remember how warm it was in lesbians' bed and how I watched them lap each other up. I get out of bed and wander into the kitchen where my zebra finches bounce from perch to perch and beep for seeds. I have named them all "Bird." I reach into their cage for the feed tray and feel their tiny hearts pumping away as they flutter from my calloused hands.

I have never fucked a woman, and I am thirty-five-years old. My body is fine and does what bodies do, respire, perspire, consume, defecate, but not fornicate. After I feed the birds and eat a bowl of Golden Grahams, I look up porno on the internet. The Saints don't play until three today, so I have time. I put my fingers on the home keys and tack out "Mexican Bride Pegs New Husband and Groomsmen with Big DILDO!!!!!" It's one of my favorites, and I reach up to touch my plastic bag filled with the crumpled notes scrawled by manicured hands. I imagine Mrs. Brewster pursing her thick, red lips, gripping a stick pen and writing to me, for me,

'Hello trash man!

Do us a favor and please don't leave the trash cans in the driveway. We appreciate it!

-The Brewster Family

The porno folds into a kaleidoscope of flesh and masculine frowns. I am imagining Mrs. Brewster unhooking her bra and those heavy breasts tumbling out. I reach for them. To weigh them in my hands, to bite the nougat-colored flesh until it softens into warm, saltwater taffy in my mouth. But my hands are covered in wingless flies that shimmy up my fingers and pour onto her skin. They track up to her mouth and pour into her orifices. She is filled with them, and I am close to coming. Mrs. Brewster is choking now and a thread of saliva spins from her bottom lip. I am coming. I am coming.

Regret. I wanted to tell her I loved her this time. That I have always loved her and can make a nest for her in my bed of bath towels and pink polka dotted sheets and feed her butter and ground meat. Everything I touch turns to flies. My tears dot the pillow, and I understand that the nothingness must be filled and that only I can fill it. All I have is their notes to stuff into the void. I clean up with an old tie and kiss my bag of notes. Sometimes, I wonder if she can feel it on her soft cheek. Like a breeze cutting through the heat.

The Saints are losing. My dad would have been piss drunk by now, knocking over two liter bottles of St. Genevieve and pissing in the closet with his hand curled around the doorknob. He would have ripped something off the wall and thrown it against the T.V. I can hear him in my head and remember he is safely in the ground now. His liver quit working, and he wasted into a pile of yellow skin draped over bones. The capillaries in his nose burst into pink fireworks across his face, and all he wanted from me was one more glass of wine. I call my mother. She is probably drunk too. The phone rings five times, and I hear her voice on the machine.

"It's Judy and Rob. Leave us a message, and we'll get back to you. Have nice day!"

I guess I should go and see her. She forgets me more than my brother who died when he was seventeen. He took her Station Wagon and drove it to California when she sent him out to get milk one day. He drove it right into a freight train. Everybody said he was on drugs, but I knew better. He used to crawl under the bed with me when Dad started hurling wine glasses across the room, and pick at the white gauzy fabric of the box spring until it tore. We drew pictures of pigs and dragons and later women with giant balloon breasts with nipples of purple crayon. When he died, I was thirteen. I crawled under the bed and wrote,

'I hate you. I hate you. I hate you. I hate you. I hate you.'

I get myself another Dixie and the butter cookies. I open the tin and shake it from the bottom. The cookies have maggots bunched around the jewel of jam in the middle. Jennings probably opened it and let them in. Motherfucker. I push them around with my forefinger, feeling their taut, cool bodies writhe away from my touch. I pick them off and turn the cookies over. I clap the lid back onto the tin and toss it next to the trash can by the television. The Saints are still losing by two touchdowns. It's the fourth quarter.

We thought you might enjoy these.

I will go see Ma. The finches flutter around their cage and cling to the gold bars. I grab my keys and dust cookie crumbs from my shirt. I'll get her some flowers. No. I'll get her a burger from Dairy Queen and a blizzard.

I finally get through the long drive-through line to the window. A pretty girl thrusts the upside-down blizzard out of the window and whips it upright again right out of my reach. I open my door and press my chest against the door, reaching for the cup. She is looking at me. She has a strawberry birthmark just over her eye and full lips. She smells like cotton candy and berry deodorant and sweat. Her name tag reads 'Allison.' I imagine her holding onto to some blond boy in the backseat of his Camaro, her knees gripping his skinny sides, panties around one ankle.

"Will it hurt?" she asks.

He's petting her, but his fingers tangle in her long brown hair, and he pulls and pulls until she's screaming, and hair floats around her like shining fall spiderwebs, and she digs into his throat, but he's grown to the size of a bear, and his spine juts, and his knuckles crack. Her creamy thighs puddle under his weight, and she bucks against him. I reach through the car window for her wrist, to drag her from under his chest.

"Sir?" The girl holds a grease-spotted bag. "Sir?"

"Yeah?" I can feel damp fabric creased in my armpits.

"I said, do you want ketchup with that?'

"No. Thank you for asking." I take the bag and start to ask her if her boyfriend has a Camaro. She's already taking another man's order on her headset. "Uh huh." She slides the window shut.

Ma hates it when I bang on the screen door. So, I set the blizzard on the porch swing and open the screen. I rap one, two, three. Nothing.

"Ma?"

The wind stirs the puffs of cat hair on the porch. The blizzard tumps over, spilling a little cookie dough in a white puddle.

"Ma? It's Hutch. I brought you some food."

Shuffling and banging. The door opens a crack.

"I don't know no Jimmy."

It isn't her voice. It isn't anyone's voice. I realize that I am not at the right house. This house is too big. Our house is smaller. It has camellia bushes, and little green lizards that dart over the walls and my cowboy bedroom, and a concrete birdbath with an angel on top. My mother is there. She's always been there, and her hard, gray eyes get soft when she spoons out butterbeans. When Dad died, she stood outside the church smoking and you know what she said? She said, "One more to go." When my brother died, she grabbed me by the shoulders and said, "At least I know where he is this time." And hugged me to her until it hurt my neck.

I cried. I cried when I remembered. I went home and set my finches free. They fluttered and beeped, and disappeared into the purple sky. I sat in the grass and thought about the women. About their notes. About Alma's lacy cursive, about Mrs. Brewster's jagged scrawl.

I could wear my father's suit and ring their doorbells. I know when Mr. Brewster is at work and when Mrs. Brewster comes back from taking the kids to school. She would see me sitting on her porch and spread her white wings and fold me to her breast. My own wings would break off and blow away to the gulf, where crabs and seagulls would huddle in them until the loud boats pass. She could forgive me for my trespasses and kiss my brow. She could show me how to fold a fitted sheet. I could tell her about the sparkling landfill filled with dolls, and microwaves, and her children's diapers.

I could return Alma's tin with warm smile, and she would invite me in, and we would drink some kind of fancy tea. She would put her small hand on my wrist, and I would follow her into every single room of the house, watching the fabric of her dress cling and swish around her hips. I could fix her sink and take out her trash. She could tell me about Sandy and together we could flip through photos. I could show her my hands, creased with black. I could drink her up.

I could tell them my name. No more trashman. No more garbageman.

I will.

About the Author:

Rachael completed her undergraduate degree at University of Texas and my MFA in creative writing at the University of New Orleans, where she received the award of Best Thesis for a collection of her short stories. Her work has recently been published in the Crack the Spine, Furtive Dalliance, and Literally Stories literary magazines.

LET'S MAKE A DEAL
by Nicolette Munoz

"I want to renegotiate the terms of our relationship."

What the actual fuck?

"I—okay?"

"I say this because I genuinely want to be your friend. I just don't want to pursue a romantic relationship anymore," Reed says, in a distinct and weird business-like voice that is so distant from what he actually sounds like that I can't fully focus on what he's saying.

And 'renegotiate'? Are we reevaluating a fucking business deal?

He's looking at me expectantly, with a blank expression on his face and no depth in those eyes of his that are usually so emotion-filled. He's sitting in my desk chair, with his leg crossed over his other and his hands folded together in his lap and he looks like some vague business man giving an intern the time of day in his fancy office.

I didn't know coldness could be so visibly depicted until now.

I guess I need to say something. "Alright."

Reed raises his eyebrows at me. The first hint of him that I've seen today; he does that when he doesn't know what to say. I guess his speech practicing didn't prepare him for a lack of talking on my part. Silence isn't exactly typical for me.

I can't take him just staring at me. I say, "This is sudden." I avoid his eye contact like the plague and fidget on my bed.

"Uh—sudden?"

I look at him now and nod. "Yeah."

"I, uh—sudden. What do you mean, sudden?"

What does he mean what do I mean? Two days ago we spent the day in bed, having sex and talking for hours until I thought my voice would give out. I had never felt closer to him and didn't realize I could feel so strongly when it wasn't being felt by the other person too.

"I mean, we see each other all the time. Nothing has been different in the past week then it was in the beginning."

"Yeah," he nods, stoically, all emotion absent from him again. "I mean, how long has it even been?"

Is there a worse thing he could have said just now?

I shrug and furrow my eyebrows together and take a long pause to feign thinking about it. "A few months, I guess."

"Yeah." He nods again in that stoic way that is starting to drive me insane. "I don't know what to say to that. I'm sorry it seems sudden."

I scoot myself back farther on my bed. "Alright."

He raises his eyebrows at me again and I want to close my eyes to avoid feeling that stare of his.

"I just think—" He starts again.

"Why?"

"What?"

"I want to know why. You haven't said."

He nods. "Of course. I just don't feel romantically enough toward you. I like you very much as a person . . ."

Reed continues but I lose track of what he's saying, as I start to sink deeper into myself, a numbness that taking me over from the inside out.

I think he just complimented me — you're a (insert adjective) (insert adjective) (insert adjective) person. Each adjective making his sentiment less and less genuine. Being overly verbose is just a way to make something fake seem real.

He's staring at me again, he must have finished up Part 2 of his negotiation speech. I'm sure he anticipated having to address the "why" question.

"Alright. I . . . get it."

"I want to reiterate how serious I am about wanting to be your friend. It's not an empty statement, I mean it, truly. I've broken up with people and people have broken up with me and it's something that's always said and it's always empty, but it's not empty now. I can't stress that enough."

Yeah, but he's overly stressing. Overly compensating again, I don't believe his sincerity at all. It's not empty, it's not empty, it's not empty. But I've never seen someone act in such an obviously empty way. I feel like I could pick him up effortlessly right now, throw him over my shoulder and carry him out of my apartment. He's so glaringly hollow.

"I don't know about being friends," I manage to get out. "I guess I would have to think about it."

I can't think of anything more unpleasant, actually. Like yeah, let me just come over and hang out with you on the couch we've had sex on. That sounds fun, right?

Reed nods. Again. "Of course. And I'm leaving that entirely up to you."

Wow. You're so generous.

Reed sighs, leaning forward on his knees now. "I really do care about you, but I felt like I needed to do this. And I wanted to do it in person, of course. Over text would have been so flat."

Do you want a fucking medal for being a decent human being? Of course he did it in person; you can't make a business deal over text.

I nod, long and slow, really emphasizing the fact that I'm nodding. All of his excessive nodding put into one. He doesn't know I'm making fun of him but it pleases me. "Okay."

He (surprise, surprise) nods and leans back into the chair. He raises his eyebrows at me and I focus on not screaming.

"So," he says, "should I go now?"

No, actually, this seems like a good time to watch a movie together. Don't you think?

"Yeah, Reed. You should go."

He nods and stands up and I drag myself off my bed. He's standing off to the side, like he doesn't know how to open the fucking door himself. I avoid eye contact, walking past him, to open it for us and lead him out through the living room to the front door.

As I'm opening it for him, he says, "So, contact me if you want to. If you don't, I'll understand."

Contact me. Yeah, I'll have my people call your people.

I nod and open the door wider. He steps through, giving me the most forced smile I've ever seen in my life.

Is he going to shake my hand now? Close the deal?

He begins walking down the hallway.

"Wait," I call out. "Reed, wait."

He turns around and raises his eyebrows again.

"Wait a second, okay?"

I don't wait for an answer before turning and heading back into my room where the book that I borrowed from him is sitting on my desk. I've been meaning to give it back — I finished it ages ago — but I hadn't felt any rush.

I walk back toward the front door and see him

standing with his hands in his pockets barely on the other side of the doorway, lingering vacant expression. This is the last image that I'll have of him.

"I was speaking emptily before," I say as I approach him. "I don't need to think about anything, I don't want to be your friend, so this is it." I hold out the book to him and look straight into those blank eyes. "Thank you for David Foster Wallace and Neutral Milk Hotel."

He looks down at the book, hesitating. He looks back up at me and I see a glimpse of some kind of substance in his eyes — nothing I can place, but it's there. He looks back down to the book, grabbing it, finally.

I shut the door before he can say anything else and lock it behind me.

About the Author:

Nikki Munoz is currently a student at University of California, Berkeley where she is working on her Bachelor's in English, with a minor in Journalism. When she is not working on her creative fiction, she is writing for the Daily Californian's Arts and Entertainment section, focusing on theater. For her fiction, she is interested in pulling both from her own life and those around her to create realistic fiction that is compelling in the mundane.

HILLSIDE STREET
by Abby Obenski

My music blared as I screamed my lungs out singing, coasting down the windy backroad leading to the little haven I created for myself. I sang along to the words that sat ingrained in my mind from time after time of repetitive listening. The words were a process, just like everything else in my life. I believed there was a process to everything. There was always order and it was always applicable.

I just moved from a small town in upstate New York to start my freshman year at the University of Boston's School of Medicine. I was coming home from the wedding of a distant cousin, more of an obligatory function than a desired one. I was tired but driving meant time for myself, which so seldom arose. I was generally reserved, but I used driving as a form of unconventional therapy. A time to reflect, a great peacefulness to block out the sound in my not so peaceful mind. I leaned my head against my hand as my elbow laid propped up on the small ledge of window and I quieted my singing to a dull mumble, reaching forward to lower the volume as I neared the last bend before my little house on Hillside Street.

As I looked up from readjusting the knob, a child who appeared to be of grade school age simultaneously ran across the road, directly in my path. "Shit!" I screamed, as I slammed down the clutch and the break in synchronous unison. My car slid on the wet pavement, snow gently falling in large, wet, heavy flakes, enveloping me in a dark cloud of miserable weather and near darkness. I could feel my heart pounding against my chest and I struggled to remind myself to take a breath. I reached for the Ativan in my purse and looked around, flicking on my high beams. My hands were trembling, but I didn't know if the cause was from shock, anxiety, or a combination of both.

It was getting dark and there was barely enough daylight to see unaided. I fumbled for my water bottle from the bottom of the passenger floor, where it flew from the momentum of the stop. I couldn't comprehend what I saw, or where the girl materialized from in the first place. I couldn't even remember the full details of the events preceding what happened. I could only muster the white blonde hair and neon pink rain jacket darting out of what appeared to be thin air, as she ran for what appeared to be her life.

Among the rest of my packed belongings, I grabbed my second North Face out of the backseat and engulfed myself in the warmth as I stepped outside. I could feel my hands shaking in response to both the freezing weather and my anxiety. The snow melted as it fell upon me.

"Hello?" I called. No response. "Are you okay?" I heard my voice echo off nothingness. I happened to look down and felt myself skid to a stop. A small amount of snow had begun to accumulate in a thin layer on the road, a thicker layer dusting the woods where it stuck immediately to the base of frozen dirt lying underneath. However, there were no tracks on the road. No footprints in the snow.

"Uh, okay Cal," I said to myself. I talked out loud. I did often, in times where rationalization was a necessity and coherent thoughts needed to be formed with a more direct impact. I brought my hand to my head and rubbed my eyes, looking again in case some sort of self-induced error was inflicting my vision.

I couldn't help but think it was materialized by my own subconscious, as a result of sleep deprivation, or the long duration of driving I was just subjected to. Could I have manifested that bright pink? That flee of desperation? Of terror?

I slowly got back in my car but it felt like an unconscious move. My mind remained fixed in the set of actions I just found myself a part of. I tried to rationalize further, to make sense of what I saw.

I had a long and busy weekend, stress was continually looming over me, I had a headache from excess caffeine coupled with lack of caloric intake, and I was exhausted and just drove for what seemed like an eternity. Any combination of these factors could have lead me to believe I was seeing a girl running away from an imaginary unknown. A figment of my own imagination. I drove slowly, my brain clouded with a thick fog. I tried to force myself to remain conscious, looking around for any potential signs for the remaining two minutes I had left of my trip. However, I didn't know what I was even searching for.

I left my bags in the car. That could be a problem for tomorrow, I was too tired anyway. My joyous mood from ten minutes prior had long evaporated. I set the thoughts of the incident aside and trudged to my bed, passing out before I could think of it further.

I sorted through the toppings of my salad with my fork. I hated cucumbers. "What's up Cal?" I heard. I could hear the smile in his voice, and I didn't even need to look up to know he was flashing the biggest smile at me. I felt mine brighten, as if his were contagious. "Hey, Jack! How was your lab practical?" I asked, looking up at him. "Eh, I got really confused on the one part, but I think I did okay. How was your exam?" he asked, as he plopped down next to me. He unwrapped his sandwich and applied mayonnaise with what appeared to be the most meticulous caution. His sandy brown hair flopped down in front of his face as he examined his sandwich once more before taking a bite. He turned to look at me with the greenest eyes I've ever seen. "Uh, I probably got a B, but I'm hoping for an A," I said with a laugh. "Oh please," he said, taking another bite of his sandwich. I watched as shredded lettuce tumbled over the edge of the bun and fell to the crumpled tinfoil lying below on the table. He continued, almost to himself, "as if Cal could ever get anything aside from an A." I laughed to humor him, even though I was still preoccupied with the events of the preceding night and wasn't much in the mood for conversation. I dumped my trash on top of my salad, realizing I wasn't hungry and merely subconsciously destroying the cucumber at my fork's whim.

I pulled my North Face over my hoodie as I waited for him to conclude eating. I walked towards the trashcan with Jack trailing behind me. He pitched his trash from where he stood, several feet behind, laughing as he made it. I watched the ball of tinfoil wring around the rim of the trashcan like a basketball being thrown in for the win at a championship. He did everything with perfection. "Nice," I said, as he caught up to me and laced his fingers through mine.

I led the way, halfway dragging him down the escalator. We had class in thirty minutes and a long way to walk. I was always cautious of time because running late gave me anxiety. I pulled the hood of my sweatshirt up with my free hand. God, it was always snowing. We walked out to the sidewalk and I became increasingly aware of my surroundings. I was a big proponent of mindfulness. I liked to live in the now, enjoying life as I came across it, and paying attention to every moment so I could access it later.

I saw the most beautiful courtyard among the buildings. We never came this way, but the snow led us on a detour through the clearest path. Huge oak trees lined the perimeter, the snow on the branches preserved with a layer of ice. Cement benches were woven through a vast expanse of flowerbeds and a tall cement waterfall stood at the center, but it looked more like a sculpted masterpiece than a functional item of reality. Everything was covered with snow, but it just furthered my amazement. An untouched, preserved beauty.

I felt entranced. I needed to get a closer view of the stretch of beauty that stood before me. "Hold on, I want to see that," I said, letting go of Jack's hand. It felt like my soul was being pulled towards that courtyard, a marionette on strings. I heard an audible sigh. "Cal, we're going to be late," I heard distantly behind me. I momentarily didn't care. I walked faster, my duck boots trudging through the unplowed sidewalk, the snow piled grass. I was on a mission. I was nearing the outlet when I heard someone speak, seemingly to me.

I slowed briefly, not in the mood to be bothered. "Hello?" I heard again, as if it were a question. I stopped and looked. A man presumed to be in his late fifties stood before me, his white hair a nice complement to the snow that was enveloping us. He was wearing an old tan suit with a dark purple tie, and his smile radiated happiness despite the dreary weather.

"Uh, hi," I said. I could hear the confusion in my voice and I felt the compulsive hold on me from the courtyard vanish. "Do you go here?" "Uh, yeah, School of Medicine," I said, but it came out sounding like a question. What was he doing standing here in the cold and soliciting strangers? A professor, perhaps? A lonely old man looking for simple conversation? "Impressive, your name?" "Uh, Calista, Cal for short." "Unique, nice to meet you Cal, names Reggie," the man said. I felt a smile break across my face and I reached my hand out to meet his.

I jumped as Jack came up behind me, wrapping his arms around my waist as if I was under a surprise siege. He leaned down and kissed the side of my face, and with a slightly annoyed tone, "what the hell are you doing? It's freezing and now we're late." "Oh, I just wanted to see this and the-," my voice trailed off to nothing as I again regained consciousness of my surroundings and noticed the man gone from my peripheral. I whipped my head around. No one.

"Yeah, but who were you talking to?" he asked, a look of concern flashing briefly over his face. "Uh, the- there was just a man standing here. Uh, Reggie, his name was Reggie. Wh- where did he go?" I stammered to get the words out. I felt panic rising. Jack just stared at me and after a second, "Cal, are you okay? What are you talking about? No one was there." I opened my mouth to speak but didn't. What was happening to me? Was this the beginning of my mental deterioration? Or maybe just a severe stress-induced mental breakdown?

I tried to focus but it was hard with him looking at me as if I was one of his future patients in dire need of critical help. My mind reverted back to last night, driving home from the wedding, the neon pink jacket, the owner vanishing into nothing, and not even footprints left behind in her wake. I glanced down slowly, afraid of what I might see.

There were footprints, but they belonged to Jack and I, stretching back to the direction we came. Nothing else. Nothing.

I left Jack at the lab and I trudged home in the forever-falling snow. I couldn't stop thinking about what happened earlier. I couldn't be going crazy. I wasn't losing it. But this couldn't be chalked up to tiredness, not twice in a row. So what was the explanation? And yet at the same time, I couldn't help but think Reggie was leading somewhere with the conversation.

Why had I been pulled to the enclosure? Almost magnetically, as if I had no will of my own? Why had that compulsion vanished once that man began to speak to me?

I turned the volume up to my music, trying to blare out the noise and background thoughts that were beginning to consume me. It was a failed attempt. I tried to analyze and work out a rational explanation in my mind, but I couldn't come up with one.

It was Wednesday. I was driving home from the library, exhausted, stressed, and once again preoccupied within my own head. I felt my eyes fluttering closed. My subconscious screamed at me to stay awake. I needed to focus. I was almost home, nearing the final bend, and that's when I saw it. The bright shock of pink darting through the woods.

I immediately slammed on the breaks in an attempt to get ahead of the cycle. I was grasping desperately for any sort of clue as to what was happening to me, and if she was real she might have an answer.

My ancient tires skidded and slid, sweeping over the road in a counter-clockwise fashion down the path of the windy, snow covered, treacherous route. I felt my heart rate skyrocket, up to the 140's....150's... I forced my eyes shut, directing the last ounce of my strength to praying.

I didn't believe in God. As the great Sigmund Freud said, religion is an infantile dependency, fulfilling something for someone as an individual. Of course that is the surface value, but I see a truth within. Just the thought of an all-being individual, dictating evolutionary ideals and overall whole world decisions is ridiculous, or at least I thought. The so-called mentally-dependent turn to this. But was I becoming mentally-dependent? It didn't matter. In that instant, I prayed.

I was in control just as quickly as I had lost it. It had only been the span of a second or two but it had felt like years. I reached for my purse but I forgot it. I closed my eyes and tried to remind myself the solution to the terrible situation that has been routinely finding me could potentially be within that girl.

But what if it isn't?

What if this is in your head?

What if this isn't real?

I snapped myself out of it. I saw the pink coat. So familiar, yet so distant. I couldn't think. It felt like my mind was in the gloomy haze we were standing in. This simply just couldn't be real, how could this possibly be explained? What the fuck is happening to me? The same white blonde hair whipped in the vicious wind of the bitter cold Massachusetts evening as the manifestation ran past an unescapable horror into the vast woods beyond.

I struggled to open the door. Desperation battled panic, but desperation eventually won as I staggered out into the cold. "Hello?" I screamed. Nothing. She was too far by now to hear me, and I had no chance of chasing after her. I missed the opportunity, to no success, no avail.

I looked down at my feet. It was snowing harder than the last time I found myself in this situation. My dark hair was masked with white, and the front of my black jacket was matted with snow, the heavy, wet flakes meshing with the faux fur.

I felt my feet propelling me forward, but it was merely a mechanical motion. I was there, but I wasn't there. I walked the remaining few feet back to my car, the door left open in the manic desperation that consumed me two minutes prior.

I watched in horror as a figure emerged from the woods, barreling down a path identical to hers. I froze. I was paralyzed by fear, although I couldn't help but to tell myself that this was not real. He didn't acknowledge my presence, too preoccupied with hunting his prey. Or was I simply no longer a product of reality? Was I a witness to some sort of secondary dimension? Or worse, was I horrifically mentally ill?

He bolted after her at full force, soon dissipating from my view. All I had left of the unreliable encounter was the vision of his red checkered jacket, worn and faded jeans, knife in one hand, and black boots leaving massive prints in the snow.

Prints in the snow.

I was enveloped with confusion, mystery, fear. I saw this three days ago, or at least a fragment of the horrible encounter that just played out before me. I felt my body carry me the rest of the way to my car, only then realizing the paralyzed state that previously took hold of me had evaporated. Simply the mechanical motions corresponding to my cerebellum's control. I was still not yet present, not consciously there.

I was stunned. What I had thought was a figment of my imagination had been manifested once again, but with a more gruesome context. I was sick, in need professional intervention. A chemical imbalance in the brain can spontaneously appear, heightening especially between the ages of eighteen and twenty-five in psychotic disorders. This was the after-effects of some terrible disorder. Was I schizoaffective? Psychosis? I didn't know, but there was no other explanation.

I was shaking so much I couldn't even muster the coordination to start my car. On the third try I succeeded and drove slowly the rest of the way home. Once again, a mechanical motion.

I preheated the oven and sat in the cold, metal stool at my kitchen table as I watched the clock. I felt lost. I picked up a book but I couldn't focus, my mind wandering to the potential sensibilities that were happening to me. It was debilitating. I left my books as they were and crawled to bed, forgetting about my food entirely. I shut off the light, as well as my phone, tapping out from reality. I'd wake up early and make up the work I missed out on tonight.

I couldn't sleep. I once again found myself thinking about the prospect of ghosts and the dimensions of the unreal. I gave in and let my thoughts carry me away.

Rationalization was a part of me. It was in my nature to question, and I mentally could not push the thoughts aside within the workings of my mind. Ghosts and alternative dimensions were the things of movies, imaginary things individuals fashioned as part of their darker subconscious. Except come to life, haunting, and associated with delusions. Part of me refused to allow myself to succumb to those ridiculous ideas, but I also would refuse to believe my questionable mental health unless I saw a brain scan proving my delirium. I was in medical school to become a psychiatrist, not because I needed one. I couldn't decide which of the two outcomes was a worse fate so I forced my brain to shut off and drifted into sleep.

I hopped off the bus on the way to the lab. I looked down, trying to shield my face from the snow. I watched my feet slush through the murky grey mess, the previously white snow altered to a dark smog from the train of early morning traffic. I turned on the street of my destination and noticed a young girl. She looked out of place, her dark green dress whipping ferociously in the wind and her auburn hair following suit. Her one hand was preoccupied with trying to tame her hair into a bun, while the other was holding a stack of something.

Even though she looked out of place, there was no reason for me to doubt her presence as reality. However, I did not want to draw attention to myself in either case. I turned the volume of my music down and altered my positioning so the view of my headphones were in her direct line of sight. I realized my precautionary measure to avoid intermediate socialization was not heeded as I heard a faint "Excuse me?"

I walked quicker, my instincts screaming at me that I didn't want to know what she had to offer. "Excuse me, miss?" I heard again, louder. It was beginning to sleet, the hard drops slashing against both my face and forearm as I tried to shield myself from the ice cold daggers. Almost against my will I slowed my pace and turned to look at her.

The wind was fierce. As I stopped the hood of my jacket whipped down off my face, leaving me exposed. My long hair flared around in the wind as I removed one of my headphones and got as close as I dared. "Please take this," her voice echoed out against the empty street and was far more shrill than I expected, lashing against my ear drums in the otherwise deadly silence. "What?" I asked. My voice reflected back annoyance, although it wasn't necessarily intentional. "Have you seen him?" She walked closer to me to distribute the unknown.

I prepared myself for some spew of religion, a conversion attempt, perhaps. I reached my hand out and simultaneously felt my heart stop after I realized what it was. I once again froze. It was as if my whole being fell unconscious, only to restart again. Except my body stayed locked in a robotic trance and my mind played witness.

"Is this a joke?" I asked, genuinely seriously. I remained frozen, aside from my fingers which mechanically let the piece of paper fall to the ground. The piece of paper that had Jack's picture on it with missing inscribed at the top.

"I'm with the Church of the Brethren. We are trying to spread a search for this man, his mother is a member. He went missing about three days ago, proclaimed after two. His body is still undiscovered but pictures surfaced of his intestines ripped out of his body. The rest shoveled out with a spade. His limbs were hacked off, next. We don't know why or who or where, but we need help to find the body so he can have the proper burial with Christ. Please, take this."

I began trying to rationalize. I hypothesized with the idea of a potential experiment being conducted on psychological torture. I was left standing there, consumed within my own horrific thoughts of the worst. I tried to tell myself to walk away, that this wasn't a reality, but my body wouldn't correspond to my mental will. My head fell forward as I stared at my feet and the sullen grey snow we were standing in. My glasses fell to the bridge of my nose and I regained control as I slowly brought my hand to my face to wipe the moisture from my eyes.

When I looked at her again her eyes were brimming with tears, as if she genuinely cared. "Please, at least just take this," she pleaded. "This isn't real," I felt my mouth move in conjunction with the words but it didn't sound like me. "This isn't real."

I woke up shaking but my mind and body felt numb. My heartbeat was climbing in my chest and I couldn't breathe. I tried to get up and reach for my purse but I couldn't. I was in a shaking, paralyzed state. An oxymoron from Hell. Unable to coordinate, unable to move. A small will from the back of my mind screamed at me to get up, the epinephrine surge coursing through my bloodstream propelling me upright.

I scrambled for my purse, falling over myself. I got the Ativan and took two right before crumpling into an unproductive lump on the floor. I laid there and within a few minutes I felt a wave of calm wash over me. It felt like I lost every ounce of strength in my being. I couldn't imagine moving at that moment, or ever again. My eyes drifted closed and I didn't wake for a long time.

I woke up disoriented and confused, my back aching and stiff from the cold wooden floor. I had no gauge of the time and it was freezing. I slowly pulled myself upright and sat there for a minute staring at nothing. I crawled to a hoodie lying on the floor and pulled it over my head. As I waited for warmth to envelop me I walked slowly to the nightstand where I left my phone, and flicked the power on.

It was two in the afternoon. I missed class and I knew I probably wouldn't be able to come back from the amount of work I've been putting off, that I probably wouldn't find success in trying. However, part of me didn't care anymore. What was happening to me? I was so focused, so driven, or at least I used to be. I felt myself getting embedded within my thoughts as my phone loaded and a flow of texts came in. Various numbers with various forms of "Where are you?" Where were you Cal? I asked myself as I scrolled further. My heart stopped. I slept through the 9 A.M. biomedical application exam.

I sat there staring at the wall. Desperation coursed through me. I was going to have to forge a family emergency or something. I felt like I was going to wither away in the pit of despair that all other failed doctors felt when they realized they weren't cut out for it.

I thought about praying in that moment, to beg for a second chance and pledge my supposed being for the supposed knowledge of God. Since when have I turned to religion? I felt pathetic doing it. I thought this might be the lowest point in my life. The point where I simply didn't know what to do anymore. The point that I turn to 'God.'

I pushed myself up and went to my desk. I opened my laptop and slowly typed my professor's name under compose. I didn't even try to lie, just a simple, "I'm so sorry, Sir. Please give me another chance." I'd do anything and I meant it. I just stared, my pointer finger refreshing the page every five seconds.

I had to remind myself that hysteria wasn't doing anyone any favors. I opened a new browser and went on Facebook, trying to occupy myself with triviality for a few minutes. The second the page loaded I regretted my choice.

"ELEVEN YEAR OLD ADDISON PARKER FOUND DEAD IN BOSTON WOODS."

No. No. No. This wasn't happening. I frantically clicked the link, skimming over the fragments. "Never returned home from school...bright pink rain jacket... Light blonde hair.... Found by Hillside Street in woods.... Multiple stab wounds... pneumothorax.... Blood loss.... Killer not yet found..."

I slammed my laptop closed. I got up and started pacing. No way was this real. I was going to wake up at any moment. I was there. I saw that chase. I thought it was in my head. But it wasn't.

I couldn't get the idea out of my head that I could have had some kind of agency. I could have done something. I could have chased after him and stopped the brutal act of useless murder.

Reason soon followed as I got lost in my thoughts. I liked to think of myself as an embodiment of reason, always my priority. I was constantly thinking, trying to rationalize, which might play a prominent role as to why I was left so bothered by what was materializing, literally, right before my eyes. There was nothing I could have done in that situation. I didn't have a weapon. I didn't have anything. If I would have tried I would only have gained my name right next to hers in the article. Gone from the world. Nothing. But it didn't stop me from the guilt, the shock, the despair.

After about twenty minutes I found that I was able to breathe again without effort. I refreshed my email and discovered a rare reply. I could retake the exam only under the conditions that I take a harder version, and by the time he left his office at 4 P.M.

It was 2:48. I got up and ran.

I've never excelled in the athletic department, but somehow I found myself nearing the turn of the last street before my destination. My heart was hammering against my chest to an almost unbearable degree. I felt like I was going to collapse, my central nervous system kicking in and putting me to an end before I reached fatigue.

I forced myself to slow as I neared the building. Without hindering my pace, I reached behind me in the pouch of my backpack and retrieved my water bottle, downing the remnants. An epinephrine surge propelled me up the stairs at the quickest pace I could manage. I slipped my way up the ice coated concrete which was haphazardly coated with salt.

I was half-running through the hall, my hair matted to my face with sweat and snow as I collided into Alyssa. We both fell, tumbling to the ground. "Shit!" I screamed. "I- I'm so sorry, I h- I have to get to Dr. Robert's. Dude, I miss-missed the exam this morning!" I was panting so hard I couldn't even manage to get the words out. She had a look of shock and concern on her face both at once.

She opened her mouth to speak and then said nothing. "What? Why are you looking at me like that? I have to go and take this, I'll catch up with you later!" I once again struggled to speak as I simultaneously pulled myself up. "Wait," she said. "You don't know what happened, do you? I know you missed the exam. We all though Jack was with you but he was just proclaimed missing."

NIGHT OWL

by Robin Wyatt Dunn

That all the last daylight should have passed; not only in the sky but in our daydreams; for night in slipping closer says we're freer than we were; or more closely tied to one another (which is what freedom is).

All the last lights should come over to us; here in our hearts, where we have been keeping them, on this last echo of our time here, La-Z-boy on derriere and Schlitz in hand, for the dereliction of our national duty, the sweetest thing.

No one offers any reservation, or much comment, other than

"What a nice evening."

Not only the hour, magic, not just dusk but the evening of accounts; the evening of the sights; the evening of the odds.

What a nice evening it is, made just by the simple reason of it, and held to on account of its righteous splendor, almost mathematical in its ordinate simplicity.

There are no other options; nor any wanted; no other avenues of escape, no other people on this earth but you and yours, on blankets with picnic baskets and the end of the world.

The end of the world is a daily occurrence; though some feel it more than others. Some days feel it more than others. We feel it here today; for a number of reasons I can't or shouldn't explain, nor do I suspect the reasons are very interesting.

The interesting thing is the feeling; those things which are more difficult to describe. Of course we have names, outfits, nationalities, languages and curses and histories; lovers and destinations; occupations; identities. The feeling is something else, some ur-stuff that waits hidden under the earth, inside of stars, in the darkness of the heart, whose rich ichor not composed of platelets but ideas and universes, the scape of the night, and other nights beyond this one, whose vast blanket covers our women in their quiet splendor.

No one can say otherwise; because it would be too rude, and no one can invite anyone else in either; it is too late. We are already here to watch it; already here to say what it is we have seen; and, well. You've been here before.

I only want you to remember it. I don't think it's too much to ask. I don't think it should be too much for me to ask.

Perhaps there's the questioning too, that we must do; or I feel I must, set under the grave and dignified expanse of the gathering night, to inquire why it is we're here.

James Agee wanted to know too; we have invited him, with his cigar and cape, and his hat. All of the past is here with us, to see why we have come; and what it means. Who is in love, and who is out, and on which courses we are trying, trying, trying, our souls to fire the needful engines underneath, to stars within.

"James, tell us, --" but he's already gone.

We are alone here under the night; swirling above. I can see everything I ever wanted to see, except for you.

About the Author:

Robin Wyatt Dunn was born in Wyoming in 1979. He is a graduate student in creative writing at the University of New Brunswick, Canada.

FAST LANE

by Katie Rose

I start slow, creepin' down the dirt road in first gear, my bare foot just kissin' the gas pedal. I need my fix though, so I press down harder on the pedal. First, second, third, fourth; I'm slammin' through gears, out on the main road now. I turn the radio up as loud as it goes and roll the windows down. The A/C in this old truck don't work no more and I'm sweatin' bullets, but I don't care. I feel the thrum of the tires on the road through the floor boards. I'm doin' 120 now and I feel alive again. Outside, cornfields are flyin' by faster than a jumbo jet. My fingers are tinglin'. My nerves are electric. I'm livin' this moment fast and free. I hear the chirp of the siren before I look into the rearview mirror to see a quick flash of red and blue. Shit.

***

I climb out of the cruiser, preparin' for the usual "license and registration" bit, but then I see the familiar white-blond hair tucked up into a Nascar cap. Now, my heartbeat quickens, and I'm preparin' to be the one gettin' chewed out. I lean up against the truck and duck my head down through the open window.

"Do you know how fast you was goin' ma'am?" I ask.

"Aw hell, Buzz, I thought you wasn't gonna pull me over no more," she says, pullin' the cap off her head and down into her lap.

Her hair falls down around her shoulders and she's lookin' at me with her big green eyes. I just can't keep it together any longer. I burst into laughter.

"It ain't funny, Buzz. You damn near gave me a heart attack," she snaps, but she's smiling and I can tell she's tryin' hard not to laugh too.

"But honestly, Carolina, you could be more careful," I say. I'm still tryin' to control my laughter, and it comes out soundin' less serious than I meant it.

"Now Buzz, ain't nobody ever had any fun by bein' careful."

I know she'll never slow down.

***

I'm relieved that its only Buzz. I can't afford another speeding ticket. I reach my hand up and gently shove his head back out the window. His dark hair is soft between my fingers. I lean out the window, catch his sweet blue eyes with mine, and snatch a pen from his shirt pocket, wagglin' it in front of his face with a grin. It's a challenge. Before I can say a word, Buzz is racing back to his cruiser. He knows the game I wanna play. I start the truck back up, throw it into gear, and slam my foot down on the pedal. I tear off down the road, throwin' dust onto Buzz's windshield. In the rearview, I see him tryin' his best to keep up in hot pursuit. Buzz is fast, but I've always been faster. Though there's never been any hope of victory for him, Buzz has always tried to keep up with me. I look down at his pen I have stashed in my cup holder and remember the day I met Buzz.

I was just a little thing, no older than four. My mamma had taken me to the playground. My favorite thing in the whole world was goin' down the slide. I liked the covered slide the best; it was like slidin' through a tunnel. That particular day, I shot down the slide and crashed into a little dark-haired boy who musta been tryin' to climb up through the tunnel. We fell onto a bed of woodchips in a tangled mess.

"What's your problem, kid? Didn't your mamma ever tell you slides ain't for climbin'?" I yelled. I was furious. How dare this kid ruin my fun?

"Didn't your mamma never tell ya to look before you go down?" the boy said.

He was right. My mamma did tell me to always look before I went down the slides, but I wasn't gonna tell him that. I was fumin'. Suddenly, I noticed the boy was clutchin' some kinda action figure in his hand. I snatched it from him, stuck my tongue out and took off runnin'. He took off after me. We ran around the playground for near twenty minutes before I took mercy on the kid and tossed his toy back to him. He leaned down, hands on his knees, and puffed out a quiet "thanks". I decided then that I liked this kid.

I laugh at the memory, realizing that Buzz has been chasing me since the day we met.

***

I'm speeding down the road outta town thinkin' that Carolina Barnett has gotta be the most frustrating, irresponsible, beautiful, free-spirited creature I have ever known. If we get caught, I may very well lose my job but there ain't a snowballs chance in hell I'll ever turn down a challenge from Lina. I press down on the gas pedal a little harder, closin' the gap between the bed of Lina's old truck and the front bumper of my cruiser. Just when I think I've caught up to her, she stomps on the gas and is roarin' down the road far ahead of me. "Dammit, Lina," I whisper to myself. I realize she was only goin' easy on me until now, and suddenly, I'm rememberin' a sunny summer's day when Lina and I were in middle school.

It was a warm day in the middle of June. It was sunny, but I remember there had been a big thunderstorm the night before. I was sittin' on my front porch pettin' my Golden Retriever, Oggie. I heard a buzzin' in the distance and didn't think nothin' of it till Lina came burstin' out of the trees and down my driveway on a brand new dirt bike. She was grinnin' ear to ear. Breathlessly, she told me she saved every penny she earned from mowin' grass and walkin' dogs and had used the money to buy the bike earlier that mornin'.

"Now we can ride together Buzz! Go get your bike!"

So I ran down to the barn as fast as my legs could carry me and met her back on the driveway with my bike. Minutes later we was racin' through the woods side by side. Lina looked over and caught my eye, givin' me a wicked grin. She took off down the path ahead of me, and I knew she wanted to race. I gassed it. After a few minutes, I started closin' the gap between us. Suddenly, I heard her bike scream and she was yards ahead of me again. I knew she'd just been goin' easy on me. I tried desperately to catch up to her. I was so focused on her that I didn't see the huge mud puddle in front of me. I wiped out, landin' in the puddle and thoroughly coatin' myself with mud. I heard Lina turn around and moments later she was pullin' me up off the ground laughin' so hard, I could see tears runnin' down her face.

I laugh at the memory, realizin' that I've been tryin' to catch up to Lina my whole life.

***

I look in the rearview and see Buzz's cruiser getting smaller and smaller. I laugh to myself, knowin' that he's tryin' his hardest to keep up with me. I take mercy on him and let my foot off the gas just a little bit. He gets closer, but I know he still ain't drivin' as fast as that cruiser can go. Buzz has always been the careful one. If it weren't for me, he wouldn't know how exhilaratin' it is to be flying down the highway at a buck forty. I smile rememberin' the first time Buzz was in the passenger seat while I was drivin'.

It was August. Buzz had just turned 16. I was out in the barn workin' on my dad's old pickup, grease smeared all over my face. I heard someone roarin' up my drive and slid myself out from under the truck. I wiped my hands and face with an old towel and stuffed it into my back pocket as I closed the barn door behind me. When I looked up, I saw Buzz leanin' on the hood of an old black Camaro. He was smilin' real wide and holdin' up a small plastic card.

"I got my license!" he said.

"Buzz, that's great! Where'd the Camaro come from?" I asked, eyeing up the newly polished beauty.

"You like it? I bought it from my cousin this mornin'. Thought we could take it for a spin together."

"You drivin' or am I?" I laughed.

Buzz answered by tossin' me the keys. Moments later I was behind the wheel and tearin' out of the driveway. Once we hit the open road, I increased my speed. At 90, Buzz reminded me there was such thing as a speed limit. At 100, he told me I should slow down. At 110, he fell silent and gripped his seat for dear life. At 120, he was so nervous he started laughin'. I hit the brakes and pulled off onto the side of the road where we both spent the next few minutes laughin' until our insides hurt. As our laughter subsided, Buzz caught be starin' at his smile. I almost told him how much I loved his smile. Instead, I put the car in gear and took to the road again.

I laugh at the memory, realizin' that Buzz has been tryin' and failin' to slow me down for as long as I could remember.

***

I think I'm startin' to catch up to Lina. I'm not sure if I'm drivin' faster or if she's slowin' down, but I'm close enough now to see her eyes looking back at me in her rearview mirror. All of a sudden, Lina slams on her brakes, veers left, and roars off down a dirt road. I don't hesitate. I throw my turn signal on and barrel down through the dirt after her. The road is rough, clearly made for trucks like Lina's and not cars like mine. She's slowed down just a little and is swervin' to avoid potholes. I'm somehow managin' to hit every single one. Her tires are kickin' up so much dust ahead of me, I can barely see her taillights. I'm wonderin' why I'd follow her down this old dirt road. The memory of our graduation day pops into my head.

It was the beginning of June. Lina and I were out on her front porch, and her folks were taking pictures of us in our bright blue caps and gowns. She leaned over and whispered in my ear, "I can't wait till this is over". I was still starin' at the camera, but I didn't need to look over to know she had rolled her eyes. I smiled a little wider. I had been thinkin' the same thing.

Later that day, after all the fus and photography, Lina and I headed down to the old pond behind her house. We plopped down on the dock and swished our feet around in the water.

"Buzz, I gotta tell you somethin'," she said, leanin' her head on my shoulder. I stiffened.

"What is it, Lina?"

"I got a job workin' at a garage a couple towns over in Janesville. I'm startin' the end of this week."

I didn't know how to reply so we just sat there in silence for what seemed like hours. Eventually, Lina stood up.

"I have to go Buzz. It'll be dinner time soon and you know how mamma gets if I ain't on time."

I just nodded my head in reply. I was upset. How could she just leave like that? She wasn't just my best friend; she was my only friend.

I didn't talk to Lina for a whole two days, the longest we'd ever gone without communication. On the third day, Lina came to say goodbye.

"Please don't hate me Buzz. I gotta go."

"I could never hate you Lina. I'm just gonna miss you is all," I replied while kicking a stone around in the dirt. I couldn't look her in the eye.

"Promise you'll come visit. I'll call you every day. I would just die if we weren't friends any more Buzz."

I promised to visit often, but I was still upset. At the end of that week, Lina was gone. A week after that, I turned in my application for the police academy. It was no coincidence I had chosen the one in Janesville. In the weeks that followed, I could hardly sleep. I was so nervous to hear back from the academy. When the letter arrived in the mail and I opened it to see the words of congratulations, I think the whole county could hear my shouts of excitement. I called Lina right away to tell her the good news.

I found a cheap little apartment a few blocks

from the academy. Every day I would wake up early to study. I worked harder than I ever had because I had a vision for my future. I pictured comin' home from work, kickin' my boots off at the door, and wrappin' Lina in a big bear hug every night. I worked through the program real quick and graduated earlier than I had originally planned. Then, I put my application in with the Janesville Police Department.

I swear, all my hard work paid off when I saw the look of utter surprise and amazement on Lina's face as I pulled up in front of Billy's garage in my new cruiser.

"Buzz, don't tell me you stole that!" Lina said.

"I didn't steal it, Lina. This here is my very own police cruiser," I replied.

I laugh at the memory, realizin' I would follow Lina anywhere.

***

This dirt road was a little rougher than I thought it would be, and I'm worrin' about how Buzz is handlin' the potholes behind me. I glance up into the rearview, searching for Buzz's face behind me, but I can't see anything through the thick cloud of dust I've kicked up. I know this road connects back up with the main one soon, so I press down on the gas a little harder, hopin' that Buzz is doing the same behind me. A few yards ahead, through the trees, I see the stop sign indicatin' the entry to the main road. I hit the brakes, look both ways and then make a right turn on the main road heading back toward town. I know our favorite diner is just a few miles down the road, and since Buzz is never gonna to win this race, I decide that I will treat him to lunch as a consolation prize. I look back to make sure that he's still behind me, and I see him flash me a thumbs up. I smile and turn back around in my seat. And then I see it, a car pullin' out onto the road without a single glance in my direction. I slam on the breaks. I hear the screechin' of my tires on the road. I feel the truck do a complete 180 before comin' to a halt on the side of the road, facin' the opposite direction I had just been goin'. Shit, that was close. I breathe a sigh of relief that's cut short by the sound of a loud crash. I remember Buzz behind me flashin' a thumbs up and my breath is caught in my throat. I leap from the truck and make a mad dash for Buzz's mangled cruiser.

***

We're out on the main road again, headin' back toward town. Our favorite diner is just a few miles ahead and I decide I'll treat Lina to a victory lunch. I know how much she loves the chocolate milkshakes there. I see Lina turn around. She catches my eyes and flashes a smile. She must have thought she lost me back on that dirt road. I give her a thumbs up to show her that I'm okay. I see her slowin' down a little bit. She must have the same idea about lunch that I do. I blink and all of a sudden, I see Lina's truck spinnin' across the black top. My breath catches in my throat. I see the car she had swerved to miss, and I slam on my brakes, but not fast enough. I see the night I almost told Lina that I love her flash before my eyes.

I was sittin' in the passenger seat of Lina's old pickup. We'd spent the whole day together, hiking through new and unfamiliar forest trails. I was starvin' and, we had been drivin' around for half an hour tryin' to figure out where to eat dinner.

"I'm so hungry," Lina complained.

"Then just stop somewhere," I said.

"But we don't know if any of these places are gonna be good," she replied.

I fished around in my pants pocket and pulled out my phone. I searched "places to eat in Janesville." A moment later, a list of restaurants appeared on the display. I picked the first one on the list and spent the next fifteen minutes readin' the directions off to Lina.

When we arrived at the diner, Lina ordered a chocolate shake and a cheeseburger. I had the same. As soon as we took the first bite of our food, we were in agreement that this diner was our new favorite place. Lina looked up at me with a mouthful of cheeseburger.

"I'm really glad you're here Buzz," she mumbled through a bite of burger.

"Glad to be here Lina. This burger is great," I said.

"No Buzz, I mean I'm glad you're here; in Janesville. I'm glad you got that job," she said.

"You didn't really think I'd just let you run off and have all this fun without me, did ya?" I said with a smile.

Lina gave her head a quick shake and grinned, her straw poised on the edge of her lip to finish off her milkshake.

Watchin' Lina slurp down her chocolate shake that night, I almost told her that I loved her, but I was too scared of what she'd say back.

***

I'm in church. I never come to church, but today is different. My body is here, but my head feels like it's somewhere else entirely. I'm sweatin' in this scratchy cotton dress. I can't focus on a single word the preacher's sayin'. I fidget with the pamphlet in my hands, not even noticin' that I've cut my finger on the edges and I'm bleedin' all over the paper. I have twenty more minutes to go. I can do this. But then the choir starts singin' "Amazing Grace." I look up at Mrs. Aldwin in the front pew. She's wailin' and there's tears just pouring down her cheeks, and I can't take it. I spring up from the pew and run for the door as fast as a I can. I barrel towards the old magnolia tree with the stone under it that reads: Brandon "Buzz" Aldwin, a great officer, but an even greater friend." I drop to my knees and rest my forehead on the cold stone slab.

"I love you, Buzz," I whisper.

I cry harder than I ever have, because for the first time in my whole life, I'm all alone. Buzz ain't on my tail no more.

About the Author:

A native of Altoona, Pennsylvania, **Katie Rosa** is currently earning her bachelor's degree in occupational therapy at Saint Francis University.

THE PHOTOGRAPH
by Marcella Meeks

Last week, my husband Gene and I went to Santa Fe, New Mexico for our fifteenth anniversary. Santa Fe is where we met and we come back here every year. Gene and I have a strong relationship, and he understands me. We get along very well together and we have a wonderful loving relationship, and I have never had reason to suspect him of chasing other women. I have always prided myself in taking care of my man at home so he don't have to get his needs fulfilled elsewhere. We've been very happy together over the years, and we both work and have a really good home life. What more could a man want?

Gene is quiet, kind and compassionate. One word that describes him better than any other is 'gentleman.' And gentleman he is. He is considerate and loyal to me, as well as smart.

I love stopping at yard sales and going to thrift stores. Gene, on the hand, would rather spend his time at the pool or watching a game on TV on his off days.

We went out to dinner last night and I read a sign on one of the street corners near the motel that read: Estate Sale - All day Friday. It gave the address with an arrow pointing down the street.

"Gene, I am going to run down the street to that Estate Sale. Do you want to come? It's almost ten, they should be open by now."

"No, I think I will stick around here and watch TV. If I get bored, I'll stroll down to the pool. You go ahead - get out of the room awhile."

I drove along the street until I came to the house where the estate sale was going on. There was a lot of nice furniture and paintings for sale. A really pretty Mexican lady who looked to be about thirty-five walked up and said, "There is a lot of stuff inside. If you need help just let me know. This was my mother's house. She passed away last month and the house has been sold."

I went inside after thanking her. There was stuff on tables everywhere that had been marked down. I saw four real nice picture frames made of oak that were marked down to a dollar each. There were photos in each one. There was one of the pretty Mexican lady, one of her and apparently her mother, one of her and a little boy who looked to be about five or six, and then there was one with her and a man standing together with the little boy in front. The man was none other than my husband Gene.

I dropped the photo, breaking the glass. No one was around so I took the back off the picture frame and took out the photo. There was an inscription on the back that said, "Gene, Cynthia, and Martin." Below that was an inscription that read, "With Love, Gene." It was dated three weeks ago. It was Gene's handwriting.

I put the photo back in the broken frame and picked up all four photos. The lady walked back over to me. "Are you alright? You look like you seen a ghost," she said, smiling.

"I...uh... I dropped this frame and the glass broke. But I want to purchase these frames."

"Oh no, I forgot to take these photos out before I put the frames out to sell. If you don't mind, just take the pictures out and leave them on the counter," she said before walking over to another customer who needed assistance.

My hands were shaking so bad that I could barely remove the pictures from their frames. When I went to pay her for the frames, I asked, "Is this your husband and son?"

"Yes," she said. "My husband is gone so it is just me and my son Martin. He is six years old. I gave these photos to my mother but she passed away. I am from El Paso, Texas - just came to close up the Mama's old house," she said, wiping tears from her eyes.

"How long ago did your husband leave you?" I asked.

"We broke up two weeks ago," she said. "But he chose another woman over me and I will never have him back. Maybe I will go back to El Paso or to Mexico after I sell this stuff."

"My husband and I are also from El Paso," I said. "So, this is your son?" I asked feebly, with shaking hands as I handed her the picture.

"Yes. Martin looks just like his father."

"He sure does," I agreed.

Some other customers had gotten her attention. Slipping the four photos in between the frames was easily enough and since no one was watching me, I eased my way out.

I drove around for awhile before going back to the room. This was the last straw for me. How on earth could Gene have another family? But it was true because I had the pictures to prove it. How did he meet this woman Cynthia? When did he have time to cheat on me? He never wanted children with me. Why her? How could he do this to me? They couldn't be married because he was married to me - or could they? What made him do it? How would I tell him what I found? Should I tell him now or should I just pretend nothing happened and let it be? Or should I get a lawyer and turn the photos over to him? Should I leave him or ask for a divorce? Tears filled my eyes and I pulled over in a parking lot and cried. Questions without answers were plaguing my mind.

After an hour of driving around, I made my way back to the motel. Gene was watching TV when I got back. "Where on earth have you been? I thought you got lost or something?"

"No, I wasn't lost," I retorted hotly.

"What happened to you? Why are you in such a bad mood. You were fine when you left."

"Do you know a lady named Cynthia? She has a son named Martin?" I decided to throw it out there and see how he responded to the question.

"Never heard of them," he said and started flipping channels.

"Is that so?" I asked. "That's not true and you know it. Look at these pictures."

"You've made a mistake, Melinda. I'm going for a swim," he said nervously.

"Gene, we need to talk." Tears filled my eyes. "Gene, please tell me the truth about this woman Cynthia and the little boy," I pleaded. "When did you start seeing her? When did you two have a son? She said you was her husband.. Is that true?"

"I have nothing to say." He walked out the door.

Grabbing my purse and starting out the door, I was going to that woman's house and talk to her one more time. It was useless trying to talk to Gene. He knew he had been found out and he was a closed book. I must go and talk to Cynthia one more time. Maybe this is a big mistake - maybe it was somebody else. It can't be real - this is Santa Fe. How did those pictures turn up here? And why? It seemed as if they were set there for me to find. How could that be possible?

I pulled onto the street where the estate sale was earlier that morning. There was a large truck in the driveway from a thrift store. I walked up to one of the guys as he was loading the stuff and asked, "Is Cynthia here?"

"The lady who owns this house left about an hour ago to catch a plane. My boss bought everything she had. He's right over there."

I walked over to him. "I need to talk to Cynthia." I said feebly.

"She left earlier. She had a plane to catch and we are locking up the house when we are finished," he said. "Sorry," he apologized.

"Do you know where she was going on that plane?" I asked.

"No ma'am, she didn't say. But she was in a big hurry and didn't have time to talk very much. She told me her mother owned this house but she passed away. I never knew the family, or where they came from." He went back to loading boxes on the truck.

"Thank you."

I tried calling Gene on his cell phone but it went straight to voice mail. I sent him a text and asked him to meet me in the room. He never text me back.

When I arrived at the motel, the receptionist at the front desk said, "Mrs. Melinda Parker, may I speak with you for a second?"

"Sure. Is there a problem?"

"Mr. Parker came down about a half hour ago. He checked you guys out and told me to tell you to head back home as soon as possible."

"He can't do that," I muttered.

"Well, yes ma'am, he did. If you'd like to pay for another night, you may but he had me to cancel the payment on his credit card so you will have to pay again."

"No, that won't be necessary," I said, tears rolling down my cheek. "Excuse me. I need to get my things."

"Housekeeping already packed your things and brought your bags down. Check out time was at eleven."

"I can't believe Gene did this to me," I said, now sobbing. The receptionist helped me carry my bags to the car and I loaded them in the trunk.

"Who did he leave with, or do you know?" I asked.

"Yes ma'am, he left in a taxi."

"Thank you."

I drove out of the motel lot crying. "I just know he boarded that plane with Cynthia. He probably planned this all along."

I pulled into a station for gasoline several hours later. I tried calling Gene's cell phone once again but again, it went straight to voice mail. He wouldn't answer the phone or the texts I sent. Why did he leave me without a word? Why didn't I see this coming? He never gave a clue that he was unhappy with me. Why did he chose to have a child with Cynthia and he never wanted one with me? How long had he been seeing her? How could he make love to me knowing he was making love to someone else? The questions just kept going through my mind. How could I have been so stupid? What am I going to tell my friends and family back home?

Later that evening, I stopped for a salad before finding a motel for the night. Once in the room, I cried again, this time they were giant sobs. How could Gene do this to me? We went back to Santa Fe where we first met to celebrate our fifteenth wedding anniversary and he ran off with another woman that he apparently been sleeping with for years. I sobbed into my pillow. Why? How? How could I have been so blind? Why didn't I see it coming? Was I that naive?

About midnight, I got up and opened my overnight bag and took out the photos. Tears filled my eyes again. Why Gene? I asked. How could you do something like this? We had a good marriage, I whispered, angrily shoving the photos back inside my bag.

The two of us had a good relationship and we did a lot of things together. There were days he had to work late and occasionally he had to take weekend trips to different parts of the country, but they were business related trips. Or were they? Was he flying somewhere to meet Cynthia and spending the weekend with her and lying to me? How could he do this? Why didn't he just ask for a divorce?

I arrived in El Paso late that Sunday afternoon. After unloading my bags from the car, I went to our bedroom and noticed right away that things had been moved around. Gene had apparently came and got his clothes. The dresser and closet was empty. The study door was open and all his things were gone. The file cabinet where we kept our bank account information was empty as well. Immediately, panic set in. On Monday, I'd have to call the bank to make sure that Gene didn't take all of our money. He could have left me a note saying he was sorry - anything to ease my pain but he didn't.

The phone rang that evening but it wasn't him. My aunt called to see if we'd made it back safely. I let it ring until the recorder picked it up. I just wasn't in the mood for phone calls right now and have to explain that Gene left me.

On Monday morning, I called the bank only to find that Gene had emptied our checking and savings account. Panic set in and I called my job and took the day off. I went to the bank and closed out the accounts and reopened another one with the only twenty five dollars I had left in my name where my check from work would be deposited every week. The banker was upset after she found out what Gene had did to me. Later that evening, I stopped for gas only to find that my credit card was declined because of insufficient funds.

Not wanting to go back to the house alone, I stopped at my friend's house for awhile and broke down and told her everything that happened this week.

"Melinda, oh my gosh. How could Gene do this to you? Do you have any idea where he is?"

"Katie, all I know is that he is with her. They have a six year old son named Martin."

"I can't believe you found out by stopping at a yard sale in freaking Santa Fe, New Mexico. This is really weird, my friend. You need to divorce the Bastard," she said angrily.

"What am I going to do, Katie?" I sobbed.

"You're going to make it, Girlfriend. Here, take this and use it," she said, writing me a check for five hundred dollars.

"I can't take your money, Katie."

"Melinda, take the money. You can pay me back later. I'm going to shoot that prick if he shows back up around here. I can't believe he had the balls to do something like that. Why don't you stay here tonight and try and get some rest"

I'll be okay. Thanks for everything, Katie."

Several weeks passed, and not a word from Gene. I called his job and asked to speak to him one day and they said he no longer was employed with their firm, and he left no forwarding information.

Late one night, I got a call from a woman from Santa Fe who said she was Cynthia's aunt. "I know you don't know me, Melinda but I am Cynthia's aunt. I have some bad news about the two of them and I thought you might like to know it."

"What is it?" I asked sleepily.

"Gene and Cynthia were on their way to the Belize and their plane went down. No one survived the crash."

"What about the little boy?" I asked.

"He's here in Santa Fe with his aunt," she said.

After she hung up, I called Katie and told her the bad news. "I can't believe Gene is dead," I told her.

"He got what he deserved," she muttered. "I'm sorry, honey but he did you so wrong. He was living a double life, one with you and one with her. The only thing I am sorry for is that he died on a plane when I should have been the one to kill him for hurting you this way."

"Katie!" I scolded. "Don't say things like that."

"I'll be over shortly. Put some coffee on."

About the Author:

Marcella Simmons has been writing professionally since 1988 – she has over 650 published credits in over 350 small press publications nationwide, and continue writing for local newspapers. In 2005, her first book of poetry was published entitled Bittersweet Morsels, and she is currently working on several romantic suspense book projects at this time. "Writing is a way of life for me. I couldn't imagine 'not' writing." Marcella commented. "One of my many passions is writing fiction and children stories - some of my children stories appeared in Pockets Magazine, Primary Treasure and Christian Educator." In 1991, Marcella graduated from THE INSTITUTE OF CHILDREN'S LITERATURE: Writing for Children and Teens; WRITER'S DIGEST SCHOOL: Nonfiction Writing; and ICS School of Short Story/Journalism

IN SICKNESS AND IN HEALTH
by Emily Wanko

This is that thing you see in the news, and you think, "That will never happen to me". Your mind has to disassociate yourself from it in order to protect you because tragedy like this does happen in reality. In reality, it is my family you saw on the Saint Louis news on Friday. Those are my two cousins embracing my aunt who found her son, daughter in law, and three-month-old granddaughter slaughtered by a revolver in their own home. The police called it a murder-suicide and we all immediately knew that there was no way Matthew James, my blood cousin, could do something like that. It had to be her.

What happened before then that led up to that point? What was the conversation that pushed her over the edge? How did it get to this? She had just gone back to work a week before. They had so much trouble conceiving that baby, and she threw it all away. She was the cancer of our family, but we had no idea. She was supposed to be his wife, the one person who would always stand beside him. "In sickness and in health", right? Wrong. Apparently, you suffer in silence, let it all boil over, seek no treatment, and then you kill your family. How pathetic. I've met her several times, once before they were even married, and she seemed sweet and normal. How was I supposed to know I was brushing shoulders with a killer? I guess you never know someone. Or what goes on behind closed doors.

I wonder if Matt tried to calm her down. I wonder if he prayed while he laid on the floor awaiting death, or if it was over quickly for him. I wonder whom she killed first. Who could fathom making that choice between their baby and their husband? My mind wanders to these questions, and I try to pull them away. In my mind I see the scene from every angle, every possibility, and in all that wondering I was still wrong. I pulled my brain away all weekend. For three days I've been ignoring everything about this that I could. My time for ignoring it was up, we flew to Saint Louis the next morning. The services were the next day.

I was pissed off. I hate traveling. It makes me extremely anxious. I'm missed class, I'm missed work, I'm missing my dog and boyfriend. My parents are missing running their business. They had to trade in all of their credit card points for us to get plane tickets to go to this disaster that is currently our lives. No Florida beach vacation for us this year. She ruined it for us. We are wasting our vacation on this bullshit. My longtime boyfriend was supposed to go on this next family vacation with us. A huge step in our relationship with my parents, and something we have already been doing with his parents. She destroyed that too. It's was freezing cold in Saint Louis, and I hate the cold more than anything. I hate her for making me go up there in that awful weather. She ruined my week; she ruined my aunt and uncle's lives.

We arrived in Saint Louis. I had been crying since 7:00 a.m. because I hated traveling, and because I couldn't run from the reality of the situation any longer. My mom held my hand in the airport as if I was a child. She sat next to me on the plane, and distracted me from my thoughts and anxieties. An hour and a half later we landed in Saint Louis. With that first step off the plane my breath ran away from me with that brisk whip of cold air. I pulled my hat down farther over my ears as I walked up the ramp to the gate. All I had to do was put my head down and follow my dad. Bathroom. Bus. Rental car place. White Castles, which is always our first stop in Saint Louis, but I was too shaken to eat anything but French fries. Dad gets me a medium fry and a medium Sprite. I envy how much food my brother can eat. We headed to Aunt Jodi's house, which is our place to stay for the two nights we were there. We usually stayed with Aunt Kathy, but that's obviously a burden they couldn't bear. We put all our stuff down in our rooms; mine only has a blow up mattress and a chair. I sit down on the blow up mattress and pull on another pair of socks. "We're ready to go" Mom calls up the stairs. I put my black Nikes back on and leave the safety of the bed.

Information came to me from my mom, from my aunt, from my other aunt that there was video evidence of her buying that handgun two days before the incident. She also bought the wrong ammunition by mistake, went back, and bought the right one. Any idea that I had before of this being a desperate, emotional, sudden situation was blown to pieces. We were all hoping that this was a heat of the moment accident because you don't want to believe that someone you know is a cold-blooded killer. You wish for a fatal accident that can't be taken back and can't be undone, but an accident nonetheless. No. This was planned, this was plotted, and this was intended. There were plans made, money moved, time hidden, and she knew exactly what she was doing. She bought the gun, and then went to my Aunt Kathy's to pick up Taylor Rose. She hid her intentions hours before she ruined my Aunt's life. This is a person with hatred inside of them, and I can't help but think that maybe we are better off without her here on earth. I feel nothing for the loss of her life; similar to if you would see on the news that police killed a gunman. You think, "Well they got what they deserved". I wish there was a gunfight. I wish she was brought to justice, maybe do fifty to life for the death of her husband and child, but no. She was a coward above all other cowards. She could not face life herself, but worse, she could not let them face life without her. Fuck her for that. Not everyone has to suffer because you are suffering.

Aunt Kathy's house is new since the last time I was in town. They downsized just like everyone else at their age is doing. Their children are grown and there was too much room for her and my uncle in the old house. I hear a dog bark. Aunt Kathy and Uncle Jim don't have a dog, but she and Matt did… Tears flowed as we greeted each other. Brian, Matt's brother is there. He greeted my brother and I, and tears welled up in his eyes. Aunt Kathy embraces us, and she says, "I'm so glad you're here, but you make it all feel real". I know exactly what she means. My family only flies in when it's something serious, usually a funeral.

On Wednesday at a Catholic church I said my hello and my goodbye to a second cousin I never met. My mom was so upset over the death of the baby, and I didn't feel that attachment because I never got to meet Taylor Rose. Maybe it was because I am crushed enough already from losing my cousin so suddenly that I can't stand to add another person to that hill of grief. It was best for me to keep this distance from a life I have never met, probably better to protect myself in that way. There wasn't a tiny baby casket, with little pinks bows, because she is being buried in the casket with her father, which I am grateful for. My grandfather says that an infant sized casket is something you can never forget seeing. I'm glad I didn't have to see one that day. I feel that Matt deserves to have his baby with him in eternity. It brings me at least a little peace, even now, to know that she isn't going to be alone in the afterlife.

Her services should be completely separate. I do not want to grieve for her. She is not a poor, lost soul to me. She was a killer, a murderer, and there is no repentance for such an evil. I hope she rots in hell. I hope she knows that she fucked up. Unforgiveable. I have wiped her from my memory. A murderer does not deserve a service; she should be buried alone with only her psychotic mother to mourn for her. My family, my parents, my aunt and uncle, my other cousins should not have to attend a funeral on a freezing Wednesday in February. Especially not for a healthy thirty-two-year-old, new dad.

About the Author:

Emily M. Wanko is the Thesis and Dissertation Reviewer for a state university in Texas. Earlier this year she graduated from Sam Houston State University with a Bachelor's degree in English. In the spring, she will be pursuing her Master's of Library and Information Sciences to become an academic librarian. This is Emily's first published piece. She resides outside of Houston, Texas with her boyfriend and dog.

THE CHURCH

by Marc Frazier

Et cum spiritu tuo, Habemus ad Dominum, Dignum et justum est.

The sound of Latin phrases echo in my head as I sit in class trying to attend to

Sister's geography lesson. I'm memorizing responses for the liturgy of the Catholic mass: a clear expectation for an altar boy.

I enjoy dressing up to assist the priest, relishing wearing a cassock and surplice a little too much. To partake in such a ritual is comforting and calming, a sensual experience in many ways: the scent of beeswax candles, wine, the lingering odor of incense and father's aftershave.

I ring the bells when the hosts are consecrated, the devout silence in the church making me drowsy. Holding the Communion plate under worshippers' chins feels like a huge responsibility.

When a host falls on the floor, it takes quite a ritual to make things holy again.

In late elementary school, I thought I might have a religious vocation; thus I went on a couple of retreats at the archdiocese headquarters, enjoying this time surrounded by males for a weekend, sleeping in dorm rooms and sharing prayers and meals together.

I possess a black and white photograph of me in front of our house in Sycamore, my hands in front of me in prayer position, little black prayer book pressed between them. I have clunky eyeglasses and am wearing a child-size version of a trench coat. This was taken before I headed out to a retreat. I wanted to become a holy brother, as I didn't feel worthy enough to be a priest, which said something about my self-esteem.

One of the most solemn times in the calendar is Forty Hours Devotion when the consecrated host, or Blessed Sacrament, is displayed in an elaborate monstrance the priest places on a side altar before which parishioners pray.

There is a schedule for altar boys to follow during the devotion period so that someone is always present. I was paired with my classmate Jeff for a few sessions of devotion. In between times, we hung out at his house near the church. I had a big crush on him and was bereft when our time together was up.

Though she died before I was born, my paternal grandmother converted to Catholicism from her family's German Lutheran religion. I never met her as she passed when my father was serving in World War II. This caused a split in the family, as everyone was Catholic except for this set of relatives. The topic of religion could be a touchy one in our family. During one Thanksgiving dinner, Tante Edo called the tail of the turkey the Pope's nose. Thankfully silence ensued.

I guess I thought everyone was Catholic really, and if they weren't, they just hadn't yet realized they needed to be. As a boy, I gathered neighbor children in our front yard, proselytizing by telling them stories of martyrs and saints. I don't know how deeply my devotion went because the next moment I was rounding the same kids up for theatrical productions to be performed in our garage. I remember when the songs from Oklahoma were on the tip of my tongue for hours and days on end. One of my friend's mothers taught me, "You Are My Sunshine," and I created a musical number for all of us kids to sing.

My father was obsessed with the rules and regulations of Catholicism, more so than my mother for whom it all seemed more natural due to her Irish Catholic background. She said converts were stricter and more vigilant than those brought up in the Church.

One pilgrimage my father liked was to a place called Holy Hill. It wasn't a very long trip, but we would pray the rosary on the way to the National Shrine of Mary, Help of Christians. It was a basilica with all the bells and whistles.

First, the outdoor Stations of the Cross, schlepping from station to station in all weathers. I enjoyed looking at the colorful brochures displayed in the entrance to the church. My sisters and mother pulled out their chapel veils and we entered the hushed nave of wooden pews, genuflecting on our right knees and making the sign of the cross.

"I don't feel well," I told my parents. "My stomach hurts."

I was having a meltdown and they were clueless as to what I was feeling. I often had strange physical sensations I think were tied to the intensity of religious fervor, of my own investment in it. I wanted reassurance. All this piousness and I just wanted a hand to hold.

I had psychosomatic health issues. I was a fainter. It seemed somehow tied to church. I would feel like passing out, and one of my parents would take me outside to get some air. I sat in the passenger seat of the car facing out, put my head between my knees until lightheadedness passed. I remember one time passing out on the sidewalk in front of the church as we left mass.

From her pew, mother watched my face whiten as I assisted the priest say mass, worried I would pass out on the altar. My doctor tried giving me iron for a while thinking I might be anemic. I spent a couple of days in the hospital for tests. I was mean to my mother who brought me a poor, cheap substitute of a kind of primitive block printing press I'd been wanting; I was fascinated with words and writing even then.

"This isn't anything like it," I said.

"I thought it was what you wanted," she uttered in a tremulous voice.

"I don't even want it," I added rolling onto my side away from her, oblivious to the effort this act of kindness took when she also worried about a husband and three other children.

My parents never thought of a shrink for a kid, but that is what I needed. Was there something so oppressive about the whole religion thing I couldn't handle, and the warm enclosed space of a church filled with parishioners made me lose consciousness? Was this a form of experiencing the fear of God?

The examination of conscience was central to the religion. I did mine before I went to sleep every night, so my conscience was clear in case I passed in the night. Not a festive childhood. On Saturday afternoons, we'd pile in the car and head to church for confessions. How scared I was during my first confession! I was afraid of the dark, and the unlit confessional booth was frightening.

There were small, lit red bulbs above a confessional booth when someone was inside. When he or she got up from the kneeler, the bulb went out, signaling that the booth was available for the next person in line for Confession. I had a set menu of sins to confess. I, of course, feared committing a mortal sin that meant certain damnation.

It was comforting that I could estimate my venial sins with a conditional "about." I talked back to my parents "about" three times; I disobeyed my parents "about" two times. As my parents stood in line, they seemed like different, vulnerable people. After kneeling to say their penance with bowed heads, they became themselves for another week.

There were some lighter moments, but not many. I loved spring, for the month of May was joyful. Some chosen girl from the eighth grade was given the honor of crowning Mary in the church during a ceremony. My proclivity to pageantry truly enjoyed this. At home, we built a May altar. A small glass vase filled with lilies of the valley and violets. We each vied for the honor of picking fresh flowers and changing the water. We'd kneel on the hard floor and say bedtime prayers together. There was something calming about such rituals.

I also found solace in the lighting of the advent wreath during the short days of December. Christmas was my favorite time of year and the rite of lighting candles was a reassuring lead-up to it. It was a reminder of the true meaning of Christmas which back then meant something to me.

It did sometimes seem Christ and the Bible played second fiddle to the Pope, to the dogma and rites of the Church. Our little black and white prayer books were used much more than the Bible which wasn't much studied.

I've always been drawn to stories of religious devotion and the extremer aspects of it: the stigmata, self-flagellation, the mystical, including hallucinatory episodes. As youngsters, we watched The Miracle of Our Lady of Fatima almost as much as The Wizard of Oz, and later The Nun's Story with Audrey Hepburn. As an adult, I'm drawn to films, usually foreign, that explore the mystical aspects of religious fervor. One such movie is Vision: From the Life of Hildegard von Bingen.

I mellowed out in high school due partly to attending public school for the first time. There were no Catholic high schools in the area. The Catholic students really stood out to everyone, as the public-school kids had not had contact with them before. I felt left out in this Protestant environment.

I went to CCD classes on Wednesday evenings at the Catholic school I had attended. It was the sixties and we mostly watched black and white episodes of Insight that were contemporary morality plays. This wasn't the church I had grown up with but something more concerned with poverty, civil rights and other social issues that really hadn't affected the small Republican town in which we lived. (Most of the Democrats in town were Catholics as were my parents). The whole sin thing took a back seat and that was a nice respite.

I attended a group of weekly meetings at various churches in town that dealt with teenagers and sex. In retrospect, it seems very progressive for that time and place, and especially surprising that my father really wanted me to go to them. I think he wanted to help ensure I would be straight and make babies. While driving home from one of these gatherings, we had a very uncomfortable talk.

You know if you ejaculate in the night while you're dreaming, that's not a sin."

"Uh-hum."

"Losing your seed in that way is okay, but that's the only way."

I couldn't believe he was using that archaic saying, "lose your seed." I don't know how I even knew what it meant.

"Sex is meant for procreation within marriage and that's a good thing. That's the way God intended."

"Uh-hum." It was a roundabout way of saying that masturbation was a sin.

As long as we lived at home, we were required to attend weekly mass. Late in high school and during my first couple years of college, my mother, siblings and I often attended Saturday night mass held outside in a little amphitheater. These were guitar masses meant to appeal to younger and more progressive Catholics (thus my father didn't join us). When I stopped going to confession every Saturday, my father would sometimes ask me when I last went. I was gradually falling away from the faith although I never lost my belief in God.

In some ways being brought up strictly Catholic is always a part of who you are. It is difficult to explain. I deeply respected how much the Catholic faith meant to my parents and to others, but eventually I couldn't tolerate the official dogma and politics of the Church. Millions of American Catholics ignore much of this dogma and its political implications; they do not see that by going to mass, they are expressing an implicit belief in everything the Church stands for. As Thomas Mann said, "Everything is political; nothing is not political." I can't even understand how a woman or a gay person could be Catholic.

Of course, there were Catholic funerals for both of my parents. At my father's, my siblings and I sat during the parts of the mass when people knelt. It was clear we had all fallen away from the faith. An old deacon made it clear from his little speech on the altar that non-practicing Catholics were not welcome to receive Communion. This really angered my mother who was known to speak her mind, and she later cornered him one day after mass and let him have it.

When my mother was in her late eighties, I started prompting her to make sure she had written down her plans for what she wanted for a service after she passed. I was concerned that my older sister who was completely type A would take charge and do what she wanted rather than honoring her wishes. Mother always said she didn't want people gawking at her, so we knew she didn't want an open casket.

One of the biggest influences of Catholicism was the parish school. We carried our books in rubber-lined bags carried by strings pulled snug at the top. In winter, I unhooked my blacker than black boot buckles, slush sliding through metal clasps, and set them to rest among boots multiplying in the narrow room of damp coats.

Father Shanahan rolled in the piano to teach us, "Who Threw the Overalls in Mrs. Murphy's Chowder?" His words sprawled across the board in sloppy script were so unlike Sister's perfect Palmer Method. She glanced disapprovingly at his unbridled animation, more comfortable with her pitch pipe—a second heart in the dark folds of her habit.

Ancient Miss Lawler talked of enzymes and proteins, reminded us of the body's fallibility: burst capillaries, faulty chromosomes. Mid-morning—cartons of white and chocolate milk neatly stacked on a wheeled cart. Sister Hiltrudis stretched logic: fornication as a crime, the trinity.

Morning's end: girls filed through the cloakroom, retrieved lunches, followed by boys. In the dark of each brown paper sack: a sandwich, chips, cupcake or piece of fruit. Then to pages of new math, strangely bright and smooth. After, geography transported us: hordes of tulips, hats like wings, water in between everything, or dogs with barrels, snowy mountains.

Finally, under the eyes of Saint James and Jesus, we were sorted and sent our way.

About the Author:

Marc Frazier has poetry in journals including The Spoon River Poetry Review, ACM, Good Men Project, f(r)iction, The Gay and Lesbian Review, Slant, Permafrost, Plainsongs, and Poet Lore and excerpts from his memoir WITHOUT in Gravel, The Good Men Project, decomP, Autre, Cobalt, Evening Street Review, and Punctuate. Marc, an LGBTQ+ writer, is the recipient of an Illinois Arts Council Award for poetry and has been nominated for a Pushcart Prize. His book The Way Here and two chapbooks are available on Amazon as well as his second full-length collection Each Thing Touches (Glass Lyre Press). His website is

www.marcfrazier.org.

CLOSING TIME

by Sidney Burris

I've been obsessing recently about eschatology, the kind of word you shouldn't use in a first sentence. It's too stuffy. But I'm obsessing about it because I've reached that stage in my life when I spend entire days trying to understand a "belief in last things," which is how some dictionaries try to un-stuff the word. I'm worried because a good day to me now is all about endings, wherever I find them, and I can find them nearly everywhere. And then a day has passed me by, eschatologically speaking. My obsession has worked its way into every corner of my life; my radar for finality pings continually now.

For example: I get out of the shower, a drop of water falls from my hair and lands on the tip of the shadow thrown across the bathroom floor by the maple tree outside the window, and since the shadow's retreating as the sun rises, I figure that'll never happen again: that drop of water on that shadow's tip as it slides across this white-tiled floor. All around me, things are happening for the last time. And it's a chain reaction. Books can help. I might read Arthur Conan Doyle and see that in Sherlock Holmes's world, things end neatly, naturally, loose ends get tied up, but then I read one of the heavyweights, like William Faulkner's The Sound and the Fury, which ends with Dilsey proclaiming, "They endured," and I realize that sometimes things also end with over-sized apocalyptic pronouncements, because while it sounds vaguely epic to speak of cosmic endurance, I know full well nothing really endures.

I won't. You won't. My father didn't. My mother won't. We come, and then we go.

But stories and novels are one thing; statistics are another.

So I did some snooping recently at the Bureau of Justice Statistics' website, which gives you an accurate statistical record of life's comings and goings, and I found a trail there of botched endings, fugitive conclusions, missed opportunities. The fact is that in 2016, for example, most "violent victimizations" didn't even get reported (fewer than 42%). On the other hand, 60% of the 480,940 nonfatal firearm victimizations that occurred that same year were reported. And guess what? With all of this victimizing going on—both reported and unreported—only one in ten of these victims received victim-services after their violent ordeal was over. The good guys and the bad guys, and the rest of us too, we all live out our lives in a fire zone of compromised principles, mediated ideals, and available services. Closure's something that happens in fiction. I mean, whose life is a string of neatly solved narratives anyway?

You've got to go to literature to find one. And when my own life has been desperately in need of some kind of closure, that's where I go. Often, as I said, to the Holmes stories, where the superior, brooding intellect of the detective pounces on the crime scene, swaggers into action, catches the deviant, and then collapses in a malaise of cocaine bliss after his campaign's done—Holmes's life is driven by the alternating forces of intellect and despondency, lines that radiate from 221B Baker Street, and his life characterizes much of what was best and worst about the imperial center of late Victorian London. And his citizens are grateful for the one-man security force: everything will be alright, the center will hold, Holmes is here, he brings real closure to the community, and he bestows the clarity of conclusion that's scarce in our own lives, particularly in those communities in crisis where only one in ten victims of violence received any type of help or counseling. Any kind of conclusion to their conflicts.

Two stories show up in our culture, then, two ways of ordering time and the events that unfold within time. Each of them aims at a different end, but both of them hold true to our experience. One the one hand, we depend on long-term, system-thinking, and we trust in the outcomes that an extended participation in such a system produces. We trust—to take one example—our legal system because we believe in its orderly movement over time toward a consensus of our peers. We also call this consensus a verdict, a formal, publicly declared conclusion to all of the contingencies that defined the trial and its proceedings. We trusted the process, and we have the option to accept its result. On the other hand, we also know that these endings and verdicts, these final chapters, are often scripted to accommodate the contingencies, special interests, and even oppressive agendas of those who would privilege their short-term well-being over the expense of other peoples' rights and liberties. Better to secure one group's short-term profits and security than work to establish the long-term health of the whole community.

It's really a kind of double time, two versions of how things often proceed toward their conclusion. Grand Scheme vs. ad hoc. It reminds me of the first time I read Othello in that massive Riverside edition, the one that makes you feel well read just to carry it around. Frank Kermode wrote the introduction to the play, and in it he talks about the famous notion of double time in Othello. The play unfolded in a day and a half, a fairly busy day and a half—this is known as the Short Time—but enough time for Othello to believe that Desdemona "the act of shame / A thousand times committed" with Cassio. And this, predictably, is called the Long Time. Did Cassio and Desdemona sleep together a thousand times in 36 hours? That's over twenty-five times an hour for a day and a half. Impossible for the two time schemes to coexist, but there they are.

It didn't bother Shakespeare, and it doesn't bother us. "The richness of the tragedy," Kermodes writes, "derives from uncancelled suggestions, from latent subplots operating in terms of imagery as well as character, even from hints of large philosophical and theological contexts which are not fully developed." Uncancelled suggestions? Latent subplots? Contexts not fully developed? That's my life! What I want is closure; what I get are suggestions, subplots, undeveloped contexts.

All of us have a sense of the Long Time in our own lives; it's what allows us to imagine ourselves old and wise, bright and fathomable. It's the time scheme that leads us to a desirable ending. But then there's the Short Time, and we know how that works too, how we have enough passion in us for a thousand acts of shame, but can't ever quite manage to cash in on it because we have streaks of goodness within us, and we fear the morning-after, Long-Time consequences. But somewhere deep within our passionate hearts we know that plain old human desire over and over again outwits and disrupts the grandest, noblest schemes that we imagine for ourselves. Ever tried to diet? Sin's a pleasure, after all—think doughnuts—because sin's disruptive of the law.

But two kinds of closure in one play, in one life: the grand plan that extends into the future and the daily map that we draw up for ourselves, the one that has to be revised hourly because we can't fit ourselves and our passions to the demanding contours of the grand plan.

I'm fascinated now by these closures, I want to control them, and yet still they happen all around me without lifting a finger. When my father's suicide attempt failed, he said, "I'll try it again too." So I a signed the legal papers and put him in a nursing home because I figured he'd have a harder time making good on his threat. But he died the first night he was there. Cause unknown. So I was implicated in his own ending, and I still resent it. But as a result of my starring role in his final chapter, I'm sensitive now to conclusions of all sorts.

I was naturally interested, then, in Kermode's little book, The Sense of an Ending. In it, he argues that just because an Apocalypse—the biggest ending of all—is "disconfirmed" by not arriving when it was predicted to arrive doesn't mean it's been "discredited." After the early Church Fathers saw that Christ didn't make it back on time, these delayed arrivals meant only that you had to recalculate the ETA further into the future, apologizing to your congregation for having missed one of the essential clues. Under this scheme, the lousy hermeneutics were just another sign of our fallen condition and another reason the Apocalypse ought to arrive and renovate everything in sight (and out of sight too, like our ability to decode texts and predict the future).

My father, I've come to believe, did his own refiguring, saw his opportunity, and took his life the first night he was in the nursing home. He told me the last time I saw him that he'd never pass a night there, and he didn't. So I'm anxious about how things wind down. I'm concerned about how our short-term actions—signing papers—intersect with long-term schemes—enabling a father's suicide.

I thought for a long time that worrying about endings was a middle-age problem, the kind of thing that goes with hair loss. But then I said, "What about that afternoon years ago when you were a boy, and you were suddenly terrified in Mr. Griffith's Soda Shop? What about that?"

It was late afternoon, and the winter darkness was closing in early. That day, I'd had a succession of brief black-out spells, the black-drops, my friends would later call them, and I'd gone up to our local drug store to buy a few comic books, hoping that the latest Flash had arrived. At that age—maybe twelve?—I'd said nothing about these small spells, afraid of what they might entail: doctors, pain, needles, embarrassment. But I'd discovered that the balm of reading—books, comics, cereal boxes, anything—settled me down, and so I self-medicated with books: isolated, alone, going down with my words to the healing ground of imaginative solitude.

Once engaged with the book, the tremors faded, my fear of them simply curled up in the corner of my concentrated attention and went to sleep, and I began to recover my life. On this afternoon, as I'd later discover, I'd come into the store just after the woman at the front had announced they'd be closing soon, so I didn't get the warning.

Overhead the bare bulbs that hung from the pressed-tin ceiling sputtered out, front to back. A man with a massive ring of keys was locking the doors, and through them I could see the lights of cars, arcing by. I felt weight, the kind of loneliness that settles in when you look too long at the stars and want to quit even though the sky is velvety and gorgeous. A cold loneliness settles in that you can't do anything about. It happened that afternoon in the Soda Shop: a brief blackout, and then an equally quick recovery.

I grabbed the new Flash, and ran down a row of Ace bandages and Q-Tips, up to the counter in the front where the man with the keys was staring out at the traffic, distracted, until he finally saw me.

"Boy, what are you doing here? Didn't you hear the woman?"

I don't recall what I said, but I threw some money on the counter, the door opened, I stepped out, and the air was icy on my lungs. The light of the passing cars curled by in a seamless ribbon; they seemed fast and fleet and determined to be somewhere else. I felt suddenly lighter, way lighter, than I had felt standing by those bandages, by those weird ointments and salves—another kind of medicine for another king of healing I didn't need. I was breathing easy; I was free.

And now, even today, I don't want to be in a store when it's closing down.

I always figured it was a private anxiety, a local application of the huge fear many of us have of dying. Maybe. But I know now it was also intensified by the black-drops, an internal, neurological sputter that mirrored suddenly and dramatically the store's closing down—a fearful symmetry between a boy's flickering brain and a store that was going dark, a grim kind of sympathetic response. I opened the comic book, and under the street lamp, I saw the Flash, resplendent in red, who could vibrate the molecules of his body so fast that he'd pass through solid walls, and with a solidifying pleasure I watched him disappear out of one frame of the comic and appear in the next frame in another room entirely. A fine fugitive spirit I remembered for the rest of my life whenever that life called for escape, invisibility, safety.

Twenty years later, I had one of the central reading experiences of my life, and it was a direct descendant of that afternoon in Charlie Griffith's Soda Shop. I was in graduate school, reading the Penguin edition of James Joyce's Dubliners, which had that jaunty photograph of the Irishman on the front: dark coat, white shirt, striped tie, signature specs, a fedora tilted at a slightly rakish angle. "Araby" is probably the marquee story of the collection, and what got me about it was the ending where the little boy arrives at the bazaar just before closing time, intent on buying a present for Mangan's sister. He has a crush on her. So he looks at a few vases and tea sets, notes the English accents of the women, which makes him feel Irish and inferior, of course, and decides not to buy anything. He's intimidated by those accents, and he's about to learn that desire, even his boyish desire for Mangan's sister, often dwindles down like a great epoch: with frustrated hopes and a general sense of malaise.

And the bazaar's closing down too. A soul shuts down in a store that shuts down: double the drama, double the pain. For me, there's real horror in that, the way the story's setting and the boy's life collapse into one another. Because it was around the time that my father killed himself that I began to have the big seizures, the muscular descendants of the black drops I'd had as a boy, at some point I felt that my father's ending was part and parcel of my own seizures, my own neurological suicides, which I would, of course, survive. But not without a lot of reclamation work, of getting back what I'd lost—memory, identity, vitality.

Two streams, then, my father's suicide and my seizures, feeding into one another; two narratives building their own conclusions, and making a torrent in the process: swift, forceful, uncontrollable.

I fear those kinds of conjunctions in our lives.

Kermode helped me again. When the lights went out in the back of the drug store, I felt what Kermode called an "eschatological anxiety," and as he pointed out, there's nothing unique about it—all people, to one degree or another, have been anxious about their ending. In the nuclear age, the evidence looks pretty good for world cataclysm, but it was equally frightening too when you thought you were going to sail off the edge of the earth into a dragon's mouth. For me, it's not about anything as spectacular as dragons hanging over the horizon anyway; it's about the closing times of darkened department stores, and when the little boy's eyes started burning in the bazaar, I recognized the frustration he was feeling. So let's say I've got an end-of-the-world disorder: the end of a ball game, the final chords of a song, anything can kick it off.

As my neurochemistry regularly sputtered and faltered, and as I regained my stability through reading, I became intimately familiar with the resuscitative powers of my books even as I learned a thing or two about the sudden disruptions, the violent breaks in the temporal stream that a seizure causes. Questions accrued. How could something as warm and friendly as the Soda Shop suddenly shut down on you, without warning? How could a single consciousness shut down and return, leaving me without memory or identity? How could a father hand a suicide-watch over to his son?

As the questions accrued, so did a few tentative, if obvious, answers. We die alone, and loneliness, I suppose, is the price we pay for self-awareness. But we also read alone, and through the willed loneliness of reading, I've fought off the burden of my father's death, and by implication, my own death. I could call this "solace," but I don't want to. Solace is temporary; I want a Holmesian solution: clear, permanent, done.

That afternoon long ago when I finally stepped out of the darkened store and into the cold air, I escaped briefly the feeling that the closing down of the Soda Shop was somehow linked to the closing down of my consciousness. As my brain winked backed into life, and I escaped with my comic book, I began to forge connections, deep instinctive connections, between reading and staying alive. Years later, "Araby" showed me, though, how my inner world, so thoroughly constructed of reading's artifice, often collided with the world around me, gaining strength as it did so, or alternatively dissipating in the collision.

Do I have an authentic fear of stores closing down because this fear leads me to a close and intimate inspection of my death? Is this, then, a useful fear? I hope so. When I finally got out of the store, the distance between me and the frigid night momentarily collapsed: I was happy to be out of the store and in the world, I was one with it and cavorting with the Flash, I could go home, wash up for supper, the kinds of things that stitch a day together, bring it in close with its vibrant textures of a rustling parka or a wool sweater—the kinds of things that give our days substance, stability, and an unexamined coherence. The kinds of things that hold dying, or the thought of dying, at bay.

It's as if these endings allow me also to spy on my own death—I'm looking through a keyhole at something I'm not supposed to see. I feel this detachment in Joyce's story; there's a touch of voyeurism in "Araby" as the boy waits in his front parlor for Mangan's sister to come out of her house and head off to school: "Every morning I lay on the floor in the front parlour watching her door. The blind was pulled down to within an inch of the sash so that I could not be seen." When I consider myself, contemplating my death from a distance as the drug store closed down, or a leaf falls to the ground, I feel similarly voyeuristic. Why can't I turn and embrace my dying, hold it closely, and understand it intuitively without fretting about eschatology? Maybe I can do that. Maybe my dying can create for me another kind of knowing.

What's clear to me now, though, as I reread the story recently, is that voyeurism amounts to an erotic loneliness, an acceptance of the distances between us without the payoff of arousal that an embrace might bring. A self-inflicted exile: we lose the dream of consummation but keep the habit of gazing. And so with eternity, death's antidote—we lose confidence that we'll enjoy it, yet we continue to look for it, to develop the gaze that might one day discover it.

I'm one of those people who suspects that our lives have portals scattered throughout them, odd events that shake us up for no apparent reason, like a store closing down, and that they bear thinking about. I take being in a store at closing time to be one of my portals, and what I see through this portal is that the universe, which appears more and more to be a massive, self-sustaining and expanding household of sorts, has built into it those gaps of knowledge about our dying that situate each of us, like it or not, in rooms of this household, flashing semaphores, beaming dots and dashes down long hallways as if to ask, "Are you hiding out in your room too? As I am? Have you figured out this business about how our lives close down? How each of us dies?"

At times, the message gets out so clearly, so well, and is so happily received by others that these distances are diminished, and in our confessed ignorance we come to learn a thing or two about building real community. A community based on knowing what we don't know, on organizing our compassion around our shared mysteries.

Narratives, particularly the stories we tell ourselves, span these distances, forge these communities, and it's why I'm so concerned to finish the story between me and my father. I find bits and pieces of it in many of the things I read, and so without knowing it, I have been reading with freighted agendas for many years. The ending of "Araby" is like a hyper-textual link to me: I read it, and up pops my father; I'm linked suddenly both to his conclusion and to the helplessness I felt as I unwittingly helped him end his own life and write the conclusion to his own story. In her Nobel Prize acceptance speech, Toni Morrison began by stating that "narrative has never been merely entertainment for me. It is, I believe, one of the principal ways in which we absorb knowledge." Absorb it, manufacture it, and guard it jealously too. The final story that my father and I make together, the one that I hold deep within myself, has yet to be fully written, and as I find pieces of it in the books that I read, I recognize them almost intuitively as I might recognize a long lost cousin simply by the family resemblance. And then I see them for what they are: accurate formulations of several feelings that I haven't had the courage to assess and articulate for myself. And all of them concern endings.

As the film version of The Hound of the Baskervilles (1939) concludes, Holmes asks Watson for "the needle." It's one of the few revelations of the man's inner life that we encounter in the stories and novels, and finally it's mysterious because it's unexplained. Holmes is a cog of empire, a rationalist in service of the Crown. I first read the Holmes canon in graduate school, and although I never thought much about it at the time, I know now that I was attracted to Doyle's sense of an ending.

Unlike espionage fiction, which revolves around the possession of knowledge in an amoral way—splitting the atom is neither right nor wrong; it's only a matter of who has the knowledge to do it, who misuses that knowledge, and who doesn't—Holmes's stories are played out in a community that has suffered a moral outrage in the form of a crime. We know that Holmes's investigation will return to the community the moral certainty, the unambiguous sense of right and wrong, that it had once enjoyed. Crime in espionage fiction is a matter of treason and failed national allegiance. It has nothing to do with absolute truth. Crime in Holmes's world has to do with an imperial notion of right and wrong, the dominance of principle, English principle, over the diverse and changing cultures the Empire oversaw.

So as Holmes begins to explain to us how the disparate clues that he's considered—the ones that have baffled both us and Watson—have led him unavoidably to the criminal we'd never suspected, we're allowed to view social aberrance in its proper context. Paradoxically, misbehavior leads us under Holmes's guidance to the truth. Endings in Holmes's world are opportunities for an explanation and justification of a way of thinking. They're victories for a popular English empiricism; the stories are deeply eschatological because their endings are based on final revelations arising from logical deduction. Those are the kinds of endings, the sorts of closings, that I coveted after my father died and I was reading my way through graduate school—I wanted my endings neat and tidy.

But what about that needle? Holmes developed the cocaine habit, we learn, when he wasn't working on a case. The whirring machinery of his intellect needed constant lubrication, and when he had no cases to keep the cogs turning, he found his solace in the balmy vacancy of the drug. But the needle represents a dark, anarchic mania in the luminous order of Holmes's ordered conclusions. As Morrison says of the griot—the old storyteller, the daughter of slaves—she was among her people "both the law and its transgression." So with Holmes's talent for conclusion and his insistence on the transgressive needle—the law of logical reasoning bundles with it the transgression and lawlessness of cocaine.

At some level, the great detective knows that conclusions, his strong suit and which occur in Long Time, are really temporary and provisional, a momentary stasis in the volatile arena of daily human experience, which unfolds in Short Time. I have rigorously inspected my father's life, as well as my own, for clues to his decision to kill himself, and so far, I have only bits and pieces. And I suspect I will never have more than these. Perhaps my father, a fanatically controlled man, a creature of invariable habit, erupted one night with his own needle as a final show of defiance against his own stifling self-control—he was a diabetic who took twice-daily injections, and there was a suggestion after he died from the on-duty nurse that he'd "gotten too much insulin."

Endings, then. Closing time. Short Time, Long Time. It comes down to two ways of looking at the world, and I don't think they're excusive of one another: attend to the swollen bud on the azalea in the front yard, its first curl of color faintly visible through the tightly wrapped green petal, how quickly it comes and goes, or feel the larger force that drives the flower, year after year, decade after decade. Either or both describe our dilemma.

We are inalienably part of what seems to be a vast, impersonal universe, and yet the mystery that awaits each of us, our dying, is personal, focused, now. The narratives that Morrison spoke of, the ones that bear the freight of meaning, conclude, stop for a moment, start up again, and finally have no ending. My life takes its contours from the lives of those who've influenced me. I live now in a middle-class neighborhood, I was raised in a middle-class neighborhood, white male, twice married with two children, and health insurance from my employer, a state university. I subscribe to Rolling Stone. These are my quadrants, and I've never really left them.

I'm not talking genes here as much as I'm talking narrative. That's my story. Much of it was written without my permission, and some of it I am attempting daily to adjust, rewrite, and rebroadcast. But stories have conclusions. And they also refuse to end. They bear us along.

We are all making stories deep within us that we're telling no one, and our griots, our inner historians, live there. But I like Morrison's notion of the griot as both the law and the law's transgression. Dead now, my father and his narrative, much of which I would alter, revise, and reject, I have listened to for years and absorbed without question, but now I see in the plot line, in the arbitrary decisions that molded and made his life, the opportunity for my own arbitrary decisions, my own transgressions. My father, among many others I've loved, is both my law and its transgression. So these inner stories don't end, they don't die, although if I log enough time listening to them, I might transgress them, and give them new life in transgression. I might write another chapter, a stronger one, and break another law.

About the Author:

Sidney Burris teaches at the University of Arkansas in Fayetteville where he is also the Director of The TEXT Program (Tibetans in Exile Today), an oral-history project dedicated to recording the stories of Tibetans living in exile in India. Professor Burris teaches classes in post-colonial literature, non-violence, and the history of human rights. His poems and essays have appeared in The Atlantic, Poetry, Agni, Five Points,The Kenyon Review,The Virginia Quarterly Review, and other journals and magazines. A poem, "Strong's Winter," was selected by Adrienne Rich for Best American Poetry in 1996. Three of my essays have been listed as a "Notable Essay" Best American Essays.

FULL CIRCLE
by Jim Bolone

Maybe it was fate that the transfer to public school from parochial school marked a first and a last in my family. I was the youngest of seven to attend the local Catholic school, which had sort of become a tradition. And by no doing of my own, after fourth grade — together with the nuns, the morning prayers, the Ave Maria — it all ended. I wasn't so sure about it, but I knew change was inevitable because I overheard Dad complaining to Mom about how things were changing in the church and after all he did to raise money for it, after all the days he'd volunteered, joined clubs, donated money, carried the bricks that made it (literally), etc. that they had the heartlessness to double tuition and deny the last of his seven kids the same eight years all the other six had gotten. He said whenever the church wanted a handout they were nice, but when it came time to give back they weren't so nice. "It was time," he said. "Time you go to public school in the fall. Besides," he added, "your new school has an all wood gym floor...and there's band." It was an easy sell because I had wanted to learn to play the drums. In the end we all won.

At public school I got more than wood gym floors and drums. I got new friends in new neighborhoods. Before transferring to public school I could walk the four blocks to class. All my classmates lived in the neighborhood. We could spit as far as we lived from each other. Changing schools meant I'd be riding my bike almost two miles away in what seemed like another country with streets I'd never heard of or seen.

One of the first friends I met my first year at public school was John Taylor. This was a kid who by all accounts was more than a kid. John was a hunter! He had his own shot gun and every fall hunted duck and partridge with his father. John was the youngest of four and the only boy. His personality was magnetic and his looks just right for the girls to notice. He played every sport and was not small by any means, and yet he wasn't a giant either. His strength was probably twice mine and he was someone you wanted on your side in a fight. In library class John and some of the other boys and I paged through issues of Boys Life and Outdoor Life. It was exciting to argue who'd get the next best shot gun or fishing rod, even though I had none. Sometimes we'd look through National Geographic to find photographs of topless tribal women. Or we'd open the fat unabridged dictionary to find the really bad cuss words and marvel at them and their definitions and at the presence of such a book in our own library. The best thing I liked doing with John was playing catch, which we did at school during recess or after school at either his house or mine. Playing catch with John might as well have been the same as playing catch with Mickey Mantle for all I cared.

It was in the eighth grade, my final year at school and my last with John when I first laid eyes on Teresa Monticelli. She was sitting high on the bleachers in a cluster of popular girls at our first junior high pep rally in the school auditorium. That moment is a water-marked memory in my life pages. It wasn't lust because I knew what that was and felt it strong when I saw those topless tribal women in National Geographic. No. It was something else. I mean, it was her face. Too young for beautiful, Theresa's was fresh and bright. She was heaven personified. Instantly I fell for her fully knowing she didn't have any idea who I was. John was with me that day. I found out later through friends that Theresa had noticed him.

Funny how obsession closes in on teens and wrangles them to the ground, how it causes unwanted night terrors, how it makes every song played on the radio suddenly about the girl or boy, while every other girl or boy they see gets compared with someone and never matches up. That's how it was with me and the idea of Theresa. You could say I was in love. She was different and so was everything about her, even her smell, which was a unique blend of perfume and a peculiar hint of cigarette smoke. I did my best to get to know her, and that included what I was good at to get her attention: being funny. And it worked. Until one day in study hall she said to me "You're hilarious!" but in the kind of way that made the whole thing feel more like a service, like I was her jester.

One of the great ironies in the course of my life was how John made it clear he wanted nothing to do with Theresa. He was dead set against ever dating her. I couldn't understand it, but at the same time was overjoyed. Problem was as much as John avoided Theresa, she became more obsessed with him. I mean notes in his locker, candy in his coat pocket, greeting cards secretly placed in his binder, all to my self-embarrassing envy.

After eighth grade most kids took different paths to a mix of high schools. Some, like John and Theresa, went to Parochial ones. (I didn't even entertain the notion of asking my dad if I could go.) Sadly, after this John and I didn't hang out as much; I really missed playing catch with him and talking about camping or hunting or reading Outdoor life and National Geographic magazines. I really missed just John.

Late in the fall of my ninth grade year I mustered the guts to call Theresa Monticelli, though now what once was complete obsession had subsided to an idled attraction. I'd heard through friends and acquaintances she didn't have a boyfriend so I figured I'd see what she was up to at her new school and other stuff. She was very happy to hear my voice and told me it would be awesome if I stopped by any night of the week "But only after dinner," she emphasized.

That's when those old junior high feelings for her returned from out of a bottle filled with yesterday.

After dinner the next day I threw on my hoody and started out on my bike for Theresa's house. The late afternoon sky was wide open, clear, and just cold enough to be uncomfortable in the hoody, but I wasn't about to waste time going back for something warmer. I pedaled on, my hands and face reddening from the cold. By the time I rolled up her driveway they burned with chill. My lips felt novacained.

Her house was small, but nice. I knocked at the door and an older man — her father I guessed — answered. He wore frayed and faded flannel paisley pajama pants, a stained and worn tee shirt, his feet bare, dark, and hairy.

"Is Theresa home?" I said. The words labored through hypothermic lips.

He smiled at me then turned. "Theresa!" he shouted into the house. He opened the door wide and invited me in. I watched him silently and slowly drag his hairy feet to a recliner chair, next to it jazz music played from a hifi unit; he lit a cigarette, crossed his leg and moved his hairy foot up and down with the music with a large grin on his face and his eyes closed. "She'll be down, don't worry. She will be," he smiled, eyes still closed, retreating to his music.

"Hello? who's there?" a woman's voice called from downstairs in the kitchen. "Who is it Sam?" She showed herself. She wore black high heels and a beige skirt with a floral top. Her hair the results of a perfect permanent. She looked proper, but didn't look in place standing in their small tri-level kitchen. She disappeared for a while then showed herself again. "Oh. Who are you?" she said.

"I'm Theresa's friend from school. David, David Fleming," I said.

"I've never seen you at St. Al's," she said. 'St. Al's' was short for St. Aloysius School.

"Uh no. We met at Clark Junior High," I said.

"Really? I don't remember you. That, that was a couple years ago." She put her finger on her lips to think. "Where are you now?"

"Northern."

"Poor boy." She shot me this grandiose patronizing look. "Your parents won't send you to private school?"

I was unprepared for that question and equally unprepared to answer truthfully. Soon as I made the attempt she interrupted.

"So you've met Theresa's dad. I apologize for him in advance. He's not dealing with a full deck and as you can hear; lives in his jazz world. I'm sorry."

Theresa came down the stairs. She saw her mother, but said nothing to her. Then she saw me and greeted me.

"You smell like the cold," she said. "I love that smell."

I never thought about that smell until she said that.

"You two can come down here in the kitchen. I was on my way up anyhow," Mrs. Monticelli said as she made her way up to the living room, wiping her top with a wash cloth. "Dad needs company," she said with a note of sarcasm. Theresa ignored her.

We sat at the kitchen table. And for just the right amount of time we made eye contact.

"Let's play something," Theresa said.

"Sure, what?" I was hoping we'd talk or something but I wasn't going to push the issue.

"Circles," she said.

She explained it all and it was simple. We took turns circling words in the newspaper that matched our feelings. "Go ahead, you start," she said.

I started first and from the lead story on the front page chose Excited.

Theresa circled New.

I circled Interesting.

She turned the page and scanned until circling Lapse.

Then I circled Unknown.

"Theresa your friend needs to leave by eight thirty, that's in half an hour," her mother said. Oblivious, Theresa only hummed as she hunted down her next word and while we played the game, her parents conversation grew louder. It was very awkward and difficult not to listen.

"Please turn down the sound; I'm not listening to it tonight," her mother shouted. "I want to hear my shows!"

"Awe c'mon. Just a little longer?" Sam pleaded. He cleared his throat then mumbled something. I heard the hinge of a steel lighter squeak open and then snap close.

"Dammit Sam!" she said, "Why's it always about you and your blasted jazz music. I don't like it. And while I'm at it I won't be home till late tomorrow so unless Theresa makes you dinner, you're on you own."

"Awe hell," he said. Then the telephone rang. "You gonna get that?" he said.

"Why don't you," she said.

The phone rang until the caller gave up. Theresa pursed her lips then circled Psychological. The parent war continued.

"Don't you ever get tired?" her mother said. "Don't you ever want more than just sitting on disability checks?"

There was an audible sigh. Theresa turned the page. I searched. This entire situation was starting to get weird, like somewhere in between imagination and reality. When I saw the word Disrupt I circled it. I thought for a moment the bantering stopped. I was wrong.

"I mean don't you want more? I'm worried about you. You're like this giant codependent baby we have to watch and feed every day," her mother said.

"I'm not co-dependent."

The hell you're not."

"I'm. Not. Fucking. Co-dependent!" he screamed. "I'll tell you what I am and that's sick and tired of hearing the same old shit come out of that exhaust pipe you call your mouth every goddam day!"

"Yeah well welcome to the club asshole. Should never have married you. Should have listened to my mother."

"You don't know shit," he said.

"Right back at ya," she said.

"To hell with you."

I nervously swallowed and was glad the music was up to cover sound. I circled Time. Theresa smiled. I noticed her mother walk up the stairs.

Theresa circled Difficulty.

I nervously circled Genuine.

"Don't think you're going anywhere this weekend young lady," her mother shouted.

Apathetic. Tired. Theresa broke the rule of one word at a time and circled both.

Amid the quarrel, we continued to focus on the game, and didn't talk much; the game was beginning to lose steam.

I noticed two empty wine bottles standing on a corner table, its surface marked with beverage ring stains, one still fresh. I was thinking how Theresa hadn't changed much since junior high. I wondered where she got the strength in a situation where I'd be crazy sick with embarrassment.

Eight thirty arrived. Mrs. Monticello came down to the kitchen. "I feel sorry for you kids," she said. Theresa didn't raise an eye. "Do yourselves a favor and never marry," she said. She walked to the corner and grabbed the two empty bottles and threw them into the garbage. "And if you do," she continued, "marry well and you won't end up being the bread winner like me scrounging every goddam penny every goddam day for a daughter who never says a thing!" The volume of the music rose.

"Probably a good time to go," Theresa said.

"I know," I said.

Our goodbye was civil and courteous. I was grateful for seeing her. She was pleasant about the whole thing. She never once mentioned her parents. We went to the back door. Then it all changed, as if I'd been struck by lightning and brainwashed. She immediately appeared to me as less, less than what I thought she was.

"Come over again," she said. "Oh. Something else," she continued. She seemed reluctant, nervous. "Do you still hang around with John?"

"Not much anymore," I said.

"That's too bad," she said.

"Yeah," I said. "It is." I opened the door and a cold rush of air streamed in and closed it behind me, pulling on the knob to make sure the lock engaged. That was it. I was out of the house of the girl I had loved since I could remember and felt disconnected. It wasn't what might have been puppy love anymore as much as a very deep sense of pity, even if she was in Catholic school.

My ride home was cold and dark. There were lots of stars out, and I made them into all the kids I knew in grade school now and maybe for the rest of my life. I promised myself the next day I'd call John Taylor to see if he'd play some catch with me, even if it was going to be cold outside. And neither of us would think about Theresa.

Years later I heard through the grapevine that John Taylor was living in Georgia with his husband, that Theresa Monticelli's parents were eventually divorced, and sadly Theresa herself had a short-lived marriage with some rich oppressive guy, and not too long after her divorce she was struck by a car and killed while carrying the Thanksgiving groceries she bought to make dinner for her father.

About the Author:

Jim Bolone has been a bartender, dockporter, bouncer, and for the past twenty-three years, a teacher. He grew up in Detroit, d from Wayne State University with a B.A. in English. Jim and his wife share their home in Toledo, Ohio with three great kids, a dog, a cat, and lots of books.attended the public schools, and ultimately graduate

BECKY AND AMY

by Kate LaDew

You were doomed, of course (the two of you) from the beginning. But you had to live out those years (eleven for her, eighteen for you) before you ever knew it.

Because it was you (the two of you) who would be in that car, driving to that grocery, at that moment.

And it would be them, the two of them, who would find the two of you, though it was not you for whom they were particularly looking (and, ultimately, could be no one else). An opportunity, an impulse, a spur of the moment decision without premeditation (there's no such thing, in any case. It happens, or it doesn't, is or is not, and in your case, particularly, is and is and only could be). It was always that particular tire on that particular car, those particular hands slashing into that particular rubber with that particular knife, obtained in a particular place without any of you knowing it would be used here, particularly, in this instance that doomed all of you (they two, you two) when you became four, never together but not ever, since that moment, separate.

Because your sister was dead the moment her body hit the water. Because you were dead the moment you could no longer find her. Because they were dead the moment they took your arms and pushed you both into the car. All of you dead, on different days in different years but gone, one way or another.

The moment you finally collided, late September, 1973, on a nighttime grocery run, with Amy tagging along to the Thrifty in Casper, Wyoming. Walking through the parking lot, paper bags against your chest, the flat tire bringing them to the ground. Digging into your purse for change to call a mother who had no way to get to you, and then. There they were. Right on time. Some vague promises of help you didn't quite believe from slurring smiles (a smell like the nail polish your mother just decided to let you wear gusting from them) sent your arm curling instinctively around Amy. And then. You were in their car. As if teleported, a sudden reforming of your cells, pressed into a backseat, greasy with hair oil and old food and your sister tight against you. The fat one saying in long drawn out syllables, there will be a reckoning, a reckoning, for it was your car, or one that looked just like it, which struck his friend, and it will be up to him, the friend, to decide your fate (the two of you). The thin one saying nothing, turned around in the passenger seat, looks at you, a starvation in his eyes, and you wish, as loud as you can without opening your mouth, to become invisible, to cease to exist, to fold in on yourself until you are nowhere at all.

The story isn't true. There is no friend, no man waiting to decide fates. You know this. The men know this. The men know you know this. And that is the moment you realize: there is no need for a convincing lie when the people hearing it will soon be bodies.

You drive for a long time (you two, they two, you four). And then. You recognize the bridge. You've been here, somewhere in the Before, on the other side of the jagged line separating eighteen years lived from the nineteen you will live After (though you do not know this, not yet). Amy has been here too, surely, and you almost lean your temple against hers to ask, a reflex, as if it is only an ordinary car trip on an ordinary night, watching scenery, pointing out the new, the familiar. An ordinary scene from ordinary lives and not an attack, a violation, a messy elbowing in of the outside world where anything can happen. The shaking of Amy's little body vibrates under your jaw, where she has tucked herself, as if you were all she needed to save her, and the words sink into your tongue, letters you will taste in the morning when everything is over and done and irretrievable. As your eyes drift back to the bridge, the night seems to stretch over them like fingers, a darkness you can feel (you don't know but the police will tell you, standing in front of your hospital bed, that it was already after midnight, already the next day) and the moon is absent. You think, Where did it go? Why tonight, of all nights, has it left us? Because there is no one else in the world except the two of you, you and Amy (and the two of them, of course. They will say each others names, sure of your death, and you will remember and you will tell the police and it will change nothing that happens tonight, the only one that matters).

And then the thin one is pressing his right hand against your face, driving it into the seat, as his left hand grabs one of Amy's pigtails, pulling. A sharp little shriek of surprise hits the roof of the car and, as if by magic, Amy is gone. The door slams and your own hands slam against the window. The fat one tells you, deep and dark, don't move, don't make a sound and you press your ear against the glass, searching for noise, for Amy (hours later the police will say that while your ears, your hands, your body were pressed against the inside of a stranger's car, your little sister was dragged 100 feet, picked up and thrown over the side of the Fremont Canyon Bridge and into Alcova Lake. Years later, you will read Amy's spine was driven into her brain, and she couldn't have lived more than a few seconds. They do not say how many seconds).

And then the thin one is back, opening the door and pushing you down, pushing your legs apart, pushing, pushing, and then the fat one and then the thin one and then the fat one and your brain says Where is Amy? Where is Amy? Where is Amy? until nothing is alive but that question because you die, right then and there, while your heart beats on and on and on and the fat one and the thin one keep pushing and pushing and pushing and your body is in the air, hoisted over the thin one's shoulder and you are at the bridge and the fat one says, Make sure she dies and your arms fall and your legs fall and your torso falls, as if separate entities before crashing together all at once, Where is Amy? Where is Amy? Where is Amy? following you down.

It might have been minutes or hours (there is no one to know but you). Your shoulders raise, lower too quick as everything whirls. Your entire self is drumming with an agony so mean and deep you are certain you have split in two. There is nothing in your head but pain and your chest heaves with the weight of it, sending out sharp little currents through every cell. And then there is cold, down to the bone. You have teleported again into some place where only water exists. It is consuming you, filling up your throat, invading your lungs and you choke and gasp and your hands are paddling, paddling, a muscle memory, swim, swim, swim until there is no more water. As your hands reach a gritty solid, everything slowing, that certainty comes back. You have been split in two. Your legs are gone, your feet are gone, and as you roll yourself over, the shards of what used to make up your lower half spark and crackle, convulsing every inch (at trial, the medical examiner tells the jury your legs were broken, your pelvis bashed into pieces. It was a miracle from God you were able to get to the road at the top of the canyon, and the yelp of a laugh you kept from spilling out in the courtroom hurt all over).

You don't decide to live. You just don't die. Tapping your thumb and index finger against your chest, the heart underneath keeps beating and beating. There's a flash of a thought, Amy's out there somewhere, but it isn't what moves you, it isn't what puts one hand in front of the other. You simply keep on existing, and if you are going to, you have to find your way out from under the bridge and to the road and back to where you came from.

It is only much later, after you are in a hospital bed, the doses of morphine less frequent, that anything like guts or will or determination or all the other grand words for just not dying are spoken aloud and register in your brain as possibly true. All the reasons you must have lived:

Because Amy was out there somewhere.

Because your mother was out there somewhere.

Because someone had to tell about that night, about what happened, about what you had and what was taken.

Because, because —

And all the reasons you did live:

Because it was always going to be this way.

Because your sister was going to die and you were going to live.

Because your whole body shivered with blood, lapping at the dirt in waves.

Because the sun came up.

Because you turned over, digging and grasping and holding (like the rope in gym class you could never make it up).

Because you were unsure at first if the pain was from the two of them moving inside you or your shattered pelvis rocking up and down, piano pedals vibrating every bone, making your whole body a sympathetic string, moving without you.

Because when the old couple found you face down, left hand just touching the yellow line of the road, and they put you in the backseat (marveling at the strength in you, yelling, no, no, just formed memories of cars and backseats and what they held splashing) and found a phone and called the police — it is was too late to turn back. You had saved yourself. And now you must live with it. (The police didn't believe at first. How do you know she crawled from under the bridge? Because we saw her trail, the old couple said. The blood from her body spanned the ground entire).

Because, finally, you did.

. . .

Ineluctable, you discovered later. An SAT word. Not to be avoided changed or resisted; inevitable. After the trial, deemed successful by the town of Casper, the two of them sentenced to death, then life in prison, you watched your family dwindle until they disappeared (all living longer than they cared to, that moonless night an obstruction they could never see over).

You graduated from high school, became a meter maid, working for the Casper Police Department (seeing the same men who were in your hospital room that day, those days, those weeks) and your friends (you had them, still) singing "Lovely Rita" at you, voices high in Beatles harmony.

You got married, had a baby (a girl whose hair you never put in pigtails) living an ordinary life in an ordinary way in an ordinary town in which nothing about you was ordinary. You were the Girl Under the Bridge, a cautionary tale to keep kids home and safe at night. A story told around campfires, on Halloween as all the little children covered their little faces and all the parents grabbed at all the little hands, watching, watching. There are bad men in the dark, they will catch you, they will eat you up, they will drag you under a bridge and no one will save you (and it was true, after all).

You moved on from writing parking tickets (all those eyes, your clothes from that night still in the evidence room) and on to sales at Casper's radio station, KVOC and then KTWO. You were pretty and sweet and smart (though not in that order) and if anyone asked, you tried not to notice the gleam of excitement in their eyes, presenting the details as if reading from a list. Grocery. Tire. Men. Car. Driving. Bridge. It was only the ones you loved, the ones you trusted, who did not ask, whom you told everything (mostly). How you waited under the bridge, sure the men would come back, covering your body with rocks and your waist length hair. How, as you crawled backwards, up and up the canyon, your stomach was falling out, hands clutching at the slippery insides. How after everything you prayed to a God you didn't quite believe in anymore, asking to die and send back Amy.

Then there were the parole hearings. The fat one and the thin one demanding to be set free, to come back to the world where you were and

Amy was not. Where part of the money you earned went to keeping them alive. Where the night that had begun to recede, flooded back, full force as you told the story, calm and cool. Grocery. Tire. Men. Car. Driving. Bridge. Every time you left the prison, and every time they did not. And every time, nothing got better.

Then you drank. You drank and you drank and you drank and you were under the bridge and then you drank and you drank and you drank a little more and were nowhere at all, exactly where you wanted to be. When your husband left, you didn't blame him. He knew what everyone knew. And he knew you were trying to be the girl from The Before. And he knew you could only be the girl in The After.

19 years from the night you died the first time, you died again. In the heat of July, 1992, you and your daughter and the man you were dating (no paper ever named him, and you suppose he was thankful) drove to the Fremont Canyon Bridge, three sets of hands sliding down the steel 112 feet above the North Platte River. Why that day at that moment, you don't know, except it was always going to be this way. Tears falling so fast and so hard from your eyes you heard them hit like bullets and the man is picking up your daughter and for an instant your throw out your arms, blocking him, sure he's going to throw her over. But of course not. She shouldn't see her Mommy cry and he's walking away, back to the car and you are alone in the huge, complete way you were alone that night, without even the moon to find you. Then, as if by magic, you are gone.

Because it was always you (Becky) it was always her (Amy) as the two of them waited for the two of you in the doom stretched out long and forever. Maybe your foot slipped. Maybe your fingers opened just enough to let go. Maybe late September found you and pulled you down. Maybe you saw your sister in that deep dark, pigtails loosened and spreading until they took up the whole world. Maybe you reached out your hand, braiding your fingers until you felt the heat of her heart under them, alive, finally and again at last. Or maybe it was something else entirely. There is no one to know but you.

About the Author:

Kate LaDew is a graduate from the University of North Carolina at Greensboro with a BA in Studio Art. She resides in Graham, NC with her cats, Charlie Chaplin and Janis Joplin.

TWENTY FIRST CENTURY SLAVES
by Naya Antoun

Despair, loss, feeling hopeless, being abandoned. Those are a few words to describe my nannie's childhood.

At the age of twelve, she was obligated to surrender her education, and simply give up on her future because her father didn't have enough money to support the family. Financial aid was not something common in the Philippines. The only common aspects in the country include death and cruelty. According to an article written by New Mandala, it states that "Violence is rampant in the Philippines." This explains how the Philippines is a country which is constantly exposed to violence.

Soon after, 3 years have passed by, and a family of 10 became a family of 8. Maryannes youngest brother died when he was 1 years old because he was infected with a deadly disease called Pulmonary lung disease.

When Maryanne was 15 she was exposed to the horrific experience of having to watch her father get stabbed. She witnessed as the killers knife repeatedly punctured her father's chest, and resulting in an extensive amount of blood to pour out. That moment, November 15, was one of the worst days of her life.

At the age of 18 she made an oath to protect the ones she loved, thus allowing her to become a security guard for about 3 years. At the age of 21 she managed to envision a better life for herself as she found love.

A dim of hope shines upon her life. Although Maryanne believed that this man would be the life preserver in the ocean that is her life's misery, her husband did not return his wife's feelings; and proceed to cheat on her with another women.

After having a child, Maryann's sister-in-law convinced her brother to abandon Maryanne. The poor girl was at the airport carrying a newborn, waiting for someone that was never going to show up. She kept crying every single night hoping for something better, a meaning to all this suffering.

One day she heard that the women who her husband cheated with left him for a another women, and therefore making Maryanne a firm believer of karma. After having accepted the fact that her husband abandoned her, she began to look for love in different places, whereupon she accidently she gave birth to her second child 4 years later with a strange man she never married. Till this day Maryanne is still lawfully married because a divorce costs a lot of money.

Within the topic of money, Maryanne stated in the interview that although she is currently working for my family, she does not have enough money to properly support her family. However, she is not willing to send money to both of her children, because she is frustrated with the fact that her children only reach out to her for money, and they use her as a source of outcome.

At the age of 39 maryanne made the extensive decision of leaving her family and work as a maid abroad. That same year her mother passed away.

At the age of 42 she went to work in Dubai where she worked for the sheik. When she turned 45 she came to Kuwait and took her cousin with her.

Now, Maryanne is happily working for my family. Unfortunately, her cousin which she brought along with her, was sent to a bad family; who abused and mistreated her.

According to "Reuters," a website that talks about social issues, it states that "The Philippines suspended sending workers to Kuwait on Friday, a day after President Rodrigo Duterte said abuse by employers there had driven several domestic helpers to suicide."

Furthermore, the president of Manila has declared that the Philippines will no longer send workers to kuwait because of abuse, much like Maryannes cousin. Additionally when the maid was being abused the owner broke her arm, and made her cry out all of the pain. Abuse should never be tolerated, some maids have lived a worst life than Maryanne, yet they still get abused. Nannies are not the 21st century slaves.

Over the passed few years my nannie has become apart of our family, she treats me like her child and I view her as a second mother, she's very dear to my heart. I am glad that I have learned so much about her life and her childhood, it makes me cherish her even more.

About the Author:

My name is **Naya Fadi Antoun**. I was born in Lebanon and now live in Kuwait and attend the American School Of Kuwait (ASK). Being only fifteen years old I have a lot to learn and even more to experience. However, being so young gives me the opportunity to want to achieve a lot in my given lifetime. Coming into high school, freshmen are expected to have a partial idea of what they want to achieve in their lives. Personally, I view the future as an intimidating topic of discussion. It has only been recently where I have truly given thought about what I want to achieve in the following years. As a female pupil I have the opportunity which many women before me did not, which many women have fought for; the right to have a strong basis of education. With this privilege, I aspire to become a lawyer or even get possible admission to the science world by working in NASA.

DISCLOSURE
by Megan Sandberg

My instinct was to leave. I did, at first. I got out of my car and sped across the parking lot into the lobby of a Marriott Hotel. Keeping my swollen eyes away from the receptionists, I scurried in my Target flip-flops, disgracing the pristine linoleum accustomed to Jimmy Choos. I raced towards the first sign I saw, hoping it would direct me toward the bathroom. My contact lenses were fuzzy from the tears, so I had to get up close to see the word, "Restrooms." An arrow pointed in the opposite direction. I kept my head down and rushed toward the familiar lady in the dress.

My instinct was to vomit. But I also really had to pee. I decided to relieve myself first, flush, then turn around and stick two fingers down my throat. Worried about germs, I covered my fingers with my sweatshirt sleeve, then shoved them toward my gag reflux. Even though I had just eaten at the Souplantation at the other end of the parking lot, I couldn't get anything to come up. God, I just wanted to vomit. I wanted to feel completely empty — of everything. He couldn't even grant me that. After a few more unsuccessful attempts, I turned around and sat on the toilet lid. My hand grabbed at the toilet paper dispenser, and I suddenly wanted to pray for the first time in years. I think I felt the need because I was hyperventilating enough to faint; I couldn't distinguish my breath from the blast of the air conditioning vent. I looked up, pleading with Him. Please, tell me what to do. Stop this feeling.

But he was waiting in the car.

Leaving him would've been the easy way out. I knew it was the easy way out because a lot of other people would've left. Once, when I was in a novel-writing workshop, I based my fictitious story on my own life. The conversations and events in my book were all constructed, but the one-line premise rang true: a girl in her first relationship with a Marine who struggled with PTSD and the remnants of an ex-wife. I didn't tell anyone it was based on reality because I didn't want to explain which parts were or weren't fictionalized. This gave people the freedom to judge the protagonist: "Why did she even go out with him again when he said he was divorced? I would've left right then!" or "I just want to tell her, 'oh honey, there are plenty more fish in the sea. Keep fishin.'"

I remember laughing, shrugging it off. I tried to shake the eerie feeling after class, reminding myself they did not know him, or us. Back then, I thought the biggest obstacles Jordan and I had were in my own head: I needed to get over my jealousy of the ex-wife; I needed to get over his judgmental father. In the space between a Marriott Hotel and a Souplantation, those seemed inconsequential.

He asked if I was okay the second I got back in the car. I've accepted my own moral failure by never answering this question honestly. I lied and said yes, then continued to cry. I felt like there was a vertical, metal bar in my stomach. It had hooked onto a valve of my heart, pulling it down every few seconds to cause an audible reaction.

"Megan, breathe."

My pain gave way to a flash of anger. "How else do you expect me to react?"

I knew I could never fathom what he had seen

on his two deployments. But hearing the images from someone you love sears them in your mind. Knowing he had witnessed atrocities we skimmed over in war novels throughout high school caused an electrocution of pain. If I felt nauseous by merely hearing it, how had he survived seeing it? And here he was, asking if I was okay.

Once, he told me in boot camp they made the aspiring Marines watch videos of beheadings and torture sessions. A crash course on desensitization. How could he know how jarring it was for the sensitized when he was trained never to flinch?

He rarely tells me graphic information, probably for this reason. It only surfaces when I squeeze it out at the very end of an argument, like a stubbornly infected blemish. These arguments are usually started by a joke or comment about politics, and I judge him for only being a feminist, not an angry feminist. We circle and circle each other, not realizing we're in the same ring until the end. Tonight, it started with a joke about reclaiming language. He saw me making a pussy-hat for the Women's March and I explained it symbolized the reclamation of the word "pussy" after Trump's infamous line. He joked, "Did he steal it?"

I stared at the wheel as my fingers touched the same strand of pink yarn again and again.

I still hadn't figured out how to knit. But it gave me something for my hands to do, an excuse for my eyes to look away from his. I hoped with each stitch I would become more articulate, and be more capable to prove, prove, prove. I was on the left, but I had to be right. He was in the middle, trying to bridge both sides, so I played for the defense.

At the forty-five-minute mark of our conversation, when I kept justifying and explaining, he said he shouldn't have joked. He should've "just kept his damn mouth shut."

I didn't entirely disagree, so I kept quiet.

He pinched the bridge of his nose. I knew the gesture; it was a request to his body: please don't let me cry.

"I don't mean to make fun of what you're doing, because I love that you're doing this and trying to change the world," he said, gulping for a breath. "I do. But for some reason I saw that yarn and thought of this yellow ribbon a few other Marines and I gave to this five-year-old girl.

She put it in her hair. And on her fifth birthday...," he trailed off, his words replaced by a choking sound.

I was not supposed to know what happened to this girl, or what country she was from.

But he didn't need to worry about breaking his non-disclosure agreement because I knew I would never tell anyone. I wouldn't curse anyone else with her fate because what happened to this girl warranted my reaction. I kicked open the door of my dumb American car, sped away in my dumb American flip-flops to the nearest door I saw, and landed in the blindingly lit lobby of the dumb American rich.

I hate when people ask him, "But you didn't really see any combat, right? Like you were just there in case something happened?" I watch as a microsecond of pain scatters his face, then, to protect them, he tells them they're right. Little do they know of the lacerations whipped into his mind, branded in the skull no one can touch.

For Valentine's Day (I requested we get each other "funny gifts"), he got me pillowcases that said "Big Spoon" and "Little Spoon." He took the "Little Spoon" one. It's a joke between us since he's eight inches taller than me, but I've realized sometimes "spooning" is all I can do. After talking to him and poking around on different medical websites, I learned PTSD inhibits your ability to respond to stimuli. Therefore, blocking out stimuli — closing your eyes, pulling your hood over your head — can be helpful. Once, when we were lying in his bed together, talking, we heard footsteps from a roommate down the hall. I'm not sure if it was his shoes, but the acoustics made it sound like the footsteps were right in Jordan's room. I froze for a second, looked up, then relaxed, knowing my ears merely tricked me. Jordan froze for much longer, his pupils dilating in terror.

"That gave me a heart attack," he said, his six-foot figure suddenly scrunching into a fetal position. His breathing became erratic.

"Do you want me to spoon you?" I asked, never imagining I would ask that question in such a serious tone. He pinched the bridge of his nose, then flipped over so his back was facing me. He grabbed at my wrist, almost desperately, and put it on top of his rapidly beating heart. I kissed his faded haircut until his breathing slowed and knew that for as many reasons as I was supposed to meet him, he was also supposed to meet me.

I know he's not apathetic about the struggles of women in America. He randomly claimed his feminist status on our third date over hot dogs, and he's always supported my Women's Studies, even tagging along to a Reproductive Justice panel and answering more audience questions than me. But, I can imagine, once you've seen ubiquitous violence against women in a less privileged country, our American concerns can become material for a joke.

Another time he spoke of his deployment, he recalled witnessing a woman get beaten with sticks by her husband on top of a hill. He asked his superiors if he could do something.

They said no; it wasn't worth the consequences. Watching the slight droop of his neck, I realized how much this killed him.

The "fictional" novel I started in January was a snapshot of a few emotions I couldn't process. By dramatizing them, I felt justified in my anger or jealousy. It was not a fair account of my relationship, but a way to rid myself of a few hurtful moments.

That night, running into the hotel, I found myself again swallowed by a wave of fear and frustration. I wasn't thinking about how many times he made me laugh or collected my tears on the tip of his finger. Everything washed away under one staggering shell of pain.

But I still got back in the car. Because Jordan did not cause my reaction that night. I reacted that way because I imagined the girl with the yellow ribbon. Because I knew he had to relive that sight every day. Because he told me he felt like an alien, and no one would ever understand what he had gone through. He said sometimes he wanted to quit smiling for once and shout, "I am not okay." That is why I ran. That is why my whole body wept. Because I could never abolish his pain.

He looked out the window and apologized for his "moment of weakness:" his diminutive burst of crying about the girl.

I said as sternly as I could muster: "Don't ever apologize to me for crying."

After a few minutes of silence, he took my hand. "I would go through everything again," he said, looking down. "I would go through all of it again if it meant meeting you. And not even to date you. If it meant I could have just met you once."

I closed my eyes, shaking. I thought this statement was the greatest profession of love I'd ever heard. More importantly, I thought I didn't deserve it.

Later that night, we went to the grocery store, and he kissed my swollen eyes and went back to teasing me as usual. Passing the healthcare section, he shouted, "What cream did you need for that rash again?" to the amusement of a middle-aged man standing nearby. I shook my head, trying to suppress my smile. Then I looked up at his pained yet hopeful eyes and felt another choke in my throat. But this one did not lead to tears. This one reminded me I was exactly where I was supposed to be. Fortunately, the feeling was just as powerful as the pain.

About the Author:

Megan Sandberg works as a Communications Coordinator at a school for gifted children in Seattle, WA, and continues to pursue creative nonfiction when not running or boxing. Her work has appeared in The Los Angeles Review of Books and Open Minds Quarterly. She holds a BA in Screenwriting and a minor in Women's Studies from Chapman University.

INSANE IN THE NAME OF THE LORD
by Teresa Lynn Hasan-Kerr

"And he sayed: heare my wordes. Yf there be a prophet of the Lordes amonge you I will shewe my selfe vnto him in a vision and will speake vnto him in a dreame:"

-Numbers 12:6 (Tyndale)

When I was seventeen, I gave up religion and soon after a tornado season began. There were tornados weekly, with several in the same weekend. It was like nothing I experienced before. There was a tornado that was so great it bore two other tornados. The sky rained with what couldn't be fury, but hail. Lightning crashed from what couldn't be heaven. Every storm, my believing parents praised God vehemently, believing that He was speaking through the violence of nature.

They'd turn up the weather channel to hear all of the warnings. From my room, I was not able to ignore the weatherperson booming that the closest tornado was roaring down the street where my best friend's uncle lived. Crash!

"God be praised, God be praised, God be praised," my father never said it once. My newfound agnosticism made me feel unprotected. I wanted calm. But to ask my father that the news be silenced meant that I was asking him to silence God's praise. The warnings would then be turned up even louder.

...

My father moved us to the tornado-prone, Bible Beltway in the south unexpectedly. He was due to retire from the Navy so we were going to move, one last time, to settle into a more stable life. My dad, mom, sister and I had been living in Japan for about four years, but we all agreed to settle in Italy. This option was on a list of places we could choose from. Last minute, my father called a family meeting to say that God wanted him to start a nondenominational church in Millington, Tennessee, which was also on the list. In the meeting, he told us that God's plan is greater than our own.

The first night in Tennessee we checked into a hotel and were told by a member of the staff that a tornado was on the way. As a family we had not yet any experience with tornados. We asked about precautions to take.

"The bathtub is the safest place if you hear the sirens," the hotel clerk gave us the advice and then the key to our room, where we were an hour later, huddled together in our bathtub. We made jokes about our safe flight and the potential danger coinciding the same evening. I think it was my mother who said that as we began this new life as first family, she refused to restrict her life to her new role.

"Church to home, to school, to church to home," Mom curled her upper lip in disgust at the thought of doing nothing else. I remember we all immediately agreed, but I don't know what gave my mother the idea that such a strict life was at all a possibility for us. And just as we visualized exactly what we didn't want, it came true.

...

We were looking at houses the late summer we arrived when we tried 127 Wilkinsville road. The modest property included half an acre and an abundance of natural sunlight that beamed through large windows. While it was less spacious than the others we had seen, it charmed my father nonetheless. I could tell. After we turned to give the property a final look, I felt nothing in particular. But the following two minutes YIELDEDan unforgettable event: the first of many visions.

My father put a hand on his chest and leaned over, letting out a groan. The woman showing us her house, my family and I looked over with concern.

"Are you okay?" Someone must have asked. It's not like my dad to answer on the first inquiry, "what happened?"

Someone must have tried again for him to finally answer, "God be praised, God be praised, God be praised...I just saw something. God just showed me an angel...with a flaming sword watching over this house." He showed us the path the angel took when charging past him. The owner and I weren't sure how to respond. My mom let out a few "thank you Lords" and it was decided that this was our new home.

Am I to say that Clark Simmons did not see a paranormal being that day? To say my father was lying or to argue that spiritual visions aren't real? If it was real to him, could I say it wasn't real at all? I know now that I saw nothing out of the ordinary; I am accustomed to the sight of my father testifying a vision.

Say it was not a vision, and my father had a slip in his previously reliable perception of reality. It could have been a hallucination. Or, he could have wanted the house so badly that he felt he needed divine approval, which, in our family, overrides any objections. I can't confidently say this is the case, but I can recall several times in which my father's desires were inseparable from God's.

He told me not to wear pants to church; it wasn't pleasing to God for women to look like men in the house of God. When we prayed in a group, before a meal or kneeling on the living room floor before bed, if there was a man present he had the duty to lead it, for "men are the head of the household," he'd quote Ephesians. We put our individual interests aside to worship as a family. Everything for His glory. We referred to people, and things as "good", "worldly" or, like the pop CDs I was made to throw away, "demonic." We went to service at least three times a week, with Sunday's service lasting the entire day. If I was sad or mad about something, my parents would stop what they were doing to rebuke the demons that made me so disagreeable. Of course we didn't watch satanic horror films, not in my father's house.

EVEN SO, my older sister once watched a scary movie at the cinema. She lay down on her bed and made a phone call. The door opened. She looked over. A dark figure with too many legs ran in towards her and then dove under her bed at the last second. A vision?

I think there was something dark in the house, whether it'd been a demon or a collective sense of guilt, fear, maybe shame lingering. A tension was there, seeming to open and shut our doors, and shuffle around in the attic above my room at night. An unknown voice would wake me up in the mornings. Visions?

...

Eventually, our incredible reality clashed with the systems of the rest of the world when I was ready to go to college. I asked my father where I should go. He said it didn't matter. So I applied and got accepted, with scholarships, to a private liberal arts school in St. Louis. I explained to him the tuition we still were responsible for and asked if I needed to take care of it myself. He said, "Actually, it's already taken care of," and refused to elaborate. This WHAT just is how he is. It must make him feel in complete control.

Desperate to get out of my school-home-church, school-home-church life, I had faith in my father and went to study. I had to be different from my family. I wanted to earn a degree.

At school, I saw what I'd previously believed was the secular world. It was like leaving the darkness of Noah's Ark but entering the old world of sinners who were such an abomination that they had to be drowned in a great flood. I made friends who'd never gone to church. I didn't go to church. There was a club. There was music, and there was curiosity. It was wickedly beautiful.

When it came time to register for the second semester, I couldn't. My account had been on hold for a balance due. All of it was due. I called my father. He refused to explain anything to me, but demanded to speak with the head of the business office. Minutes later, the hold was lifted and I was able to register. I asked my father what had happened. He said only, "it's taken care of." I asked the office what had happened. They said there had actually been a misunderstanding. I registered. It seemed to be taken care of.

In the following semester, the same thing happened. There was a hold not allowing me to register. They said there was a balance due and it was from two semesters and I could not register for classes until it was paid and that was final. My father, unsurprisingly, gave me no answer as to what was happening with my account. I had no choice but to dropout of college. I went back to my family in Tennessee.

...

My father never spoke to me about what happened with school, but he began to speak about a strong belief that God was going to give him eighty thousand dollars, most likely by way of military benefits. Then I understood what had happened.

When he spoke with the business office, he told them he was going to receive some kind of benefits from being in the military, meaning the eighty thousand dollars he was entirely sure he was going to receive from God. At the sound of "military" the woman in the office must have thought, "oh the GI Bill," (it usually comes in late). She made a note on the account that it would be taken care of soon and lifted the hold. She expected the money to come from the Veterans Benefits Administration. There was a misunderstanding, indeed.

I didn't have the money I owed, totalling five thousand dollars. The debt was legally in my name and no one else's. I was simply not permitted money for gas to find a paying job. The account defaulted to a third party, adding two thousand dollars to my sum. I gathered shreds of faith in myself, borrowed sixty bucks from a friend for a greyhound ticket back to Saint Louis and by autumn was moved in with a boyfriend I met through school.

Because I was the age of the average undergrad, in small talk people often asked where I studied. Most couldn't understand how I could leave school to move in with my first boyfriend. I learned to laugh off their judgment and began to lie, to say that I was still in school. To this day I still explain this era as a hiatus to find my passion. When prompted, I'd also say that my parents are just a little on the religious side.

Several years, minimum wage jobs, and borrowed sums later, and I graduated from the same college. However, I'm still haunted by our dark religion. What happened to us? Were we insane in the name of the lord?

When I ask my father any question pertaining to what God told him, I am answered with a detached but thunderous, "God be praised, God be praised, God be praised."

About the Author:

Born a Navy brat in San Diego, California, and a nomad ever since, **Teresa Lynn Hasan-Kerr** earned a bachelor's degree in English with an Emphasis in Creative Writing and a minor in French at Webster University in Saint Louis, MO in 2017. Soon after graduating, she decid-

THE EXTRAORDINARY INFLUENCE OF THE MOORS ON SPAIN
by Dr. Raymond Fenech

"The reins of their horses were as fire, their faces black as pitch, their eyes shone like burning candles, their horses were swift as leopards and the riders fiercer than a wolf in a sheepfold at night. . .The noble Goths, the German rulers of Spain to whom Roderick belonged were broken in an hour, quicker than tongue can tell. Oh luckless Spain!" [i]

The Moors occupied Spain in 711 AD, when what was described as an African army crossed the Strait of Gibraltar from Northern Africa. The Moors led by Tariq ibn-Ziyad invaded the Iberian Peninsula, Andalus when Spain was still under the rule of the Visigoths.

The Moorish occupation lasted for almost 800 years, affecting the Spanish language, and even the music scenario with the introduction of flamenco. Health and hygiene were among a list of the Moors' priorities, with the invention of the toothbrush, followed by an incredible wealth of new medical knowledge about diseases and diagnoses, as well as curing these with medicines, surgery, and other scientific interventions. But this was not all, the Moors also brought with them new knowledge on agriculture such as the cultivation of various fruits including lemons, almonds, oranges, bananas, coffee and eggplants and taught the Spanish farmers how to cultivate cotton as well as silk. They also introduced highly sophisticated irrigation systems, some of which had been installed by the Romans in the 4th century and which the Moors restored and extended. These brought water into the more urbanized areas through complex well networks, pools and fountains. Private homes and their gardens, public squares, including the public baths, all benefitted from this water supply system, some of which can still be found in Andalusia.

Hasdai Ibn Shaprut (915-970 CE), was a famous Jewish physician who served Abdul Rahman III (912-961 CE) at Córdoba. Using his knowledge of Arabic, Hebrew and Latin, he translated an important work on pharmacy. But he was not the only one, because there were other famous Muslim physicians in Al-Andalus, such as Ibn Juljul (Córdoba, b. 943 CE) who wrote on Dioscorides' work of pharmacology, De Materia Medica about the history of medicine, from the Greeks to his time in Categories of Physicians.

Famous surgeon, who served al-Hakam II as court physician was Abul Qasim al-Zahrawi (Córdoba, d. 1013 CE), who wrote about several diseases and treatments in Tasrif, a renowned medical studies soon to be found in all European universities. The book had become famous after its translation into Latin in Toledo, when al-Zahrawi was given the name of, Albucacis.

Through the translations of Ptolemy, or better known in Latin as Claudius Ptolemaeus (ca. 90 – ca. 168 C.E), Archimedes and Pythagoras, and the introduction of a new numbering system, the Arabic and Moorish society altered the modern understanding of medicine, mathematics and astronomy.

Ptolemy, a renowned mathematcian, philosopher, geographer, map-maker, astronomer, theologian, and astrologer lived in Alexandria, Egypt. Most of all, he is remembered for his development of the Earth-centered cosmological system, known as the Ptolemaic system, or Ptolemaic cosmology, one of the most influential and long-lasting, scientific discoveries in human history.

Paper and Arabic numerals, which replaced the existing Roman system were brought into Europe by the Moors, as well as the most recent wealth of new discoveries and knowledge of India, china and Arabia such as the Compass.

The most modern European City of that period was Cordoba, the very centre of Moorish territory in Spain. In this city, there were commodities that are not always available even in some cities of this Third Millennium, such as cobble-stoned streets, pedestrian pavements, street lighting, and even public baths, which were supplied with running water from a plumbing system that also fed huge reservoirs and majestic fountains. All of these 900 baths, private homes and mosques had toilets.

Cordoba boasted of the Great Mosque, Medina Azahara Palace and Al-Hakam's library, which attracted visitors from all over Spain and other European countries. According to renowned historian Basil Davidson, there were no countries in the 8th century, more admired by their neighbours, or more comfortable to live in, than the rich African civilization which took shape in Spain.

Today, my country Malta boasts of free education and medical services for all its citizens, but this was already a standard procedure in Spain, under the Moors. In fact, people from all walks of life and faiths benefited from their concepts of giving free education and medical services to all, even the poor. In June 1367, the hospital of Granada became a renowned symbol of this Moorish policy offering medical care and asylum to all its residents. The building project of this hospital was given the go-ahead by the Nasrid ruler, Sultan Muhammad V, who ordered its construction in 1365. The interior of the hospital was tiled in glazed mosaic, marble and stucco lined the interior. The bricked façade of the two storied building was plaster encased. Recessed galleries and square rooms surrounded the courtyard in which a long pool with two fountains, decorated by lions was installed. At the end of the 15th century, Granada was finally conquered by the Christians and the last Nasrid ruler, Boabdil, was exiled briefly and finally left for Fez in Morocco.

Andalusia was ruled by the Moors for 800 years from the 8th to the late 15th century. The evidence of this is clearly demonstrated in the legacy they left behind. These included the two most visited monuments, the Alhambra and the Mezquita, which were later both acclaimed as UNESCO World Heritage Sites,

The influence of the Moors' culture extended far beyond the Spanish borders, with the mighty cities of Sevilla, Córdoba, Granada and Cádiz being recognized throughout Europe and North Africa as great learning centres. These also became renowned for their magnificent art and rich architecture, and became the homes to some of the most eminent scientists and philosophers of that period.

The Moors were men with a variety of talents and the Spanish country side boasted of sophisticated irrigation systems, clear proof of their agriculture prowess, not to mention the beautiful effect created by the famous white-painted hillside villages, which the Spanish call, Pueblos blancos.

To eliminate the problem of long distance travelling from one city to another, the Moors designed these white painted multiple towns and villages along the popular paths, most travelers used to pass from to travel from one city to the other. These brought about the erection of citadels and fortresses, where many Moorish sultans settled with their families and servants. Most of these fortresses and citadels are now in ruins, but there are still a good number left which are still intact.

The Moors were clearly much more advanced than the Europeans, so much so that whilst over 90% of the European population was illiterate, education was open to all under Moorish rule, no matter where they established their universities. There were only two major universities in Europe, yet the Moors could boast of 17, all of which were found in Seville, Cordoba, Malaga, Almeira, Granada, Toledo and Juen. All of these were extremely reputable educational institutions. There were no public libraries in Europe, yet in Spain there were seventy, the largest in Cordoba, which consisted of six hundred thousand books.

Perhaps those who do not know the history of Spain, or speak Spanish would not realize that the Spanish language consists of over 4,000 Arabic words and phrases and all the words starting with 'Al' are actually derived from the Arabic language.

The music scene in Spain was also influenced by the Moors and it all started with the arrival of Ziryab, which means, 'The Blackbird', a musician in 822. Instruments such as the Lute (El oud), the Lyre and the guitar (Kithara) were all introduced by the Moors. Ziryab doesn't seem to have been solely known for his music, but was also a sort of food connoisseur who invented the new style of eating that divided a meal into courses, starting as we do today with a soup and ending the meal with a dessert.

However, it does beggar belief how a Roman Catholic country like Spain was indeed once a flourishing land in which three Abrahamic religions, Judaism, Christianity, and Islam coexisted for so many decades in peace and harmony, learning and exchanging their wisdom without ever having to seek bloody confrontations. Today, the world seems to be going backward instead of forward and unfortunately some of the current Muslim communities seem to prefer to segregate themselves from European societies because of extremists like the Jihad or Isis, all pooling in to create a situation of terror in the Western World with systematic terroristic attacks, and the incessant persecution of their own Muslim brothers, those who do not share their same extreme policies within their own lands.

The Moorish Influence on Spanish Cuisine

Especially in Andalusia, the presence of Moorish culture can be seen in every corner. One of the biggest legacies left by the Moors during their reign was undoubtedly the cuisine, which continues to be enjoyed today by the Spanish people and tourists alike.

The installation of irrigation systems by the Moors opened up harvesting in arid areas, and not only improved the cultivation of vegetables, but also improved the quality of the produce. This was supported by the introduction of Asian vegetable products, which until then were totally unknown in Spain. Today's Spanish cuisine continues to use these products, which include, fruits, vegetables and spices such as, saffron, apricots, carrots, coriander, artichokes, carob, aubergines, sugar, grapefruits, and rice. Because of the success of the cultivation of these products, Spain today is one of the leading producers of saffron and along with Iran, produces eighty percent of the crop worldwide. The above vegetables, fruits and spices are found to date in Spanish and Andalusian recipes, such as Pinchito Moruno Andaluz. This dish consists of chicken, and includes the spices, saffron, cumin and coriander. Also a very strong ambassador of the best Spanish cuisine is Paella, which is based on the main ingredients of rice and saffron.

These spices and aromatic herbs so popular in Spain, along with the culinary methods associated with them were among the cultural wealth left by the Moors. Spanish dishes still found today, such as salt crusted baked fish originated from the Moorish cuisine. For example coating fish in flour and frying it in oil in Andalusian gastronomy, actually came from the Moors. This method of cooking fish is maintained to this day and can be found in Andalusian festivities. Fish and vegetable preservation by mixing in salt, or soaking in vinegar for a very long time were techniques introduced by Muslims and still used today, such as the anchovies in vinegar and olives in brine.

But the most Moorish influence on Spanish cuisine is in the desserts and sweets. In Andalusia this is very evident. Pastry making was completely revolutionized by the Moorish introduction of almonds, now so prominent in Spanish gastronomy – such as the Torta de Almendras (Almond Cake). Many of these desserts have since then been given Christian names: the Torta Real from Motril, Torrijas de Semana Santa, which consists of deep fried toast in honey, and Tocinos de Cielo from Guadix. Some of these desserts are made in convents or Christian institutions and have been given names associated with the Christian religion such as, Angel's Hair (Cabello de Angel) Nuns' Sighs (Suspiros de Monja) and Bones of a Saint (Huesos de Santo).

Despite all this legacy, those eight centuries of

Moorish rule in Spain have passed into its historic records more as beautiful legends than historic facts. So much so, in the end these were not even considered important enough to study, or remember. But then, this attitude is a typical reaction, which did not happen only in Spain after the Moorish occupation, but also in Turkey, where for example, there are no historic records of the bloodiest epic battle of the great siege of Malta of 1565. At that time, Malta had become a great hindrance to the Turkish pirates because they were often being intercepted by the ships of the Knights of St. John and ruining their slave trade. This was when a decision was made to invade the Maltese islands and put a stop to the activity of the Christian knights once and for all.

The Turkish Armada consisting of 48,000 men came to Malta with the aim of annihilating it, but the small army of 9,000, defenders of the Christian faith had other ideas. The reason for Turkish historians to have left out this historic event was not all about the battle they lost, but more likely about the important significance of their loss, which eventually led to the demise of the Turkish Empire and their rule over many European countries. I'm quite sure the Turkish historians of that time did not want this devastating defeat to go down in the annals of their history and preferred to forget all about it, just like Spain wanted to forget about the invasion of the Moors.

Any nation that is occupied forcefully by another cannot be expected to rejoice, or highlight that period for future generations, even if such an invasion would have brought a wealth of culture, prosperity and wisdom. People would prefer to go hungry, sick, illiterate and poor, but free to run their own country as they please. It's happened so many times to conquering empires throughout history and nothing will ever change. When people come to choose between their precious freedom and living under the rule of an alien country, the former will always be their preferred choice.

References:

[i] Edward Scobie, The Moors and Portugal's Global Expansion, in The Golden Age of the Moor, ed Ivan Van Sertima, US, Transaction Publishers, 1992, p.336

Five Fascinating Facts about Moorish Spain (Lisa J. Yarde

The Moors in Adalucia 8th to 15th Centuries (Robin Lambert Lowry & Fiona Flores Watson

The Moorish Invasion of Spain and the Christian Reconquest (Daniel Medley

The Great Siege of Malta (Dr. Peter Hammond – Reformation Society, Cape Town, South Africa)

About the Author:

Dr. Raymond Fenech embarked on his writing career as a freelance journalist at 18 and worked for the leading newspapers, The Times and Sunday Times of Malta. He edited two nation-wide distributed magazines and his poems, articles, essays and short stories have featured in several publications in 12 countries. His research on ghosts has appeared in The International Directory of the Most Haunted Places, published by Penguin Books, USA. In 2009, Ray graduated with BA first class honours in creative writing and later obtained his PHD. In the same year, he was awarded a scholarship in writing therapy by the Creative "Righting" Center, Hofstra University of New York. He is a visiting professor (creative writing and parapsychology) for an online university and conducts creative writing classes for both adults and children.

BUSHKILL
by Ingrid Blaufarb Hughes

Just past the Bushkill Creek we turn off Route 209 and I lead Jay into the deep shade of sheltering trees to walk the gravel road I know by heart, every curve and ledge. This is the place I would trace in my mind before sleep during years when we couldn't visit, the place we came back to from far-off countries or not so distant states, the place where we were together, parents and children, grandparents, aunts and uncles, cousins.

It's as if the land lies under a spell-—in fact a quirk of local history: the plan to dam the Delaware, the farms and woodlands taken, the houses knocked down and buried before the change in plan, the protected preserve left to go wild, named for the Delaware Water Gap fifteen miles downriver. There are no campsites here, no trail markers. A few local people know this way to the river, but right now it's all ours.

The hill is smaller now; we're up it in two minutes. Here Poppy's black walnut trees— trunks straight and thick, disappearing into branches far overhead— still mark the edge of my grandparents' garden. I see the beds of roses and lilies and the vegetable garden, where my grandmother bends to inspect her tomatoes. Jay can see only an impenetrable welter of young birch and tulip trees, dense brambles and brush. Deep in there my grandparents' ashes feed the growth.

That's where the house was, I say. Two of the great oaks by the turnaround still survive, while another has fallen, its roots a massive disk standing on edge, their tangle holding enough earth to nurture a few weeds. The dirt road off to the right, a shortcut to the Schoonover's farm, has been swallowed up entirely.

We pass the ravine that dives down to the Delaware floodplain—the ravine I loved for its green depths, too steep and thorny to explore, then as now—and follow the road that goes over the Hogback. Poppy's pine forest slopes down on our left, pine and oak and birch climb steeply to the right. Several hemlocks by the road and a low stone wall mark the site of the bungalow where my parents and siblings and I used to stay. We shared the house with a good sized black snake who made an occasional appearance in the living room. Here too there's dense new growth, making it impossible to find the three trunked birch where my brothers had a tree house.

Down the hill again, I can just make out the tracks of gravel leading us to the river. A long field that I particularly loved used to lie on our left—an early stage forest now. In the woods along the drop-off to the flood plain, we look for the gravestones among the trees, lichened but still readable. Nineteenth century Schoonovers lie here.

The way to the river is waist high with hummocky grass, nettle and blackberry briars. I lead Jay instead through the pines, planted by Poppy for a tree farm before he found he loved the trees too much to cut them down. Here needles on the ground give us better footing. Then we have to brave the thicket, but by now I'm too excited to care about the prickers or even the poison ivy. We forge on, trampling ferns.

At the bend of the wide serene Delaware, under the great sycamores, I breathe in a deep content. I had thought to peel off my clothes and swim, to savor the muddy, rich scent of the backwater, the slow pull of the current, but even in my exalted state I can see the bank has become too steep, the earth too dry and loose to climb down or up.

All year I am grateful for this protected realm, amazed at our good fortune in the Eden we lost and regained even better—the towering old trees and new growth, the ravine and the river bank, all ours by right of loving them.

Some years my daughter or niece or brother joins our visit to Bushkill. Each year the young trees are taller and another giant has fallen. The pine woods host young hardwoods along their edges now. The walnut trees are holding. I'm seventy now: they will outlive me. My ashes will lie below them.

About the Author:

Losing Aaron, a memoir by **Ingrid Blaufarb** Hughes about her son, was published in 2016 by Irene Weinberger Books. Her poems and stories have appeared in many periodicals including Lilith, West Branch Review, Kalliope, Mudfish and The Massachusetts Review. She was born in London and grew up in Athens, Saigon, Singapore, and various parts of the US. As an adult she lived in New York, where she raised her children and taught English to immigrants and native New Yorkers at the City University of New York. She now lives in the Hudson Valley and is active in a peace and justice group there, Women in Black.

CITY DEER

by Darren Demaree

CITY DEER #13

there is play in emerging from the trees to consume to raise your head to bat your ears against the quiet that will always raise a head to meet you there i don't care that they avoid me that they avoid my dogs it's just an incredibly life-affirming entrance so often i have seen them in the light & i have been able to talk myself into leaving the house

CITY DEER #14

i dug a fire pit i placed rocks around it i collected all of the sticks from the yard i lugged the branch that had fallen from the dead tree on the property line i used an axe for something other than a mirror i am excited to see what tomorrow brings

CITY DEER #15

my thighs always tucked beneath the athletic shorts are never excited about the split of the day that can erase the red flag's movements my thighs know about the suits in my closet neither of us care much about the suits in my closet i have been incredibly fortunate to watch that expensive cloth wither

About the Author:

Darren C. Demaree is the author of nine poetry collections, most recently "Bombing the Thinker", which was published by Backlash Press. He is the recipient of a 2018 Ohio Arts Council Individual Excellence Award, the Louis Bogan Award from Trio House Press, and the Nancy Dew Taylor Award from Emrys Journal. He is the Managing Editor of the Best of the Net Anthology and Ovenbird Poetry. He is currently living in Columbus, Ohio with his wife and children.

THE RIVER IN SUMMER
by Iain Twiddy

Leaf-falls

The trees are squandering their leaves,
crisp red and gold notes, thin as smoke,
backed by a huge blue bank of sky.

They pile up, add to the childish stash
I would kick through, catch, flap away,
hoard in the brace of white pages;

they set down wealth to pension me
when I am barely memory,
when my sight is miserly

as a needle, so I can't tell
if I've reached the edge of the forest
like a rich man leaving the kingdom.

The River in Summer

I want to tell of the river in summer,
of the field grass hissing and cricketing,
of the duckweed bubbling, dragging the flow
as slow as limestone, of the stripweed
flagging underneath, sinewing like trout
which seemed like stretches of bed-mud come to life;
tell of the flirt and glug, the deep reed suck,
of the willow fountain, chestnuts ballooned,
the mill-bank an undercurrent of wasps,
of the haze of flies like a mist of thirst.
I want to tell of the river in summer,
the weight of every word hitting my tongue
with the same recklessness, the same playful
relish as the river then accepting the stone.

The Butterfly Book

Last time on Skype, he showed me
two caterpillars, green, squishy and striped,
thin as the fingers through which
they were wriggling, and to which his head
was breathlessly tilted.
He fetched the book in, opened it up,
told me all that happens with the leaves,
the sleep and the chrysalis,
or the mouthful way he says it.

Now, his fourth birthday, he's called in
from a garden loud with sun.
Words squirm through the cables, the squabbles;
I'm not sure he can hear. But I ask.
Any butterflies yet?
And he twigs, smiles brightly, rues his lips,
shrugs his upturned palms out, splitting
the winter in which I've been chrysalised,
leaving me butterflied with light.

About the Author:

Iain Twiddy studied literature at university. His poems have been published in The Poetry Review, Poetry Ireland Review, The London Magazine and elsewhere. He has written two critical studies of contemporary poetry.

SYNTHESIS

by Tucker Lux

SYNTHESIS

It can happen anywhere
all at once.
Memories bring
trees to applause
cooling, brushing skin
envelop
invade.
Summer's first whisper
brings all
wayward ghosts home
from haunting the scent
I trail.

Medicine for a fractured heart,
split so many ways
Midwestern air
prairie sweet.
If I have known you,
you are here too.
Without knowing, you
inhaled
exhaled
sent a piece of yourself
into my own lungs
my bloodstream
my heart and mind
and I pass you along again,
better for the draft.

ESTABLISHMENT

Bare feet planted
still, still,
eyes closed.
Will your pores open.
Will roots from the soles of your feet
down deep, deeper
grabbing hold, pushing up
through cold crusted soil,
through concrete,
through broken glass,
through isolation,
through resignation.
Cultures begin in the seeds
in the soil
and rise toward the heavens
reaching, straining up
like branches,
like wheat stalks,
like every green growing thing
to truth,
to light,
to love,
to kingdom come.

EXCHANGE

The quiet economy
of rubbing shoulders
takes from us
and makes us all
more than ourselves.
Let's be honest.
Our own voices
are not the only ones
we hear.
No one's vision is unaided.
We all owe more than we have
to give back.

If I have ever
known you,
called you friend,
know you
have become my eyes.

SECONDHAND

We pay good money
to watch the man
believe in himself.

Diversion comes free these days.
We are here to watch culture take shape,
hear it
reverberate and change
the world's rhythms:
resurrection chord by chord.

How many are here
with their good money
for secondhand faith?
And how many have open ears,
willing hands,
and leave closer
to living something
that can bear believing?

SPRING

Go out.
Suck this air
down deep, full
of health
laced with
hayfield and pine.
Heavy
with memories,
with prophecies
of renewal,
of sun-warmed freckled skin,
bare feet.
Inhale.
Exhale.
Close your eyes.
Repeat.
Let it open your pores
open your dreams and unleash them.
You have found
the fountain of youth.

About the Author:

Tucker Lux hails from Toledo, Ohio, where he savors his wife, and kids, and breath, and friends, and where he teaches Middle School English, and reads, and listens, and sometimes writes words of his own.

STEEL PROPHET

by Jonathan DeCoteau

The split-second cleaving of foliage—gaunt
From the haunches of marauding night—
peeks through, with lead-tongued panting
And black crescent eyes:
It is a baby deer made manifest before me
As I set my steel sites for the hunt.
Surrounded as I am by lighted misery
taken from time and thrown claylike against eternity,
stretching the bulbous moment of my nine-year-old life
out until it wrangles and bleeds—
The thick paste of dawn is a but a thin line circumnavigating my gun
As my fingers press ever so slightly—
And then freeze.

All about me are dun, twisting sequoia and the dinge of sodden dungarees;
Vines wrapping around, like the misshapen mouths of green gods of ivy,
That speak neither to the fawn nor to me;
The nascent breath of the fugitive baby,
copulating with the fat heaving of killers
All thrown up like aging milk,
Only to splatter, in thick, petulant globs,
the moment that sours beside me.
Shoot, shoot, the killers chant,
A word too naked to the touch for its primeval finality.
Still I crouch; still my fingers dance on the trigger;
Still they freeze.

I hear and do not hear
See and do not see
For words are not eyes,
pale and translucent as they rob first light,
of its pink vitality—
they cannot say, as blood can,
Please do not take everything I am away from me.
A yearling's eyes are worth all the words of the prophets
When they stare in absolute vulnerability
When I crouch, my face sweaty and half-obscure,
Holding a steel prophet in my hands
That points oracle-like from
This Delphi of shale and granite
As if imparting a mute god's decree.
Perhaps Neanderthals once stood by the same rock formation,
Sanguine spears slung about their navels
Their faces painted in the dry clay of necessity,
Chanting some lost guttural cry,
To gods both profound and bloodthirsty—
A call to the kill—
That now fills me.

But the fawn is not guttural
As it stands frozen in its own moment of pale impossibility.
There is shaking of crook and limb, the throbbing of artery,
A slight, scurrying sneeze
As its semi-spherical black eyes, lit by the same sun that nourishes me,
Search dark and light
Frantically
for hidden figures scrambling circuitously.
For a moment, the yearling's eyes leave me—
It has spotted its family—
And I shoot, God help me.
The fawn crumples at the thunder more than falls,
Its flesh,
Like its blood,
Indistinguishable from the mass of dawn and soil—
Spilling into the mouth of a long-dead tree.
And the cheers, oh, yes—
You got him! You're a man!—
Even then they shoot at me

As my crouch too becomes a crumple
Of newly minted misery,
My smoky prophet by my side
As I smile—yes, smile—crookedly,
like a Zapotec priest holding
a beating heart before the sun-cracked stairs
Of the Great Pyramid of Tenochtitlan.

But death is not neat,
A flight of breath,
A wavering of limb, or
a simple extinguishing of the eyes—
it is predatory,
and it was not done with me.
The baby deer cried, yes cried—
As it saw its own spindly legs
unable to spindle the shale and rise,
as it saw the sinewy pink of its insides spilling viscously,
as it defecated, and saw that it defecated,
and heard its mother's cry too late
to appease its misery,
lying its red-tufted head down
in the mess of red, white, and brown
caused by me, while
my father and his camouflaged buddies
jumped, hooted, and hollered
like Pan wrapped in hairy black goatskin
ravishing Selene—
so they stood before the cadaver,
breaking beers over me,
unmoved by the unholy.

And to this day,
That steel prophet speaks to me
Whenever I hear news of a kid gunned down in a park
Or see the senseless killing of a mother and child—
The image of that baby deer is ever before me
As I ask the killer that is me
what it is to be a man:
To be jumping and celebratory,
Wielding the prophet's power,
Or to be shuddering and holy.

And always in answer I see the baby deer
Crumple and fall,
Its eyes on mine
Trying to remind me of the humanity I lost that day
I went for the kill.

About the author:

Jonathan DeCoteau is the author of The Naked Earth, named 2008 Fiction Book of the Year by The Online Journal of News and Current Affairs. His work has been published in Jewish Fiction, Longshot Island Magazine, Literally Stories, Reader's Quarterly, Farther Horizons Than These, and Far Horizons.

THIS IS MY EVENING
by Diarmuid ó Maolalai

Israel and Palestine

I had put the goldfish
in a small tank by the window
and had named them
(some joke)
Israel and Palestine.
they didn't know the joke.
they lived together
as good a life as they could
bobbing like bathtoys
near a view
where
every day
nothing happened. I fed them
but never enough to kill them
and they gobbled it like morons
and looked at me
with dumb glorious eyes
and fat heads,
after a while
knowing if I came over
it would mean new food.
when I left the apartment
I left them there -
what was I to do? bring them in a sock on the airplane?
and I wrote a note for the landlord
saying

"if you have children
then these are for them. their names
are Israel and Palestine"
in hindsight
maybe a bad joke
since the landlord
who was traditional Jewish
probably had
views
we hadn't discussed.
they kept me company
for two years
and must have got flushed
the day I moved out. there wasn't much
to that flat
and I'm pretty sure I'd got it
two days after the last guy. probably
he didn't have time
to clear them out for his kids
while the next tenant
was banging on the door
and he was sweeping away
the rest of my trash.

Paddy's Day 2018

there,
it is the sweetness of the dream,
or the stickiness
anyway,
and love
comes stumbling drunk
through every doorway;
a woman and 2 men
outside my apartment,
and the men are gay
and married
(that couldn't have happened
even a year ago)
and I hear them.
they are
banging through the hallway.
it's paddy's day
2018
and they
are stumbling,
joyous stumbling drunk.
only 1 of them is Irish
and he is happy
anyway;
he has 1 friend with him
and 1 lover.
I've spent the day at home
so optimistic
something would come
that I missed it.
I should go in
deal out cigarettes
and share a drink with them
but instead I'll stay at home,
drinking here,
satisfied,
listening to music
and the sounds next door
of a party happening.

Concert

I rattle the triangle
like a bag of potatoes.
scared,
drunk,
I strum the violin
til people get up
and shut down their windows.
I'm a one man band
of extraordinary virtuosity.
no bum notes here. just arses.
wet wineglass shrieking
like a harpooned pigeon,
ploughing into sounds
you've never heard. I bang
cymbals
and scream
better than Munch.
if it takes anything at all
I'll make you notice me.

Amory

is listed in the dictionary
only
as a proper name
and an old-fashioned one at that;
a character
in Scott Fitzgerald
or some old
American play.
but it has the cadence
of a word too,
lost in time -

amory;

a memory of love
or some subtler
shade of feeling,
grassy veldt or hills in sweden
and letters
scab-written
in peasant unspelled french:
amory - from amore;
lit. the ardour felt when
your love
is in another country
or more
than a taxicab
away.

amory;

from a memory;
lit.
the feeling
when your love

This is my evening.

1 glass for ashes
the other for
wine.
1 night long
to look down the days
and think
this is deferent,
this is deteral,
this is the way
of the fox,
the wolf,
the woodhuddled animal.

this
is the deer,
poised,
ready to run at the road
if the car
will just slow down

this is the hand
that guides the pen
that inspires the sword.

the backspace key
is the only gift
and the wine;
the ability to expel mistakes
made in the moment
by the drunken finger
and only let the night move in.
smoke
accidentally blown into the eyes
and burst away,
breathed downwards

to linger
on wool.

nights like this
ring around
an abundance in which

things dance.

About the Author:

DS Maolalai recently returned to Ireland after four years away, now spending his days working maintenance dispatch for a bank and his nights looking out the window and wishing he had a view. His first collection, Love is Breaking Plates in the Garden, was published in 2016 by the Encircle Press. He has twice been nominated for the Pushcart Prize.

RENAMED

by Tom Laichas

At the Edge of Air

When the newborn inhales the Breath, flesh and clay still comingle. Between earth and this new animal, there's no hard edge.

The infant wonders where skin ends, where world begins. Loess infuses a fingertip. A breeze caresses stray bone.

The child thinks: I am not so far from this earth.

Renamed

New to the world, the animals listen for every fresh sound. Sap seeps from trunk to crown. Tidal salt crusts the crisp reeds. Grassland soil swells in the sunshine.

From such music, each beast fashions a name as long as the day and as long as the night, chanted in rhythm with all living things.

Then the boy appears. He points his stub of a finger, renaming the creatures with grunts, glottal stops, and guttural growls. All living things are now at his mercy.

The first songs silenced, the Voice revises the verse:

>   In the beginning, there was prose.

Other-man

Other-man, also kneaded from clay,
walks by himself
full grown and awake.

Hair as thick as a bear's, brows heavy,
eyes brown, large as two moons
better to see in the dark.

He knows no names, but he knows the creatures,
their ways and their hungers:
by pawprint and piss he knows them.

If he wants their company, they walk with him willingly.
He has a creaturely walk, light and lively.
They lick his hand; he tickles their ears.

As for the boy, he's furtive, hiding himself
behind trees, behind boulders.
He's hiding from Other-man.

He thinks himself clever, the boy.
But other-man knows the boy's breathing,
his odors, his footfalls as loud as a shadow's.

One day the boy calls the creatures by name.
Who can resist? They lope and they slither.
He recites their names, chaining them to him.

Other-man watches the boy claim dominion
over creatures who moments before
had told their own stories free from this magic.

On the Garden's last day, the animals follow the boy
away from the flames and into the world,
beyond Other-man's knowing.

Belonging to no one,
alone in the wasteland. Other-man runs
this way and that, lost in the wreckage.

stanza break

The Garden burns hot, hot as a furnace.
Other-man's bones crack, his marrow boils.
His skull splits, his brain pan sizzles.

Or else he escapes, running wild with grief
to the edge of a field.

He is Cain's first kill. Some say that, too.

About the Author:

Tom Laichas lives in Venice, California. His recent work has appeared or is forthcoming in High Window, Lummox, Underfoot, Panoply, Eclectica and elsewhere. Follow him at Left, Write and Centaur

(https://leftwritecentaur.com).

COMFORT IN A THEORY

by Mark Taksa

Comfort In A Theory

The watering can I hold over a daisy
is dry. Waiting for my neighbor to appear
in her window, I pose. The pocket of my shirt
hides the ripped edge of an opera ticket.

My neighbor parts her curtains,
watches the sky, quits pretending
she is evaluating clouds, and asks
if the climate is fair for a stroll to an aria.

Questions of fairness, I say, evoke enticement
and all enticement, evil or innocent,
provokes deception. In short, I have no opinion
about climate. I offer my theory that friends
walk closest when among abandoned
buildings too hollow to hold music.

To take comfort in a theory, my neighbor
answers, is to dance and hope for a cloud
to drop into empty hands.... My smile counters
her doubt, as if I am a waiter, and she,
having chosen the most pricey burgundy,
is unfolding a magnanimous wallet.

Mystery Is mostly

A cook's cap lampoons the cop's badge.
His stiff chin wavering, he scrutinizes the theater,
its seats torn out, and tells us to catch his whimsy
or be no more than a ticket in a suit.

He says we make mystery with our personal
ruin, as if undressing from familiar duds,
as if clothing in unknown notions.

Into his cupped and naked hands,
he gazes, as if into magic soup, and dares us
to see minestrone. He tells us to notice
the dry in the rainy sky, to stand among
drenched umbrellas and not get wet.

Mystery is mostly comical, so, declining
to be a fool who wastes a ticket, I rush through
the empty door, take off my wet coat,
and touch the dry in my drenched hair.
My whimsy keeps my life undressing.

Bouncing High

The clicking coming close is an iron knight
rushing to halt my march. Hurrying past
my fear of turning, I enter a clump of branches
which brushes my thought from castle days.
I slow into the hummingbird's aria.

The chain clicks louder. Though the pavement crack
might jam my sneakers, I turn and look into
a fleshless grin. The bone man lifts my hand
from dog fur. His dogs flutter their ears,
lift snouts, and sing for us to go.

Sun will not, the bone man whispers,
always decorate my stride. My sneakers, I protest,
are too scrubbed, and I am too new to dancing
to sleep in his dark house. I shout for him
to take someone eager to sleep.

Tags click. Waiting to go, the dogs fidget.
The bone man tugs me to fallow. I think of my legs
bouncing high under the sun beyond the woods.
My shout swerves me from the pavement and into
the grass deep over my already stepped path.

Borrowed Blank

I walk out of my unstitching shoes
and throw off my socks. My tuxedo floating
into the ocean, I imagine the waves
pulling my wrinkles flat.

Sitting in a blanket she folds
up to her chin, a woman with cave eyes
shifts into my shadow. Her face is free
of furrows. Pouring sand on my toes, she says

no path is unrough and no nakedness
can bring back a baby's skin;
I will be wrinkled and unstitching—
unless I occupy blankness.

My sight clutches the blank of her caves.
I turn, dress in the ocean and retrieve
my sodden and sinking clothes. Out of the waves,
I am a wet tuxedo. Covered by my borrowed
blank, I have no fear of unraveling.

Comfort In A Theory

The watering can I hold over a daisy
is dry. Waiting for my neighbor to appear
in her window, I pose. The pocket of my shirt
hides the ripped edge of an opera ticket.

My neighbor parts her curtains,
watches the sky, quits pretending
she is evaluating clouds, and asks
if the climate is fair for a stroll to an aria.

Questions of fairness, I say, evoke enticement
and all enticement, evil or innocent,
provokes deception. In short, I have no opinion
about climate. I offer my theory that friends
walk closest when among abandoned
buildings too hollow to hold music.

To take comfort in a theory, my neighbor
answers, is to dance and hope for a cloud
to drop into empty hands.... My smile counters
her doubt, as if I am a waiter, and she,
having chosen the most pricey burgundy,
is unfolding a magnanimous wallet.

About the Author:

Mark Taksa's poems are appearing in Main Street Rag, Slant, and Trajectory, He is the author of ten chapbooks. The Invention of Love (March Street Press), Love Among The Antiquarians (Pudding House), The Torah At The End Of The Train (first place in the 2009 Poetica Magazine chapbook contest), are the most recent.

LEMONS FOR CLARA
by Leslie Philibert

Lemons for Klara

for Klara Grünzweig 1957-2016

drops of river or ice patches;
all of this without your notice
      but tough and half eternal

the lemon tree grows
      cool and silent;
      this makes you remain.

Golem

unholy earth, dark with stein,
unformed loam at birth;
a worded child of mud,

fingernail skinned blacklack eyes,
peek out of a ball of wet slam;
a groundling that waves like a black branch

across the sleeping fields,
see a shadow under the cold grass,
near in sight under a crust of frost.

Tower of the Blue Horses

(*after Franz Marc*)

Four of stained glass and stars
all leftglance beyond ratio or air,
thin as tissue but strong

as a pastel visa; fated curves
guide your hand, voices drag you
into mud and steal the day.

A Night in Tenerife

the sea the skin of a wet dog,
black the beach; a ruined church,
the coastal lights a string of lesser ways;
we are as empty as a dropped shell
pulled across the ebb, a ripple of salt:

and as the night gets deeper
a dragon breathes like the tide:
no mistake, the dark needs its hours.

About the Author:

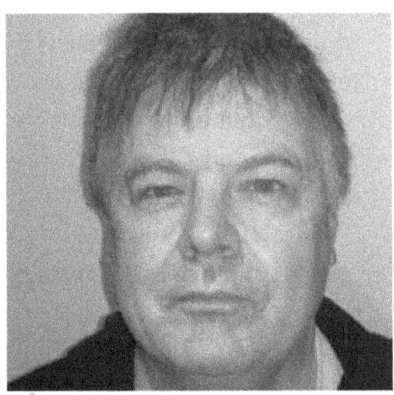

Leslie Philibert is a London-born social worker and poet living in Germany. He has published work in a number of magazines in the UK and US and has done some translations for a South German theatre group. He is married with two children.

After Reading The Bell Jar

curl up like black paper,
burning like a moth;
a glove turned inside out;

trapped too under a house,
a circle hidden and musty,
fragile under steps;

let us escape the carrying,
legions of white coats,
corridors as long as life.

IDENTITY

by Jan Wiezorek

| Waste |

removing our teeth | throwing them with the plastic utensils
into the sea | along the grid steps | the EGK
of hearts skipping | | | tripping
over | a | beat | |

careening | on cobblestones | how the boy
holds the door | and cannot smile | so we
all bow | reach down to receive |
placing refuse in his cup |

what to do next | how winds jostle the palms
fringing | naming | soundings that fit in quadrilaterals
| in triangles of refuse | nestled on the pier
of all voices | from this height dreaming again | floating
as on the water

of us | how we twist to see and stumble | we are half-dying
against a milk bottle | cap | blue as the water on the night
in which the garbage arrived | uncertain

how lovely the light reflects
that which we toss away | spangles
as innocent as straws for the pelicans | stripes
for the screams of birds |

Identity

Who knows that he's
a young male,
though all muscle

and inbred so much
as to make problems
managing identity.

He hears tree frogs
click open the legs
of a wetland.

No one hears
the swan unfolding her neck
against bills sucking up

the slop like a windup toy
ending its cycle, revealing
the perfect duck

near short hairs of a bulldog.
Look up under every cardinal
hugging this tail of nature,

showing its sex in color
of mallards floating up-butted
across brown and black fuzz.

Who marks identity as a caterpillar
wishing for wings and milkweed?
Kelly green ferns spring,

but some could be asexual:
what secret thrill
the warble water

toasting algae among the spots,
asking for a friend
with whom to float,

dreaming
the words
"identify as."

The Flame Against the Bayside

Like him, we all wear
our own versions
of a black bow tie
and white shirt,
dark coat and trousers.
The night matches intensity
in our eyes. What light remains
shines on almond skin
and broad forehead. We carry
dark leather portfolios
and a demeanor that stands
tall along flat stones.
Flash of fireworks,
flame against bayside,
a romantic candle—
all these sources
light our faces
in the sway of shoulders,
staying pressed in night
turning our sweat to skin:
seeking adventure
in delightful purpose,
our spirits walking
within the sounds of our steps.

Out the Window

More about the reflections of yourself
than the weight pulling at your gut,

a waist as loose as a goose, stretchable,
knowing the affirmation of a brown belly,

large and distinctive, without noticing
the turns and pauses held in glass,

interrupting the grass and the bruised orange
of a brown worm taking afternoon sun,

appearing to move as light moves,
heating the shadows fled from branches

to scatter the lawn. One end investigates,
as a worm moves with wonders

finding its way, grounded.
A robin looks thru the window

into the eternal now, and as long as you look
and the robin looks, future is put on hold,

commanding the present
like a growling stomach.

Think about eating,
but before turning,

the bird takes the worm—
the end farthest away.

It does not suck like you suck
noodles, but the movement

appears for effect. One can only see
this happen by using an index finger

and tracing the route of a supposed
worm inside the throat, imagining

the route a worm takes beyond a beak,
a mouth, vacuuming the five-inch worm,
as an Asian noodle dish
appears to the collective mind.

You leave the window
and enter the kitchen. Sublime,

awesome, monstrous, exciting,
filled with an attitude.

Adventure as patient as a robin,
an endgame of love for a worm—

and an empty stomach.

About the Author:

Jan Wiezorek writes from Barron Lake in Michigan. He has taught writing at St. Augustine College, Chicago, and his poetry has appeared or is forthcoming at The London Magazine, Southern Pacific Review, L'Ephemere Review, Yes Poetry, Scarlet Leaf Review, Xavier Review, and Modern Poetry Quarterly Review, among other literary and online journals. He is author of Awesome Art Projects That Spark Super Writing (Scholastic, 2011) and holds a master's degree in English Composition/Writing from Northeastern Illinois University, Chicago. Visit him atjanwiezorek.weebly.com

NEW TESTAMENT
by George Held

New Testament

And the land shall open like a giant vagina
allowing the re-birth channel to swallow
all the detritus of our sick civilization –
the fossil fuel-guzzling auto-mobiles,
the stone mansions and cardboard shacks,
fences and fence-posts, the livestock released
from their diabolical enclosures and gruesome fate,
the squealing, sobbing, cursing masses of so-called human
beings – the self-deluded masters and mistresses
of the universe – and they shall be digested inside
that hole after the land closes behind them,
as after birth, and is sewn shut by the mighty
Weavers of Gaia, who police the land
every few millennia to allow it to heal
and to re-grow its original organic
cover of whatever plants best nourish it,
like clover in a spent field...

Schiele's Portrait of Dr. Erwin von Graff (1910)

At 20 Egon is on a roll,
Convinced a style's in reach.
In art school he stands out –
A weirdo even among young
Bohemians but with enough
Crimson ambition to try
To curry favor with Herr Doktor
Profesor Christian Griepenkerl,
Young Egon's nemesis.

O that we had a portrait of him
Done by Schiele in the style, say,
Of his Portrait of Dr. Erwin
von Graff, Gynecologue
of Vienna, with his colorless
Eyes and hairy forearms
Revealed by his short-sleeved
White tee under a pinkish gray
Sleeveless surgical vest.

The white bandage on the tip
Of his right ring finger contrasts
With the swarthy skin and black moustache.
This is a man of stature,
A man one can trust in the surgical
Theater, if not with one's wife.
Imagine Profesor Griepenkerl
Portrayed with the same hauteur
And x-ray insight as Dr. von Graff.

On Whiteness

Nazis were white
Einstein was light,

like Protestant Albert Schweitzer
an admirable white Switzer.

All MLB players once were white;
Jack Roosevelt Robinson's debut
elicited both hate and delight.

Fred Koch conditioned
his sons David and Charles
to finance the far right

while Dr. Koch found strains
of anthrax and tubercular blight,
all these men being white.

Melville's "thoughts of whiteness"
appear in Ahab's likeness
and dominate his idée fixe,
The great white sperm whale Moby-Dick.

Our own great white whale (with an orange crest),
exemplar of some whites blessed
with power and money, now inhabits
the ultimate white house.

ROAD TRIP

by Sarah Sherwood

A Wild Place

I come from a place quite untouched by fame,
Where waters flow, quiet and pure.
In this place, there's no conquest to claim.
The people are safe and secure.

I come from a distant place where flowers grow,
Their blossoms paint the spring.
Where I come from, the people all know
The magic of Earth's wild things.

It takes a whole village to raise up one child,
Yes, this much I know to be true,
But children must be raised both magic and wild,
Or else they will end up like you.

Where is the magic in all that you see,
Where do your spring flowers bloom?
If we are not wild, if we are not free
Then surely we have met our doom.

Road Trip

You say let's go, let's take the open road.
We'll find a place with pine scent in the air.
Our skin glows beneath the garish lights.
You blame the city for making me so soft.
Armed with the warmth of something just awake,
I start to wonder what you want from me.

There is a stillness in the soul of me.
Our winter proves a long and weary road.
Something inside me is not yet awake.
The darkness hovers mist-like in the air,
The ice inside my veins does not go soft.
My heartbeat matches the flashing stop lights.

In the dark I can only see headlights.
No drop of radiant day saved for me.
There's no moon in the sky, the starlight's soft.
Hopelessness and hope converge on a two-lane road.
Dark and light both swirling through the air,
Yet I still find it hard to stay awake.

The gentlest people rarely feel awake—
At least that's what they've told me, and the lights
Of fireflies dance through the evening air
As I reflect that you hardly know me.
My childhood flew away beyond the road.
No more will I be gentle, no more soft.

Maybe the city did not make me soft,
Maybe you're why I could not wake.
As I stand by the side of this long road,
I watch you head for looming neon lights.
And see exactly why you asked for me.
Your love for me has frozen in the air.

So you return to smoke and dust-filled air,
As winter melts away with spring rain falling soft.
I'll take back all the things you took from me.
Without you near, my spirit is awake.
Soon I will see the world and all its lights,
While you stay on your same old open road.

My road brings me to that pine scented air,
And softly, soft, I dance among the lights.
I am me. I am here. I am awake.

JANUARY
by Laura Foley

Swing

While the giddy bird feeder
swings over crusted snow,
Clara waters geraniums,
pots of rosemary, thyme,
a lemon tree. Come, she says,
smell the lemon tree, so sweet,
like Spain in spring, see
the fig, it grows new leaves
as if it doesn't know
we've got three feet of snow,
four months of winter left.
I bend to the replete
yellow buds she proffers,
then pivot, focusing
on yellow finches, as if
their golden fluttering
might gild me.
I have to turn away
to savor the love
one of us will lose,
our loneliest day.

The Day of the Dead

I think of her lying in the lower field,
beside the cow's grave, her coffin hand-hewn,
filled with late season flowers, weeds,
hays and grasses, her body one week gone,
buried not far from the pond
we often dipped our bodies in.
Now she flies, unseen,
lightly over water's surface,
through cow fields, horse pastures,
every inch of her beloved garden,
over tops of trees, as we, those left behind,
tread onward toward the darkest days.

January

A blizzard of cyclone-cold wind
whips snow in Elysian drifts
around Stygian pines,
builds fantastical walls around the house,
turns familiar woods otherworldly,
provides a world of reasons to stay inside,
as the finches at the feeder
grow more gold-feathered every day,
and the days, they say, grow longer,
though from inside this shaken globe of snow,
it's hard to know.

White Plains Hospital, Psychiatric Division

As Clara and I drive, I identify new highways,
upscale houses, and shopping malls sprung up
since I was young; don't mention hearing
Mom's voice from fifty years ago, You see,
they don't look like bars, as I mirror her gesturing.
The stolid brick buildings remain unchanged,
over-heated corridors, airless, quiet as death,
our footsteps echoing against the scarred wood,
passing shadowy, ancient photographs
staring out at us. Stopping us at the locked doors,
the attendant checks our gifts—
no plastic bags, no dental floss,
no medications, no shoe laces, no glass.
Inside, a middle-aged woman slumps
in her wheelchair, as an older man
complains to no one in particular.
When we reach her room,
I mourn how gaunt she's become,
but she rises eagerly to greet us
showing us, from her window,
the labyrinth where she walks,
with a group of patients and attendants,
anathema to the teen still in me,
but when we leave, she pats me on the back
obsessively, and gently,
as if I needed comforting:
my oldest sister, looking out for me.

Swing

While the giddy bird feeder
swings over crusted snow,
Clara waters geraniums,
pots of rosemary, thyme,
a lemon tree. Come, she says,
smell the lemon tree, so sweet,
like Spain in spring, see
the fig, it grows new leaves
as if it doesn't know
we've got three feet of snow,
four months of winter left.
I bend to the replete
yellow buds she proffers,
then pivot, focusing
on yellow finches, as if
their golden fluttering
might gild me.
I have to turn away
to savor the love
one of us will lose,
our loneliest day.

About the Author:

Laura Foley is the author of six poetry collections, including, most recently, WTF and Night Ringing. Her poem "Gratitude List" won the Common Good Books poetry contest and was read by Garrison Keillor on The Writer's Almanac. Her poem "Nine Ways of Looking at Light" won the Joe Gouveia Outermost Poetry Contest, judged by Marge Piercy. Her book, The Glass Tree, won a Foreword Review Prize for Poetry.

Her poems have appeared widely in journals and magazines including Valparaiso Poetry Review, DMQ, Room Magazine, McClellan Poetry Prize Website, Pittsburgh Poetry Review, Bellevue Literary Review, in the anthologies, Aesthetica Creative Writing, In the Arms of Words: Poems for Disaster Relief, Ice Cream Poems, Roads Taken: Contemporary Vermont Poets, Not My President, an anthology of Dissent, and others.

A palliative care volunteer in hospitals, with an M.A. and a M. Phil. in English Lit. from Columbia University, she lives with her wife and their two dogs among the hills of Vermont.

NEWTON'S LAW
by Lenny Lewis

He'd been raped in Tripoli
so he said. Hosted a parasite.
Given it to her without asking.
She sported a livid scar
where the worm had turned.

Soho before it was fashionable.
Before AIDS. Long before
every properly accessorized
white woman had a black man
on her arm. In those days

they threw vagabond brothers
off the roof just to confirm
Newton's Law of Gravity.
When he got back
from his maritime peregrinations

he wasn't upset his wife
had shown her conjugal cicatrix
to a young buck from the Village.
In fact - a full moon
glistened on the cobblestones.

 " Come down. Do it again.
He wants to watch."

THE SHOW

Sitting in the cupola
secluded by grape vines.
It may have been ice tea
or mint julep in May
around the Derby in Kentucky.
A perfectly Southern thing.

Women from the mountains.
Mother and daughter.
Married both in Lexington.
Daughter now a mother
of two made a bold confession.
At fifteen and a year older

than when her mother
lost her virginity
to a married man. She
had wanted "to try him out."
She had reliable information
he had "a big dick."

He recalled lying on a bed
the daughter and her
underage friend coming
into the room. A Blue Grass
beauty next to him.
Moonshine high.

Her legs in the air.
Moaning her high lonesome
like a cat in heat.
The girls left.
Mother and friends jamming
on Black Beauties and bourbon.

Engaged in extravagant banter.
Waiting for the show to begin.
The woman on the bed
later divorced her husband-
said to be good breeding stock-
and married the milkman.

About the Author:

Lenny is a jack of all trades. Frequently to be found working as a carney. South in the winter. Coney Island in summer.

NEGLECT

by Katherine Carlman

Neglect

No thing positive, effective, demonstrative -
No contacting, no sharing, no encouraging,
No remembering, no caring
No support, no approving, no affirming - -
No thoughtfulness

    No anything.

No calls, cards, texts, letters, flowers, packages, gifts…
Neither giggles, fingers snapping, movie quoting, horn honking, doorbell ringing,
Nor lyrics sharing, door knocking, song singing, message texting, phone calling…

    Nothing.

Not hugs, jokes, smiles, joy; chuckles, snickers - - laughterlaughterlaughter- -
No coffees, dinner, drinks, a movie…

None now, not ever, never more: nothingness.

The Root of All Things

"How Great Thou Art"
The woman sang,
"How great Thou Art..."

And from orbs I call mine own,
Water drizzled my cheeks.

A band marching,
Drum rumble-thrumbling,
My chest echoed the throb.

Tears pricked
My eyes then, too.

What is it, this trick?
Pluck this thing, this string - - no,
not that one - -this one!

Pull it
Snap it back
Quick you go!

With an old ballad
Or a kettle drum
With a perfect note
Or a sad, sweet tune,

With anything true.

And wall-lah!
(Barry, always Barry)

I spring a leak;
I need repairs.

My goodness ... the ache of it

Little breaths, shallow things
Like those tiny puddles
We used to avoid after a quick rain.

There's not enough oxygen.
The air has gotten thin
(Or my lungs have gotten thick)

My rib cage, I suspect, encases
Nothing more than puffs of dust.

About the Author:

Katherine Carlman is a writer living in Ojai iCalifornia who enjoys exploring the world with her husband and children. Her play, The Sixth Station, is available through Samuel French. Additional short plays have been published by Plays Magazine, and her poetry has appeared in Otto. Her essays and articles have been published by NACADA, Catholic Exchange, Twins Magazine, and Big Apple Parents Press, among others. "Exploring Kazimierz and Kopiec in Kraków," a travel essay, was recently published by BootsnAll.

IT'S THAT KIND OF DARK
by Kate LaDew

it's that kind of dark exactly

like in those silent films,

when the man tenderly puts his arm around the woman's back, under her knees,

lifts her white and black body, carrying her to a bedroom the audience never sees

if you look close enough, you can watch her soft lips mouthing

if you drop me, you bastard, I'll break your neck,

as the title card reads oh, how I do love you so.

when you arms circle clumsily, lifting my faded tan, blue-veined body,

it's that kind of dark exactly,

and I say the words out loud, no camera to catch me, I'll break your neck —

but if you look close enough, press your ear to my chest, curl your fingers under my ribs,

if you read me like braille, oh, how I do love you, how I do love you so.

one day, I break off shards of my sandwich,

careful to throw only the pieces free from egg and mayo,
watch the ducks circle, shoot their beaks down, recoil, blue-black eyes expectant.
I wonder if they're waiting for another throw,
or searching my own eyes for the names of the unborn birds settling in my stomach.
I wait. they wait. a shrapnel of bread hits the water, and we all lean back, satisfied.

one day both Bach and Handel were blinded by the same ophthalmologist,

so it's no stretch to believe you and I were ruined by the same man,
you as a teenager, me before I was born,
you ducking your head from every touch,
me watching strangers,
looking for those eyes you say you'll never forget
a man-shaped nightmare we both fall asleep to

About the Author:

Kate LaDew is a graduate from the University of North Carolina at Greensboro with a BA in Studio Art. She resides in Graham, NC with her cats, Charlie Chaplin and Janis Joplin

HAPPINESS

by Andres Mesa

What if it Were to Be?

Some loves
Are brief.
They come and go,
Like the rain,
or the years.

Others,
long-lived
and difficult;
thick,
they cling to everything
like honey.

But they too
disperse.

The ebb and flow of time
takes them away.

Although the brief ones aren't as tragic,
their echo
rings longer.

with them,
you can only imagine
What could have been.

At least,
With the long ones
You know
What was.

Shells

Time wishes to forget.
Men want to remember,
some want to be
remembered
as the tide sweeps in,
beneath houses built
on sand and stilts.

We rush,
sifting along nooks and dunes,
looking for a shell
silver-lined
and gold-plated
among the heap
of rocks,
many and ordinary.

Time wishes to forget,
and I myself
want to forget
about the lonely supermarkets
loaded with shells
and the shell collectors
who charge you interest on your shells,
or the long nights
spent thinking of
how few shells I have,
or of those
distant beaches
promising more shells,
or of the jobs
that force us to say:
"Please sir, shell out more shells!"

The sunken-eyed politicians
promise all of us more shells
in the next eight years,
as our wooden houses
sag
beneath
the load of borrowed shells.

They are building a machine
inside the Federal Reserve
that can assemble
a million shells per minute.

We just have to do our part,
and write it all off
in our tax returns
so they can
pump out more shells;
explosive shells,
concussive shells,
incendiary shells,
and shotgun shells!
to be distributed
into the wide-open mouths
of pot-bellied infants,
in some part of the world
where they have lost
all
their
shells.

Soon they will consolidate our shells,
and trade us
new plastic ones
which are just as good
but valid for only a few years
until they
finally make
fully electronic shells
so we can at least have
some in our accounts
and have
the peace of mind
to not think
about the people
who made our shells,
or the people,
distant and long extinct,
who did not have to worry
about hoarding shells
because the Earth was
thick
and
ripe
with them,
or to no longer
envy
those
who
at least
had a basket
to
put
their
shells
in.

Happiness

No one wants to talk about happiness.
One would expect,
Since there's so little of it to go around,
People would clamor to hear
of the twenty people
In the heartland
who found their true loves
today.

Some solitary academic
finally discovered
the answer
to his lives' quest
and concluded
God
Is waiting up the street
to meet us in the corner bar.

The day of judgment
Happened a hundred years ago
and everyone passed!

It was a sweet fiction,
which we took too seriously
read a comedy
as a tragedy
and,
like children,
made a mess
of it all.

But calamity
washes easily
with a little water
and good faith.

Perhaps,
after five days of only good news,
people will stop
reading the press.

They will line up
to hear about the guy
who cut his twenty lovers
into thin strips
and pieced from them
a map to lead him to his heart.

They will yearn to know
of the fifty frigates
docked and loaded
ready to take the fight
to those who grew their economy
from blood and sand.

Then,
they will look upon the stars
and realize
how far away
they are
from
the corner bar.

About the Author:

Andres Mesa is a Colombian born poet who received his MA from Stony Brook University in 2014. He currently teaches philosophy in South Florida where he resides. His work explores the themes of transience, temporality and existential longing in modernity.

ON BEAUTY: ESSAYS, REVIEWS, FICTION, AND PLAYS

by Wally Swist

Paperback: 240 pages

Publisher: Adelaide Books (September 2018)

Language: English

ISBN-10: 1-949180-32-8

ISBN-13: 978-1-949180-32-9

Product Dimensions: 6 x 1 x 9 inches

Beauty is relative—however, it is also abundant and perennial. One type of beauty may diminish and morph into a deeper philosophical truth. Beauty can take the guise of morality and define the outer reaches of what it means to be fully human—to grow into that. The film Amour, directed by Michael Haneke, which was made in 2012 and won the Palme d'Or, is, ostensibly, all about beauty and what is beautiful about life, as well as what are intrinsic elements of living that may be seen as being opposite to beauty. The film's characters are a husband and a wife, two former music teachers, in their twilight weeks and days. Jean-Louis Trintignant is Georges and Emmanuele Riva is Anne. They are retired. They are cultured. They read, go to concerts, enjoy each other's conversation, and still love each other—for the most part. Anne once shocks Georges by saying, as wives often enough stun their husbands by their appraisals of their characters, "You're a monster sometimes." However, she clarifies that declarative sentence by adding: "But very kind." That is beautiful.

After a lifetime of marriage to each other, Anne suffers two strokes and Georges cares for her throughout her decline. He bathes her, feeds her, exercises the leg on the side she can no longer feel, practices speech therapy with her. Many men, or wives, for that matter, would never have the wherewithal or the courage to brave such lengths—of true amour. Georges may be guilty of being a monster, in Anne's experience, but he is the precipitant in furthering the spark of beauty between them. The drama may seem very French, something Camus or Sartre would have taken delight in, with both Georges and Anne seeing the end of their lives in plain sight; however, instead of being grim, they rise above the end of life, in uncommon transcendence. In their amour, and its tacit veracity—there are several touching scenes regarding Georges physical care for Anne, which are truly heartrending in their depth of humanity and active loving—the viewer is offered the essence of what love is and what having an affair is not. Hence, the irony in the film's title. In today's world where greed, sex, and narcissism are common, the beauty of Georges and Anne is exemplary as not only a moral and cultural pedagogy without pedantry but, quite aesthetically and humanely, one act of beauty after another. Through another's lens this might be seen as hardship and turmoil, unimaginable spousal duty and death in life.

At the film's end, without giving anything away, Georges is clipping the flower heads from a bunch of daisies he has just purchased at the florist. He fills the kitchen sink and scissors the flowers into the water, then throws away the stems. These are meant for his Anne. Often we need to practice the art of discernment in order to see clearly. Sometimes we need to ruin the flowered stalk to create a ritual for celebration. As Anne says, in one scene, over dinner with Georges, while looking through photograph albums, "It's beautiful." Georges responds, "What?" Anne answers, "Life. So long."

That is what constitutes perennial beauty and remains beautiful. If we allow ourselves to discover the epiphany in the commonplace in our lives, we realize, to our astonishment, that all along, through every disappointment and affliction, we can say, "it's beautiful."

Wally Swist's books include Huang Po and the Dimensions of Love (Southern Illinois University Press, 2012); The Daodejing: A New Interpretation, with David Breeden and Steven Schroeder (Lamar University Literary Press, 2015); Candling the Eggs (Shanti Arts, LLC, 2017); and The Map of Eternity (Shanti Arts, LLC, 2018). His poems and prose have appeared in many publications, including Appalachia, Anchor: Where Spirituality and Social Justice Meet, Arts: The Arts in Religion and Theology, Commonweal, and North American Review.

"A novel MARTYRS, HEROES, AND FOOLS is about the WW II Battle of Okinawa from a unique point of view.

This novel goes beyond the ordinary with three parallel storylines ending in poignant tragedy. A page turner."

John Wells is a retired naval engineer living in Annapolis, Maryland. A graduate of the U.S. Naval Academy and the Naval Postgraduate School, Monterey, California, he cut his teeth by writing technical documents for Navy shipbuilding programs that resulted in his ability to express ideas clearly and elegantly, but it's been a lifelong obsession with classical literature that honed his skill to become a professional wordsmith who writes fiction that has readability and character-based dynamic storylines. A literary realist, he has developed a writing style suited to modern readers in this publishing era when novels have to compete with television and video games. He believes that "following the crowd" in writing guarantees mediocrity.

MARTYRS, HEROES, AND FOOLS

by John Wells

Paperback: 300 pages

Publisher: Adelaide Books (September 2018)

Language: English

ISBN-10: 1-949180-34-4

ISBN-13: 978-1-949180-34-3

Product Dimensions: 6 x 1 x 9 inches

A novel, following a stream-of-conscious narrative from a twenty-five-year-old man who has hitchhiked to the Maritimes in Canada and has gradually fallen away from his Christian background, finding his lifestyle to be buried in drugs, booze, and thought.

N.C. Robert has a Master of Theological Studies. His schooling and general interest has always been in theology, philosophy and literature. He began writing poetry in high school and had his first poem published in Poetry Quarterly in 2013 titled "Resting Home." After that, he was inspired to write his first novel – A Coast.

A COAST

by N.C. Robert

Paperback: 180 pages

Publisher: Adelaide Books (September 2018)

Language: English

ISBN-10: 1-949180-35-2

ISBN-13: 978-1-949180-35-0

Product Dimensions: 6 x 1 x 9 inches

AWAKENING

by Laura Solomon

Paperback: 150 pages

Publisher: Adelaide Books (September 2018)

Language: English

ISBN-10: 1-949180-36-0

ISBN-13: 978-1-949180-36-7

Product Dimensions: 6 x 1 x 9 inches

Laura Solomon has a 2.1 in English Literature (Victoria University, 1997) and a Masters degree in Computer Science (University of London, 2003).

Her books include Black Light, Nothing Lasting, Alternative Medicine, An Imitation of Life, Instant Messages, Vera Magpie, Hilary and David, In Vitro, The Shingle Bar Sea Monster and Other Stories, University Days, Freda Kahlo's Cry, Brain Graft, Taking Wainui and Marsha's Deal.

She has won prizes in Bridport, Edwin Morgan, Ware Poets, Willesden Herald, Mere Literary Festival, and Essex Poetry Festival competitions.

She was short-listed for the 2009 Virginia Prize and the 2014 International Rubery Award and won the 2009 Proverse Prize. She has had work accepted in the Edinburgh Review and Wasafiri (UK), Takahe and Landfall (NZ). She has judged the Sentinel Quarterly Short Story Competition.

Her play 'The Dummy Bride' was part of the 1996 Wellington Fringe Festival and her play 'Sprout' was part of the 2005 Edinburgh Fringe Festival.

www.ingramcontent.com/pod-product-compliance
Lightning Source LLC
Chambersburg PA
CBHW081328190426
43193CB00044B/2886